The Transformations of Man

*the text of this book is printed
on 100% recycled paper*

LEWIS MUMFORD

The

Transformations

of Man

HARPER TORCHBOOKS
Harper & Row, Publishers
New York, Evanston, San Francisco, London

This TORCHBOOK paperback edition reprints Volume VII of the
WORLD PERSPECTIVES, which is planned and edited by RUTH NANDA
ANSHEN. Dr. Anshen's Epilogue to this reprint appears on page 187.
A hardcover edition was originally published by Harper & Row,
Publishers in 1956.

THE TRANSFORMATIONS OF MAN
Copyright © 1956 by Lewis Mumford.

First TORCHBOOK edition published 1972

STANDARD BOOK NUMBER: 06-131665-2

Contents

Introduction to New Edition

THE TRANSFORMATIONS OF MAN stands midway between the four volumes of my Renewal of Life Series and three later volumes, *The City in History, Technology and Human Development,* and *The Pentagon of Power,* books originally conceived as limited revisions of those earlier volumes. But as it happens the writing of *The Transformations of Man* resulted in a widening of my own historic perspective: so it is at once a crystallization of my past studies and a digging down to deeper levels in the understanding of man's mind and culture.

While the factual descriptions in this book conform to attested archaeological, anthropological, and historic findings, what perhaps distinguishes this interpretation is the continued interplay between a mass of well-sifted specialized knowledge, a sprinkling of free but circumspect speculations, and the cumulative reports of personal observation and experience. Not least the last; for there are many significant aspects of human existence that cannot be discovered or interpreted even by the most highly qualified scientists except through the process of living.

As a generalist I have taken advantage of a license too often self-denied by the specialized scholar: that of assembling data from widely different areas in order to bring out a larger pattern that otherwise escapes observation. From region to region and age to age that pattern is constantly changing; yet the underlying fabric of culture preserved in artifacts, institutional forms, physical structures, and above all in language, ramifies upward through all the successive historic strata. What is now characterized as 'instant culture' is a deliberate effort to eliminate the most essential fea-

1

tures of the human heritage: the collective memory of past events, the perpetuation of present achievements, the anticipation of future consequences. From the standpoint of this book, accordingly, past, present, and future are not successive stages in time but form part of an organic continuum in which the 'past' is still 'present' in a 'future' that is already obscurely operating in the mind in the form of dreams, fantasies, ideas, intelligent projects.

With such a philosophic background, allied in many respects to that of A. N. Whitehead's, it is not surprising that I have found the beginnings of the so-called Industrial Revolution, not in the eighteenth century with its steam engines and automatic looms, but in the highly mechanized human machines (megamachines) that built the great tombs, ziggurats, walls, cities, and irrigation works of the earliest civilizations. This view not only rejects the notion that the past can or should be left behind, as if only new discoveries and new inventions had any importance: it likewise rejects an assumption that has reinforced the naïve belief in mechanical progress; namely, that man is essentially a tool-using and tool-making animal, whose increasing intelligence came about mainly through the cunning employment of his hands. Against the notion that man's principal concern is the conquest of nature, present evidence indicates that man is primarily a brain-using and symbol-making animal, whose first great achievement was the reshaping of his own organism and the ultimate creation of a human personality, significantly different from his original biological self.

In this transformation man's whole body, not merely his hands, were involved; beginning with the difficult coordination of a whole group of organs for the achievement of articulate speech and the improvement of interpersonal communication. The primary sources of advanced technology, including repetitive motion, standardization, and division of labor derive—as A. M. Hocart first indicated—from the culture of the body in group rituals, dances, and magical invocations.

This radical reorientation was not perhaps the least contribution begun by *The Transformations of Man*. Fortunately the proof of my rereading of man's origins lies readily at hand. At a time when crude stone tools were still being employed on the building of the Pyramids, without the aid of even such elementary machines as the pulley or the wheeled wagon, the language of the Egyptians and the Sumerians, indeed of far more primitive people, had already reached a degree of complexity, standardization, flexibility, autonomous organization, and controlled abundance far beyond the achievements of the most advanced present-day machines. Even the rigid mechanical discipline of the workers who composed the new megamachine and the marvellously exact measurements of the engineer-builders were products of refined mental organization, not merely a perfection of routine handicraft skill.

Here perhaps is the place to emphasize still another radical revision of both historical and anthropological perspectives, closely allied to the shift in emphasis from tactical advances through the hand and the tool to the strategic victories due to the brain and the symbol. Strangely, *The Transformations of Man* is one of the first modern sociological interpretations to give full weight to man's inner and outer worlds. I say 'strangely' because Sigmund Freud reestablished—some three-quarters of a century ago—the significance of the dream: so by now the fact that man has a constant dream life, active day and night, should be an essential part of every other description of the human condition. This plenitude of images was perhaps the greatest creative contribution of man's oversized brain—though like every other kind of quantification it has a negative side and it has increased the need for vigilant evaluation, selectivity, and control.

Unfortunately, those who had been strictly schooled in the geographic, economic, or technical interpretations of history had come to treat man's subjective activities as mere by-products of external forces and conditions—immaterial and insubstantial, if not inherently disorderly and irrational. Freud himself had helped to reinforce this one-sided objectivity, with its materialist illusion of an independent reality untouched by the human mind. In approaching the dream through the treatment of neuroses, Freud tended to look upon all forms of inner activity except thought as a neurotic phenomenon. This caused Freud to regard all art, myth, and religion as pathological disturbances—at best primitive survivals—which would soon be banished by the operations of the scientific intelligence.

If this book has not been received with open arms by the positivists, the pragmatists, and the behaviorists who still dominate the social sciences, perhaps the chief reason for their neglect, not to say hostility, lies in the fact that I have attempted to redress their unbalanced picture of man's actual development. Not the least offense committed by this new picture is that, by giving due attention to the effect of Bronze Age religions on the development of technics, it also gives a clue to the more life-menacing manifestations of the *Myth of the Machine* from the Pyramid Age on to the Nuclear Age.

When I began to assemble the materials for this overall view of human development, I had no preconceived scheme or climactic outcome in mind. The patterns of culture and personality that emerged at each stage came into existence without my conscious help or manipulation—though once they had taken shape I could often give them further support from the body of anthropological and archaeological knowledge that has accumulated during the last quarter century. Certainly it is not for the author himself to evaluate critically the fresh contributions made by *The Transformations of Man* especially since they are only beginning to be discovered and confirmed by other scholars. Enough if I add that more than two centuries ago Giambattista Vico, with far fewer data to support his intuitions, had at many points opened the way for such a generalized account of human development. Though my work has many other sources and precursors than Vico, I should be happy even at this late date to be found in his company.

In general, I am content to let these pages speak for themselves: all the more because many of my most ominous characterizations of Post-Historic Man have in the meanwhile turned into demonstrable realities, thanks to the automatic acceleration of the very processes that the exponents of progress have counted on to bring about human salvation. Faced with the earthquake shudders of psychotic hatred, murderous violence, and random destruction that now threatens to swallow up all human culture, we can at last perhaps recognize those deep structural faults that have been present since the dominant institutions of civilization first erupted and solidified. For that portion of the younger generation which is now reexamining and retesting both ancient practices and current routines, a clarified consciousness of the past may prove the best safeguard against wanton rejections, perverse choices, and premature disillusions.

Though I found it necessary in the later *Myth of the Machine* to deal at length with the negative components of civilization, focussed in the all-powerful and now all-pervasive megamachine, I still stand by every perception and hope set forth in the concluding chapters on World Culture and One World Man. Admittedly the prospect for an early fulfillment of these hopes has become dimmer—and would, as I took care to point out, demand a miracle —but it would be far less realistic to pin one's hopes on the technological transcendentalism of the so-called futurologists, from Buckminster Fuller and Arthur Clarke to Herman Kahn and Alvin Toffler. Fortunately, though the human race usually shows its worst side during periods of affluence and insolent power, it often behaves at its heroic best—like the British at Dunkirk—in the midst of disaster. The more hopeless our present situation seems, confronted as we are by both ecologically unbalanced environments and psychological unbalanced minds, the more imperative it is not to lose hope. The coming generation has still another option open, man's oldest one: that of consciously cultivating the arts that make man human.

—L. M.

Animal into Human

I

When we go back to the origins of man, we go back to a time before he left any records except his own bones; and all too few of them. Some day, at the bottom of a sunken ocean bed, or in caves yet unexplored, we may discover richer human relics. But it is doubtful whether material objects, bones, stones, shards, can reveal what we want most to know—by what cunning and daring, by what dreaming and searching, man discovered the germs of his own humanness and nurtured them. What matters most about man's past will remain in the realm of speculation and fantasy. Teased by this obscurity, almost every people has fashioned a myth about its origin, nature, and destiny, though too often the mythmakers ask themselves only how their kind became Babylonians, Greeks, Jews, Romans, Japanese, and not when and how they became men.

Since none of these old myths does justice to our present knowledge, I purpose to fashion a myth that will be more in keeping with the science of our time, yet more ready to venture into factual quicksand than the scientist, if true to his prudent code, can let himself be. This new myth does not, it goes without saying, profess to come from divine revelation; nor yet can the earlier parts of it be called, even by the most generous stretching of the words, verifiable truth. But in its speculative vagueness, as in its dubious flashes of illumination, it reflects the actual mystery with which it deals. Where the facts are beyond recall, our myth will seek to reconstruct them by reading back from the known into the unknown, since the historic transformation of man is repeated, in effect, with the birth and nurture of every new human being.

In significant ways, the terms of the present myth of man have changed. We no longer ask for some dramatic moment of creation that calls for an external and all-powerful creator. The extension of astronomic and geologic time lessens the need for sudden power: our creative agent is inseparable from the long process of creation itself, slowly gathering purpose and direction over the aeons, gradually 'making up its mind' and at last, in man, beginning to achieve the first glimmer of self-consciousness.

Something that may later be identified as life and mind perhaps is present at every stage of the cosmic process, though visible only when one looks backward. Certainly, long before man came on the scene, a multitude of organisms had taken form and invented ways of perpetuating that form and altering it, each after their own kind, within the life cycle of their own species, in relation to environments and organic partnerships that sustained it. Out of this cosmic web of life stepped man : the creature that dared consciously to be a creator, and that found another path to creation than that of biological metamorphosis.

Man seems to have descended from a group of apelike primates that lived in trees, when a large part of the earth boasted a tropical climate. In one or more places, at one or more times, this creature took the first steps toward becoming human. Some alteration in his metabolism, some mutation in his genes—yes, perhaps some inner impetus and need—endowed him with a bigger brain, relatively, than almost any creature but the mouse possesses; and man's sustained urge to make something of it started him on his long career. That change made it possible for man to live in a more complex world, or rather, to take in more of the complexities and possibilities of the real world : it brought with it the development of greater manual skills, finer co-ordinations, greater sensitiveness to both outer stimuli and inner promptings, a greater aptitude for learning, a more retentive memory and a more wary foresight than any of his ancestors could boast.

The overgrowth of the human brain may signify a more general condition that sets man off from his nearest animal colleagues : an abundance of unused energy not marked for nutrition, reproduction or defence. In other animals, excess vitality runs off mainly in muscular play. In man, it produces a constant undercurrent of sounds, images, exploratory actions. His infantile interest in his own body and its products includes other expressions, though his tendency to blow and bubble and babble and hum has no purpose or direction at the beginning except sheer organic activity. Arnold Gesell has shown that in early infancy a baby will turn to constructive acts, putting one block on another, before anyone instructs him in these possibilities.

In short, the undifferentiated material for symbols and fabrications rises out of man, not waiting for any external challenge, but prompted by his own maturation. And it is surely no accident that the least controllable part of this flow—but eventually the most significant, indeed the very source of significance—wells up from the unconscious. What was uniquely serviceable for man's development was his ability to fix and formalise these spontaneous images and symbols, and to attach them to objects provided by the external world.

By developing his mind, man lessened the need for other forms of organic specialisation. When Karl Pearson compared man's brain to a telephone exchange, handling incoming and outgoing calls, he took in only a small part of its activity: it is a power station, a storage warehouse, a library, a theatre, a museum, a hall of archives, a court of justice, a seat of government. The instinctive equipment of most species is sufficient to ensure their survival. By transferring authority to a controlling intelligence, sensitised by feeling, enlarged by imagination, man sometimes endangered his survival, but he opened the possibility of further development.

Nature, Dr. Walter Cannon demonstrated, has practised the 'economy of abundance' in fashioning man and many of his ancestors: hence the excess of energy that is stored up, ready for emergencies, the provision of paired organs, the ears, the eyes, the lungs, the kidneys, the breasts, the testicles, so that even if one member is injured the other can take over the burden and keep the organism alive. But this same generosity applies even more magnificently to man's central nervous system: long before man could count on ten fingers, he had enough neurons at his disposal to make possible the learning of an Aristotle, or an Ibn-Khaldun, the wisdom of a Confucius or an Isaiah, the imagination of a Plato or a Dante. Let us not forget this generosity. The wisdom of the body has further applications to the life of man in our time: for an economy of abundance brings with it, not the duty to consume, but the readiness to create.

Man's immediate ancestors possibly went halfway on this path of development: man completed it. But the ability to walk on two feet was so lately acquired that it never became part of man's organic inheritance: he must still be taught how to walk, around the beginning of his second year, and about the same time he adds to his animal vocabulary of signals, gestures, uncouth sounds, another distinctly human trait: the imitation of formalised sounds and presently the use of words to express feelings and meanings. Words pin down man's associations and multiply them. Without words he could react to environmental pressures and stimuli; but he could not enlarge this milieu into a world that stretches far beyond his immediate sight or reach.

Along with these two outstanding achievements, goes a fact that John Fiske was perhaps the first observer to rate at its full importance: man's prolonged infancy, sanctioned if not promoted by maternal indulgence. In a sense, man is a retarded animal, for the span between his birth and his maturity, when he is ready to mate, is relatively longer than in most other species. By the time man is old enough to reproduce his kind, the horse is ready to be put to pasture in his old age. This freedom from adult tasks encouraged growth: thanks to his long childhood man found time to play and experiment, time to learn, time to take in not merely the immediate environment but the remembered experience of his kind, time to grope in dream toward a distant future. Escaping in youth the pressure to survive, he had leisure for self-development. This fact sets even primitive man apart from his animal neighbours.

With the utter helplessness of the newborn infant went a prolonged period of breast feeding: this reinforced the common mammalian trait of tenderness. In addition, the shedding of the hairy garment of the apes, particularly in the female, brought about a more intimate and pleasurable contact between mother and babe, to say nothing of her mate. Breasts and lips became instruments of erotic love, and out of that happy association spread more general habits of protection, nurture, and loving attachment. The extension of the period of parental care and childish irresponsibility promoted playfulness; and play was perhaps the earliest realm of human freedom.

In sheer play and make-believe man may have made the first great advances in culture, beginning with human speech: more significant than any acts that could be described as practical invention or work. Man's use of tools, with their sharpening of his practical intelligence, came early; but the passage from the animal to the human may have been furthered even more by his rich emotional life, coloured by love, hate, fear, anxiety, laughter, tears, demanding outlets of expression and communication. Many insect orders long surpassed man in constructive facility and social organisation; but no other creature shows the faintest capacity for creating durable works of art. It was not alone the Promethean theft of fire but the Orphic gift of music that turned man into a creature so different from his primordial self.

One other trait came to mark man off from his animal neighbours besides his playfulness and his artfulness: his propensity to imitate and emulate those around him: to smile when they smile, to be doleful when they are sad, to reproduce their gestures, to articulate the same sounds. Even when the immediate occasion is absent, man's retentive memory may prompt him to recall a valued moment and repeat it in play; for repetition itself gives him a certain satisfaction and security, as we see in a child's love of ritual and his insistence upon having a familiar story repeated with every detail in order.

The impulse of imitation, the disposition to make-believe, the habit of lingering over a satisfactory response in memory and working it into a meaningful pattern—these seem to me fundamental contributions to truly human development. They were means by which man detached himself from his organic limitations and from the all-too-slow process of biological change. By daily nurture, he produced a 'second nature,' which we now call culture, transmitted by imitation and habit. This culture became more natural and proper to him than his original make-up because it included not merely what he was and is, but what he loves and admires and purposes to be. Of all the labour-saving devices that man has invented, this earliest invention, that of detachment from the organic, seems beyond any doubt the most important. This achievement paved the way for the free development of intelligence long before intelligence devised further tools for its own advancement.

In achieving culture, man's first steps were doubtless the hardest, like the first pennies that lay the foundation for a fortune. By now, man's culture has become visible in the outward world, in buildings and cities, in institutions and printed records: but for long the greater part of it was carried in the mind and transmitted only by gesture and word of mouth. Poverty of numbers, poverty of material equipment, poverty of symbols, held back further development: for long his difficulty was to hold fast to the little that he had acquired. After the first steps had been taken, man's achievement of the specifically human must have been upset by frequent relapses into his naïvely animal past. Even today violent rage temporarily brings on this result. Would man, with his new potentialities and prospects, manage to retain his adventurous ways—or would he fall back into sleepy animalhood? At the beginning of his ascent, that question may have stirred man's deepest anxiety.

Our present age, beyond any other, should understand the urgency of this question. For man's humanity is now threatened by the possibility of relapsing into a barbarism more elemental than has ever been encountered in historic times. Though culture itself tends to be cumulative, in the process of taking it over each generation starts from scratch. Without parental love, without filial veneration, without a secure sense of the future, the very effort to become human may miscarry. Through overreliance upon mechanism and automatism our generation has begun to lose the secret of nurturing man's humanness, since he gives too little care to the conditions that make each member of the community sensitive, tender, imaginative, morally responsible, self-governing, disposed to imitate human ideals and to emulate ideal examples of humanity.

Fortunately for primitive man, he was not, like us, intimidated by the cold perfection of the machine, nor did the universe seem to him a machine. And even more fortunately, perhaps, one of the first objects of his love was himself : indeed, without his excessive vanity and self-love early man might never have explored the principal paths that carried him beyond his original animal concern with survival and reproduction. It is not perhaps by accident that narcissism—preoccupation with one's bodily image and absorption in one's own capacities and desires—still marks the passage from adolescence to maturity. If in maturity overweening pride often comes before a fall, at the beginning pride and vanity came before man's rise and prompted him to greater efforts. When man loses this deep self-respect, the world itself seems corrupt and loathsome.

2

But was there perhaps some more devious path that led to man's emergency from his purely animal state? His sociability, his industry, his constructive propensities, his amorous excitements, his domestic partnerships and solicitudes—all these he shares with various other species. But there are two traits that, even if they are shared in some dim way by other species, leave no mark on their behaviour, but colour every aspect of man's existence : they function throughout human history and probably through prehistory, for the greater part unrecorded and unrecordable. One is the capacity to dream and, above all, to transform imagined projections into actual projects. The other is the sense of awe and veneration, not unmixed with anxiety, in the presence of forces that lie beyond the range of man's intelligence.

Man lives no small part of his life in the presence of the un-conscious and the unknown: he is apparently the only creature who ever had the intuition that there is more in nature than meets the eye. In opening up his specific human capacities, the unknown, indeed, the unknowable, has proved an even greater stimulus than the known, while his peculiar fore-consciousness of death has added an enigmatic dimension to his life that has carried him beyond dumb animal acceptance of that terminal event. Infinity, eternity, immortality, potentiality, omniscience, omnipo-tence, divinity, to say nothing of zero and the square root of minus one, have no counterparts in animal experience.

If the constructive use of dreams differentiates man from other animals, this faculty may have occupied an even greater pro-portion of early man's attention and interest than over-rational interpretations ordinarily allow. In the depths of the human personality, the unconscious and the supernatural are united in the form of dynamic images transcending any actual human experi-ence: demons, monsters, dragons, angels, gods take possession of the dreamer and become more obsessively real than the actual world of here and now, to which he confusedly returns. With these overpowering images, independent and autonomous, some-times as vivid in daylight as in sleep, man went farther in the direction of detachment and projection: detachment from the animal, projection of the super-human and the divine.

The feeling of his cosmic loneliness may have separated dawn-man from the manlike ape, long before he found words to express that feeling; but with it, out of the strange commanding symbols of the unconscious, may have come a sense of being favoured by powers and agents seemingly not his own: powers attached, through his sexuality, to the deepest sources of life. These happy hallucinations may have touched every conscious act with an obsessive insistence. So man's self-transcending nature prospered in the climate of the supernatural; these fantasies confirmed his own tendency to overvalue his dearest object of love, himself.

All this must have antedated anything that can be called religion. In the beginning was the *mysterium tremendum*, unfathomable, uncontrollable, indescribable: the source of light and darkness, warmth and cold, delight and dejection, life and death, not yet divided out into nature, man, and God. Man learned to live with this mystery and in time to project it, interpreting the unknown

by symbols equally incapable of rational explanation. True, other animals seem at times to have cosmic responses: wolves bay at the moon: elephants perform secret nocturnal ceremonies: chimpanzees have shown something like awe in the presence of the uncanny, be it only the image of a donkey, made of rags and buttons. But in man the sense of wonder and mystery may have been stirred in the first gropings of self-consciousness and even more than his practical intelligence may have helped lift him out of his animal state.

At a later stage, one finds these mysterious promptings surrounded by rationalisations and conceptual supports, translated into rituals, expressed in abstract forms of art; but in the beginning they must have antedated dogma and moral code, perhaps even speech. Out of this cosmic anxiety and awe, in which self-abasement and exaltation both played a part, came the sense of the sacred, which has no animal equivalent: the sacredness of blood and the birth rite, the sacredness of sex, the sacredness of the word: finally the sacredness of death, and with it the impulse to solemnly care for the bodies of the dead, and to dwell in the imagination on their future existence.

This quickening to the unknown, this widening of man's effective environment to include vistas of time and space beyond any animal need or capacity, this imputation of some more permanent value and significance to the passing moment—all this is, from the standpoint of survival or practical utility, an aberration. Yet in man's early departures from sensible animal accommodation to his visible environment we may hold a key—perhaps one of the main keys—to what is veritably human. In these reactions, man exposes himself to fearful illusions and self-deceptions that sometimes carry him beyond the borderland of sanity. But precisely because of his readiness for fantasy untouched by the here and now, he penetrates levels of existence and meaning that no other creature seems to approach.

The other source of man's veritable humanness was his capacity to dream; for this is the forward-moving counterpart to memory. In origin derived perhaps from man's anxiety, the dream took on a positive function—it became the great instrument of anticipation, invention, projection, creative transformation. Sensitive to outside impressions, which keep reverberating in him long after the stimulus has ceased, man's hours of sleep, when he is detached from practical needs, are flooded with images. While the outer world supplies the material for these images, under pressure from within they undergo extravagant transformations, which his waking intelligence would reject. Man's manipulativeness and curiosity, his trial-and-error discoveries, certainly furthered his command over the external world: but the dream has the special sign of art: it expresses the nature of the dreamer and gives him further insight into his own potentialities. This self-expression was an important element in man's transformation.

Living phenomena differ from the nonliving not only in the fact that they originate in the organism and are in keeping with its general plan of life which brings about successive modifications and transformations in time—growth, maturation, reproduction, death. They likewise differ in that they are directional, anticipatory, preparatory, goal-seeking, though at the organic level the end-in-view has become so completely structured that it cannot be separated from the creature's own nature. In man, his anticipatory reactions become detached and externalised as conscious purpose; and in his awareness of his desires, he intensifies their expression or by detaching them he may divert them to ends that partly contradict his own original nature. This is one of the functions of dream. Possibility and purposiveness, along with anxiety and prudent anticipation, all seem to cluster around man's capacity to dream, and to carry this function from the unconscious of sleep to the whole field of his waking life. By detaching purpose from organic structures and functions man both brought it into consciousness and gave it a special human destination.

In following this line, man breaks away from the purely adaptive behaviour of other species: he turns upon nature with counter-proposals of his own, which move toward obscure goals he can never fully understand until he has given them form. In this respect, one can explain the development of human culture in general only by understanding the process of creating a work of art. This act, when it is not purely imitative, transcends the knowledge of the creator and often seems to outrun his powers: it draws on capacities that could not be known till they were summoned forth and externalised. The wish, then, is not merely father to the thought: it is the parent of all man's creative acts and functions. And because the erotic impulses themselves play a larger part in man's dreams than sex itself can satisfy, the dream carries into every act and occupation an image of some further fulfilment, open to his own creation.

3

With the word and the dream man was able to pass from the limited animal vocabulary of signals and signs to the almost un-limited human vocabulary of symbols. But he did not reach this goal directly: in all probability, he moved toward it by a round-about route, by way of love and play. Before sounds took shape and became repeated often enough to be identified, man possibly had a larger repertory of expression than any other creature, if only because of his mobile facial muscles. The ancient dialogue between mother and child, which begins in gesture and facial expression, turned gurgles and babbles into formed sounds and sounds into recognisable words. As with dream images, it seems likely that man playfully cultivated his organs of speech before he turned language to the more practical uses of communication or command. Here again one can only tell plausible fairy stories. But one can watch part of the process once more in every new-born baby.

In babyhood, certainly, language begins as pure expression, as a mode of emotional communion, long before it becomes otherwise useful. Beneath its many other functions, which make for social unison and enlarge the field of common knowledge and shared behaviour, language promotes emotional solidarity: it is a bond of identification and recognition. Those who speak the language with the right tone and inflection, using the familiar vocabulary, are kinsmen, neighbours, fellows: people to trust. Those who do not are outsiders and enemies: at best, ridiculous creatures, not quite 'people,' as the ancient Egyptians openly felt. So the deepest of bonds became in time one of the greatest of barriers between the tribes and races of man; and man's most universal artifact, the spoken word, because it is so deeply steeped in the individuality of experience, became an obstacle to the union of mankind.

There is still another function of language that so far, perhaps because it is so obvious, seems to have escaped attention. Language, the most important agent of directed thought, has the special trick of inhibiting autonomous images. Once language is achieved words may indeed summon events or images into consciousness: but when they function actively they may also, as the busy, efficient agents of directed thought, halt the self-induced hypnosis of sleep. This fact is well known to those who have been sleepless. If primitive man was at first almost a neurotic victim of his own excessive image-making power, the invention and elaboration of language may have acted as a helpful inhibiting agent, which kept him from being overwhelmed. By displacing autonomous images that welled up from the unconscious with verbal symbols attached to conscious processes, he may have brought his whole life under greater control. Much primitive thinking would still remain dream-like, infantile, magical. But by the very nature of the word, thinking itself would become centrally directed, and in time, by its very detachment from the unconscious, it would serve to enlarge the realm of the rational, the intelligible, the practical.

Once man achieved the beginnings of verbal and graphic symbolism, he acquired a formal organ of detachment and projection: he could take in a large area of experience and keep it unified in his consciousness, bringing past and future, near and far, into a common field. So, too, he could, with the materials so brought together, express his own innerness in forms that were themselves permanent enough to recapture his original intuition even after the immediate occasion had passed. The wonder of the word, above all, must once have filled man's life as a whole far more enchantingly than the wonder of the atom does today; for the act of naming was a godlike process, a second creation: when one had gotten possession of a name, one seemed to exercise command over the object it identified. No other animal possessed such powers. This was not just the ability to think: it was the power to create, the magic breath of life. With its help the inevitabilities of nature were supplemented with possibilities divined only by man. No wonder primitive man thought, even after he had achieved civilised order, that the name was the essence of even divine identity, and that naming and creating were one.

So marvellous was this achievement that, down to our own day, man has persistently sought to apply the magic of words to realms where it is worthless. Since words often do bring about changes in human conduct, acting as a trigger if not as a bludgeon, primitive man sought to apply this power to non-human objects as well: were not clouds and trees alive? By word magic, he would invoke rain or fertility, health or energy. Yet even if recent experiments in telekinesis should be fully verified, there is little doubt that this method is the least profitable way of effecting a change in the raw physical environment: so this magic was doomed.

But it has not been for nothing that the word has remained

man's principal toy and tool: without the meanings and values it sustains, all man's other tools would be worthless. Man's greatest concrete achievements rest on these abstractions. By means of symbols, man was able to escape enclosure by physical circumstance and his own biological nature. What was symbolised could sooner or later be realised, either in art or in life.

4

Let us examine more closely the formation of the human self, for it presents problems no other animal faces, and discloses aptitudes no other animal reveals. Over a generation ago the French sociologist, Gabriel Tarde, sought to explain human society by the Laws of Imitation. By pushing that key into holes where it did not fit he brought discredit to the concept. But man is in fact a highly imitative animal: his 'consciousness of kind' brings with it a desire to impress, to please, to gain a response from his kind; and emulation, based in mutual admiration, is one of the paths to this social solidarity.

But imitation cannot be reduced to mechanical mimesis; and only at its lowest levels can it be confounded with drill. In man it involves admiration and love, an effort to identify the self with its beloved object in order to draw more closely to it; and distance and inaccessibility seem to intensify the effort. At a certain point in man's development, it is not the actual person, but an ideal pattern, that brings forth this propensity. This effort to achieve an imagined good or an ideal goal goes along with another human tendency, equally ingrained: that of lingering over and elaborating every natural act, so that it will have a special meaning and value detached from its immediate function, though often closely dependent upon it.

Thus the snatching of food becomes the ceremony of dining: the need for sexual companionship creates the forms of courtship and marriage; and a thousand other occasions of life are given a form that makes the original stimulus the least significant part of them. Man is born into a world of sensations and motor impulses: he matures into a world of meanings and values: indeed, his culture rests ultimately upon his ability to convert the raw materials of existence into forms that independently sustain social life and nurture the development of the person.

This tendency toward elaboration and efflorescence is not unknown on a purely biological level. There it is associated chiefly with sexual activity: the growing of ornate excrescences in the mating season or the turning of the simple mechanism of fertilisation into the aesthetic splendours of flowers. Possibly the impulse to prolong transitory acts had its origin in man's year-round openness to sexual excitation: by formal elaboration he saved himself from exhaustion and found himself in a far more meaningful world. At all events, the long circuit of art and contemplative thought replaced the short circuit of direct action. 'Verweile doch, du bist so schön!' may have been one of man's earliest demands.

Thus man does not simply live his life from day to day, in a sober, matter-of-fact way: he dramatises and enacts it. For every phase in his development, he creates a plot and a dialogue, a sequence of actions, an appropriate costume, and a special stage. In time, as with an actor who has spent his life in tragic roles, his natural face may take on the features of the mask. What is culture itself but an elaborate masquerade for confirming man's original bit of make-believe, that he was not in fact a mere animal? By losing himself in role after role, drama after drama, man explores passages that the fixed parts assigned by nature would never have opened up. As a result his performance lacks the sureness and perfection of other animals, who have had to learn only one role. But in compensation, the continued shifting of parts has made him able to master new situations that would have baffled any other creature.

These characteristics must, from the beginning, have aided in man's delivery from his 'given' self. For he is the only creature who does not without effort know what he is. His being is always involved in a becoming, and that becoming involves a self-transformation. He learns to 'be himself' only by the process of working over his original nature. Once upon a time I knew a little boy, aged three, who became a baby bird: he no longer wore clothes but had feathers: his feet were claws: his arms were wings: his nose was a beak: his home was a tree: his bed was a nest; and all his acts, for a time, were involved in this dramatic replacement of himself. This autodrama required, too, that those around him should play appropriate supporting roles. Since we often see these impulses at work in a young child, without any promptings from the outside, we may hazard the guess that they were also present in the childhood of the race; in fact, many survivals, like totemism, indicate a similar make-believe. What is important is not the animal form but the make-believe itself.

On this interpretation, then, man became man by formalising ritualising, symbolising, dramatising every natural act he performed; and in time this faculty permitted him to transform his entire environment, bring it closer to his self by giving it the same attributes. This capacity for aesthetic projection brought forth a second self, a more truly human self, one in accord with man's still unstated and unfathomed possibilities. Only at the highest stages of his culture, when he has passed through these transformations, when he is confident that the 'human' has been solidly won, does man feel as free as the Greeks did to return to his natural self in its idealised wholeness. At that moment the naked body, unblemished by decoration, appears with sudden glory in sculpture. If one accepts the conventions of make-believe, and recognises the essential part they played in man's development, many of his strangest historic acts become logical and meaningful. But if one stands outside, even many of his most rational acts seem absurd.

Today we have largely forgotten how much of man's life was fashioned in definitely human form before his technical facilities were much better than a beaver's, and long before his social organisation had begun to approach the complexities and the functional divisions of the social insects. While man was still a mere food gatherer, hardly yet a well-armed hunter, he had probably invented most of the decisive instruments of culture and above all projected a new image of himself. And if man's own body was the first object of his loving care, we should not be surprised to find that the most ancient of his arts was probably cosmetic and body decoration: an art known to the lowliest Australian Bushmen and still the subject of more lavish expense than any other art in present-day society. Perhaps, by dabbing his face with red clay or ochre primitive man sought to establish his new personality, visibly different from his untouched animal self: the sudden transformation of the mask. The very word personality derives from this formal covering for the face.

These acts of self-identification happily did not stop with body painting, scarification, and tattooing: man's artful masquerade, in time, touched every part of his society and his environment, not least his inner self. By means of his culture, he wrought changes in himself within a few thousand years that nature would have needed millions of years to accomplish by the tedious process of organic evolution. And unlike biological changes, such cultural transformations could, when they proved a handicap to human development, be modified or replaced within a similar span of time.

Now the art of becoming human by gesture and word and formal act was man's earliest and greatest art. But for a long time, I would suppose, man's sense of his new identity must have been insecure and vulnerable. The possibility of losing hold of his new self—of forgetting the key to language, for instance, and lapsing into mere gibberish—must have haunted him. In our time, we are confronted with problem children who have a 'reading block': they find it difficult to identify printed sentences with a meaningful flow of sounds. There may well have been a time in human development when the translation of sound into meaning was even more precarious; and the possibility of not being able to make this passage may have deepened the fear of being transformed by magic back into a animal, as in the ancient fairy tales. Hence the emphasis on repetition and ritual: the exact words in the exact order and no other. The fear of relapsing into animalhood is recorded in the adventure of Odysseus with Circe in the *Odyssey*; and it comes out in many other forms, including severe prohibitions against sexual congress with animals. Yet with it went perhaps a sense that, in partly cutting loose from his animal roots, man had lost a source of strength. Like the plant, he needed not only the air and light above him, but the soil beneath.

Despite the fact that man became man by creating a new world, a meaningful world of symbolic and cultural forms, which had no existence for the animal, the ancient spiritual tie with his animal past could not be lightly severed. The feeling of identification lingered in primitive societies in the cult of totem animal, and was carried over into the religions of civilisation, in the lion-headed or hawk-headed gods of Egypt, in the sacred bulls of Assyria, Crete, Persia. And if the temptation to sink back into the securities of his animal state long remained with him—indeed still lingers—at the beginning he perhaps put it behind him only by energetic repression.

'Dreams and beasts,' Emerson noted in an early *Journal*, 'are the two keys by which we are to find out the secrets of our own nature.' That has proved an even more penetrating intuition than he could have guessed. If the domestication of plants and animals was one of the upward stages in man's development, his own self-domestication was of even greater critical importance, beginning with the process of penning in his own animal self. From the beginning he knew that the vigorous animal core of him needed no special encouragement: it was rather the faint tremulous stirrings of an embryonic new self, as yet unborn, to which he must give heed.

Every new generation must repeat dawnman's original effort. But today our very consciousness of our animal origins has in some quarters given rise to the curious belief that this part of man's original nature alone is real, valid, integral, and that the forms of morality and social discipline are only superstitious impositions upon the true nature of man. Sophisticated modern man is therefore in danger of succumbing to a degradation that primitive man must have learned, after many lapses, to guard against; the threat of losing his humanity by giving precedence to his animal self and his nonhuman character over the social ego and the ideal super ego that have transmuted this original inheritance.

Yet, however far man goes in his self-dramatisation and self-transformation, he can never leave the animal behind. The blind surge and push of all organic creation bottoms his unique creative activities: his most ideal aspirations still rest on his eating and mating and seeking food and fending off dangers, as other animals do; and some measure of animal activity and animal delight belongs to his deepest humanity. Even at the Day of Judgment, Thomas Aquinas reasoned, the body would be necessary; and there is no detachment, no transcendence, that does not rest on the use of man's animal resources in ways no other animal has dreamed of.

Now that man understands these primordial connections, he must acknowledge his old debt to his partners throughout the whole range of organic creation, his constant dependence upon their activities, and not least his link with his own original nature. Though he is now the dominant species, his fate is still bound up with the prosperity of all forms of life; and he carries his own animal organs and his natural history into every ideal future that he projects. They, too, partake of the divine impetus and approach the divine goal.

Archaic Man

I

We have arrived at a truism that has so far been forgotten it has the air of a paradox: the need to become human is man's first need, and perhaps it remains his deepest one. Nature provides the materials for this change, but man himself must effect it. In essence, it rests on a constant effort at self-identification, self-affirmation, self-discipline, and self-development: if much of this is routinised and imposed by the inherited culture pattern, it still was the outcome, in the first place, of wilful effort. By becoming human, man exchanges the stable natural self, native to each biological species, for a countless multitude of possible selves, moulded for the working out of a special drama and plot he himself helps to create.

But the 'human' has never so far been the generically human: the image man coins in one culture does not yet pass as human legal tender, without a heavy discount, in other cultures. Possibly the transition from animal nature to human culture was made at different places, at different times, by stocks with somewhat different anthropoid ancestors, even if stemming from some common unspecialised line. So few in numbers were these hominids at the beginning, so widely sundered by oceans and deserts and mountains, that they separated out, in the course of their long development, into five or six major continental groups, showing patent physiological differences, beginning with differences in skin colour, as between black, brown, tan, ivory, pink, and running through a gamut of other differences, such as blood types, immunities to disease, and many minor differences in anatomy. But by two marks, one biological, one social, all men proclaim themselves members of a single species: they can mate and produce equally fertile offspring; and they can communicate by speech.

These separating qualities, deepened in isolation by the effects of climate, vegetation, food, and occupational specialisations, laid a basis for further cultural differences. Each group tended to conceive its own type, with its own characteristic expressions and projections, as the truly human one, when it encountered the members of another race; and so, too, each community, in its isolation, looked upon its own culture as in some 'sense more central than other cultures. This only means that in origin man's meaningful and valuable life was attached to a small group. 'Humanity,' as an open group that embraces all groups, did not exist even as a concept, probably, until the coming of the great culturally intermixed empires. Stoicism was its first great philosophic expression. Up to now it is still only an idea, though that idea approaches the moment of realisation.

For the greater part of human history, then, and surely for all prehistory, the differentiating and isolating elements in culture have outweighed the pressures and aspirations that made for unity. Not that marginal occasions for intermingling and borrowing were lacking: migration, marriage outside the local community, trade in special commodities, eventually travel and military conquest, all brought about some measure of cultural interchange and assimilation. But on the whole, the specific processes that served as agents in man's emergence for long remained localised and particularised: all the greater as achievements because they were the product of petty communities, limited in resources and manpower.

In this respect, early human groupings probably showed the same 'territorial behaviour' that biologists have lately discovered in many other species: a tendency associated with mating and the nurture of offspring to establish a delimited habitat, a home base, defended against the intrusion of outsiders, particularly outsiders of their own species. Within the claimed area, a local way of life would flourish, based on a local food supply, local sexual customs, local gods, a way confirmed in all its peculiarity by means of a local dialect and language, usually as unintelligible as a family joke to outlanders in the next valley. Secure in their specific human pattern, many groups must have largely contented themselves with that feat: to pass on that achievement seemed more important than to carry it any further. There are parts of the South, in the United States, where—it used to be sardonically remarked—merely 'being white' constituted a lifetime's occupation. So there were long stretches of the human past when merely being human was enough to exhaust the efforts of the group.

In regions where there were plenty of fruits and nuts, this early period of arriving at the human estate may well have been one of leisure and plenty. Hesiod, in his *Works and Days*, pictured that golden age when men 'feasted gaily, undarkened by sufferings' and 'died as if falling asleep, and all good things were theirs.' That haunting image of a period before the curse of organised work and systematic butchery had descended on man may be less of a fond illusion than scholars once thought. The recurrent hardships of the glacial periods, which accompanied the early development of man, doubtless brought forth every form of skill and cunning to aid his survival. But the interglacial periods may have been relatively idyllic periods of ease and abundance; and the legend of a golden age is perhaps an authentic folk memory of a breathing spell in the midst of tropical luxuriance.

From the beginning, at all events, there are two sides to man's life, the Promethean and the Orphic, the technical and the artistic, the constructive and the expressive: one mainly a struggle with the environment, the other an ideal expression and enjoyment of his own nature. These may even correspond in some degree to the rhythm of change, between a hostile marginal habitat, which called for external mastery as the price of survival, and a soft environment, which permitted playful experiments and rewarded them with further self-development.

uses word probably A lot (Dose nt know for sure)

2

There came a moment, probably after the lower palaeolithic period and almost certainly before the neolithic, when not only had the change from animal to man reached the point of no return, but when all the prime inventions necessary to human development had been made: language, the expressive arts, morality, the use of fire and edged tools, and a body of traditional knowledge, sufficient not only to ensure physical survival but social continuity. Man had transformed himself into a creature concerned, not only with the perpetuation of his species, but with development of the good, the true, the beautiful, and the useful, as the capital instruments in his own self-transformation, and as the further by-products of that transformation.

What was incoherent, confused, ferocious, irrational, regressive, was never entirely sloughed off, but it ceased, except in moments of disintegration, to threaten man: he had achieved the means of making and remaking himself. If we call this creature 'primitive man,' the adjective is less significant than the noun: though he had still much to learn, he had acquired something infinitely precious: the method that made learning possible, and that further made it feasible to retain and pass on to those unborn what he had learned. Even before the great neolithic revolution, man had probably, as Carl Sauer and others have shown reason to believe, achieved settled communities, living on planted tubers and shell-fish, with some of the continuities and domesticities that go with such a life.

Man cannot help leaving his imprint wherever he goes; but at the beginning, the impression he made on himself was perhaps greater than that he made on his environment. This changed when he made the great technical improvement of domestication, which we associate with the selection and cultivation of plants, and presently with the planting of crops in permanently cleared and cultivated fields. The invention of agriculture wrought a further change in man's self-culture; for domestication is a process of gentling and nurturing and breeding that demands selective care and forethought. In every part of this process woman's needs, woman's solicitudes, woman's intimacy with the processes of growth, woman's capacity for tenderness and love, played a dominating part.

As long as the old roving life prevailed, her place was neces-sarily a subordinate one: man's hunting prowess committed the group to a life almost as wild and mobile as the great herds of buffalo or deer that supplied his food. Hunting in packs for big game, like the hairy mammoth, palaeolithic hunters perhaps de-veloped habits of disciplined co-operation and physical courage that the older, pick-me-up ways of the food gatherers had not demanded: with this went doubtless the special masculine traits, long accounted virtues, the capacity to shed blood, to commit acts of violence. Even after the last glacial period, some of these brutal necessities may have left their mark upon the community, passing from the hunter to the herdsman, whose cold-blooded butchery indeed contrasts unfavourably with the more venturesome slayings of the hunter.

But at a critical moment a technical and social revolution took place, roughly some eight or ten thousand years ago. Like most human changes, its foundations were probably laid in an earlier period of partial cultivation; and in calling this new age the neolithic period, anthropologists clung to an old habit of over-weighting the importance of durable physical relics. But though there was a marked advance in technical skill, in the passage from flaked tools and weapons to the ground and polished tools of the new economy, the profounder change was in most respects independent of these mechanical improvements: it rested on an insight into living processes: the selection and cultivation of plants, in particular the pulses and the hard grains, millet, wheat, barley, rice.

This domestication of plants seems largely woman's work: instead of taking life, like the hunter, she nurtured it in the earth, as she nurtured it in her own womb. With the planting of crops, man had for the first time a secure food supply from year to year that depended upon his own efforts more than upon luck and magic. With this came hearth and home: a permanent habitation and a regular habit of life, favourable to further nurture. Though the later domestication of animals encouraged nomadry again, in search of green pastures, the domestication of plants brought human settlement. With this, human life had a visible continuity in space and time that it had hitherto lacked: such a stabilised group of families living in villages provided by their common efforts not only a more secure supply of food, but better facilities for reproduction and the protective oversight and varied nurture of the young.

Possibly domestication had side effects that were as important for man's development as more direct and visible influences. Did woman's selective knowledge in breeding plants extend, during this period of consciously directing the reproductive processes, to the human species, too? To hazard even a guess would be to plunge again into the realm of myth. But there is modern physiological evidence to indicate that improvements in nutrition hasten the state of puberty and promote fertility: so that the quantitative increase of food in early neolithic times may have acted as a double stimulus upon population increase. So, too, we know that domestication tends, in other animals, to make reproduction a year-round function instead of a sharply seasonal one associated with a spring rutting period. Man's ancient ties to organic vernal changes are of course still visible: but his susceptibility to sexual impulses at all times of the year, his desire for sexual contact out of all relation to the need for offspring, may have grown with his own domestication; and this general expansion of the erotic impulse was perhaps not the least important aspect of the neolithic revolution, energising his imagination and expanding the realm of sublimated sexuality, in art and ritual.

From the limited nature of his food supply and his technical equipment, even after the domestication of plants had been accomplished, we know that early man first emerged in very small communities, and the total population of all these communities must have been on the same order as the population of the North American continent when Western man discovered it: sparse and scattered. Agriculture made it possible for people to live generation after generation in little hamlets or villages; and as the food supply expanded, more such settlements must have come into existence, for with the increase of the population fresh land would be put under cultivation. Thus man became not only human but domesticated in an intimate, face-to-face environment, the world of the primary community: the family, the tribe, the clan, the village, the neighbourhood. The visible presence of kinsmen and neighbours, friendly, responsive people, sharing the common life: the security of a place of limited dimensions, easily explored, full of concrete satisfactions, meaningful sights and sounds and smells, familiar landmarks—all this established a common human realm, midway between man's larger natural habitat and his symbolic abstractions: a realm where nature was humanised, and man was naturalised, for the environment reflected his own intentions and purposes, even as it preserved his memories and encouraged his hopes. To preserve that balance was the better part of wisdom: hence the fear of the nontraditional, the unaccustomed, the strange, the foreign: hence, too, the love of the accepted, the conventional, the often repeated, the proved: the veneration for ancestral ways. 'This is done.' 'That is not done.' Food, marriage, child care, all the events of life, indeed, fall under these customary canons of judgment. Unless one 'belongs' one does not exist.

In this domestic village culture, there is for every occasion of life a bit of proverbial wisdom that clinches decision, guides action. In that security and inward peace, the people of the village could look across the river at another community, as Lao-tse observed, and never have the impulse to cross it. This early life was not free from severe disappointments, painful ordeals and even ordinary psychal tensions: if it were, it would be hard to account for the early invention of beer and wine, which anaesthetise anxiety, lift the depressed heart, soften pain. But compared to the repressions and conflicts that were to develop presently in the next stage of man's emergence, this phase had an almost idyllic calm. The rituals of seeding and planting and harvest enveloped human growth, though often mingled with darker rites of blood sacrifice. Feasts and festivals, crop tending and lovemaking, followed the cycle of the seasons. The Corn Goddess flourished. Economically, archaic society remains contentedly at the level of subsistence, rarely willing, while true to its own principles, to make the concentrated collective effort needed to produce a higher output. All the more, then, it welcomes the seasons of plenitude that soften its habitual penury: lucky catches, windfalls, or the occasional golden harvests that make festal leisure possible. What extra wealth he possesses archaic man reserves for the great punctuation marks of life: birth, marriage, death.

In stressing the role of memory, habit, and tradition in primitive life, we have tended, during the last century, to treat the sense of the future as an entirely modern contribution. But to do this is somewhat to falsify both the facts of history and the nature of man. Human society, from the very beginning, shows plenty of forethought and anticipation, which reach well beyond the widespread animal tendency to put by food to tide over the winter: the prehistoric practice of ceremonious burial certainly concerns the future; and all sorts of providential and forward-looking acts, the planting and guarding of trees, the planning and building of permanent stone structures, show a design, not just to meet immediate needs, but to serve future occasions. Every monument, be it only a cairn or a sacred stone, is an admonition and a pledge to one's descendants. Just as the ability to take the future into account in any immediate judgment is one of the signs, psychologists tell us, of both intelligence and moral responsibility, so a mixture of anxiety and providence has been a constant mark of human development.

In early society the long future, as distinct from the day-to-day and generation-to-generation span, was left to the gods: man lacked both the intellectual and the physical powers to project his own plans over a millennial period, or to ordain wholesale social transformations that would involve every institution of society. But the change from a mainly backward-looking attitude to a forward-looking attitude is one only of emphasis: both were present, it would seem, in the earliest cultures, and both must be active if our present culture is to endure. 'Man looks before and after,' and *plans* 'for what is not.'

3

We have followed man's transformation back to its sources, hidden in time, much of it open only to the imagination. But beneath the visible surface of history runs an underground river carried forward from neolithic times, and still bearing the silt of even earlier cultures. Following André Varagnac, I shall call this 'archaic culture.' This archaic tradition, for all its many primitive characteristics, is not to be confused with the cultures of primitive peoples that survive today, though they have many common features. Our surviving primitives, through their long-introverted development, have achieved a degree of complexity and sophistication that often approaches decadence—as in the tribe that has surrounded canoe building with so many lethal taboos that they no longer dare build their canoes.

Archaic man took form in the neolithic village; and the attributes of his culture, still alive in custom down to the end of the nineteenth century, are as widely distributed as agriculture itself. Even today some four-fifths of mankind still live in physical conditions approximating those of a neolithic village.

This communal archaic life is earthbound; its gods are the gods of vegetation; its whole routine of existence is associated with the cycle of the seasons, with the planting and harvesting of crops, with the mating of animals and the marriage of men and women. Having reached the level of skill and knowledge achieved by neolithic agriculture, the main effort of archaic man is to preserve the equilibrium of that life: he works hard enough to earn his food and lay by a surplus, if possible, for the next year; but he is not consumed by the need to pour into his working life, into mere productivity, the energy that should go into sexual play or reproduction, into games and rituals, into building and decoration. Down to our day, if Raymond Pearl's figures are correct, even American farmers, whose life has long been divorced from archaic rituals, still engage more often in sexual intercourse than their urban contemporaries.

The social nucleus of archaic life is the family. The household hearth is its altar, and the continuity of its life, through the house, the land, the children, the bounded fields, the animals and crops, is doubly assured by the handing on of the whole store of knowledge and precept from parent to child, from master to helper, from the old to the young. No small part of this lore is, when scientifically judged, fanciful and superstitious: ancient taboos, magical practices, mythical projections go along with its soundest empirical observations. But so close is this whole culture to the demands of life and the requirements for human nurture that it has met the test of reality—at least by the criterion of survival—

longer than any other culture. Where its precepts are followed, it brings forth crops, arts, crafts, and, above all, men and women, regenerating the land itself, renewing the culture, and maintaining a sound human level.

Archaic man is the conservator of life: he guards the future by holding tight to the past and, above all, to his ancestors. Both in religious cult and in the looser form of general tradition, he worships his ancestors and seeks their guidance when he is confronted by life's situations, on the sound supposition that the same difficulties must have occurred before. He does not for a moment imagine that the wisdom of the race is embodied in the experience of a single lifetime, still less that his own individual fragment of experience would be sufficient to keep him straight. Archaic man, flinching from the new and the untried, is happy to live in the fashion of his forebears, to maintain the level they had reached, to pass on to his children, unimpaired, the heritage his parents passed on to him. Hence his respect for age; for only the old have lived long enough to take in the whole heritage and to hand it on. The wisdom of the Elders binds the present to the past and so prevents the future from falling short of the past. In case of conflict or doubt, it is in the council of the Elders that the living past speaks and lays down, with the least necessary alteration, the 'eternal' way. Custom and law, education and work, government and morality, are not separate departments of life: they are aspects of the whole—intuitively grasped because vividly lived—and only within this whole has each separate life its significance.

All the elements in this archaic life are part of a carefully ordered collective ritual that punctuates not merely man's works and days, but the stages of life. In this existence, the competitive spirit plays hardly any part, except perhaps in games and sexual rivalry: only what can be shared, what can be handed on to one's family or neighbour, deserves to be cherished. So deeply are habit and custom internalised that they become second nature. But the repetition is not compulsive and uniform: in every act, there is some measure of freedom, some play for individuality. One sees this objectively in the archaic arts, pottery, weaving, basket-making, carving and even metalworking. Though the work itself is repetitive, and the general form is that of a particular village or the region, there remains a place for the personal touch, for the cherished accident (as in pottery glazes) that keeps any two products of handicraft from being absolutely uniform. What holds for useful products holds even more for art. Archaic myths and fairy stories and ballads spread from one land to another; but each version is the same with variations. Without this element of spontaneity and resilience archaic culture would not perhaps have had sufficient vitality to survive.

In archaic tradition, the land and the primeval occupations take a hold on the human spirit that is still unbroken. The land itself ceases to be mere territory, staked out against the intrusion of other creatures, though it remains that, too: it becomes a repository of sentiment, swarming with memories and projects: the place where one's ancestors are buried, whose paths were worn by their feet, whose trees were planted by their hands, whose stones were formed into walls and buildings by their labours, the place whose perpetual renewal or restoration forms the best part of the present generation's labours.

If this archaic environment was limited, it was cut to man's size and within his grasp. Its very restrictions increased his own sense of adequacy. This contrasts with our own age, whose vast expansion in every direction makes the individual feel ever more insignificant.

Though the words blood and soil have been degraded in our time by degraded men, their concrete realities pervade the archaic tradition and come down to us today even in the inflated stereotypes of patriotism and nationalism. Herodotus reports that the Cimmerians, who could have saved themselves from the invading Scythians by fleeing and finding new territory, decided instead to make a stand and be buried in their fatherland. Such an honourable attitude of piety toward the place of one's birth and nurture threads through the archaic record. Unfortunately, the loyalties of the archaic community were passed on to civilisation mainly through the collective rites of war, with the creation of a special caste, exempt from labour but inured to danger and bellicose sacrifice.

By the same token, though the basic form of work in archaic culture is agriculture, the other primitive occupations, hunting, fishing, boating, woodcutting, herding, mining, weave themselves into the archaic fabric, producing modifications in human character, and accenting its individuality in special occupational roles. Through these occupations, even earlier traits and rituals enter the mainstream of archaic culture: the prowess, the risk-taking, the playful gambling of the hunter, for example, or the dogged courage and skill of the miner, whose arts go back to the palaeolithic period. Through these occupations a variety of environments with their multifold suggestions and promptings helped further to shape the human spirit. Underneath later sublimations all these individualised primitive types remain, like the grain of the wood under paint or varnish.

The ancestors, the burgeoning family, and the household gods, the holy ritual, the cycle of vegetation and reproduction—these constitute the realities of archaic culture. A collective routine devoted to the nourishment and enhancement of every aspect of life; so that no part of human existence grew out of proportion to the other parts. All the goods of this life, however, fell within the charmed circle of the small community; and men paid a price for this security. The enclosed community produced the enclosed personality, and vice versa. Kindness was a quality one showed to the kinsman, and then by extension to the neighbour: truth, honesty, friendliness, forbearance, abstention from rape or murder, applied only to those within the community, not to those outside. This long apprenticeship in isolation left its mark, and even now tends to thwart a wider unity. We still associate stability and security with enclosure, and before the prospect of an open world we timidly shrink back with a kind of agoraphobia. Yet so central has this archaic culture been, so successful in providing norms for human development, that it has preserved itself under successive waves of civilisation, right down to the present. In other forms than those created in neolithic times, its I-and-thou relationship must be carried into every wider community, if that community is to endure.

Though it is true that archaic culture lives to itself and lives for itself, we may easily overstress this fact, and forget that by the very diversity of human needs this insulation was far from complete. Slowly, the advances made at later stages of human development infiltrated archaic culture. It is not from the neolithic village that the almanac and the laws of private property come: it is not from the cult of the household gods that the village temple or church, attached to a prophetic tradition that claims universal assent, arises. Some of the ballads that seem the immemorial possession of a folk were produced in a distant royal court, just as many of the plants in field and orchard are the exotic booty of distant conquests or explorations, undertaken by more ambitious or envious people. These additions and accretions seep in from without and slowly become assimilated by the archaic culture. If archaic cultures become somewhat 'civilised' the reverse process also takes place: the intruding civilisation or religion becomes 'paganised' in equal degree. No foreign form is used by archaic culture until it has, as it were, rotted and become part of the organic cultural compost.

4

The archaic tradition has maintained its hold, with varying degrees of tenacity, in every part of the world right down to our own time: least perhaps in North America, and most, it seems likely, in India and China. All through Europe, its relics remain in pagan festivals like Midsummer Eve and Carnival, in the persistence of folklore and sympathetic magic, in superstitions about lucky days and lucky numbers, which have defied generations of rational education.

But perhaps the deepest effect of archaic tradition was the operation of taboo: a universal trait that first drew the traveller's attention in Polynesia. Taboo affixes to this or that object or act an absolute prohibition: the canoe used by men must not be entered by women, or one who has touched the dead must purify himself before having contact with the living. Few taboos, even the almost world-wide one against incest, are more than partly rational: but the absolute inhibition invoked by the taboo was one of the great safeguards man invented against mischievous self-induced images and unconscious powers that might overwhelm him. As with a well-trained army, the generalised habit of obedience, the respect for inviolate limits, was more important than the particular occasion that brought it forth.

Precisely because taboo carries no practical or reasonable sanction, it established a strict habit of self-control. Where the young have neither veneration for their elders nor respect for taboo—where in fact they have grown up completely outside the circle of archaic culture—they easily express themselves in acts of juvenile delinquency, for whatever senseless violent impulse may seize them passes directly into action. No sacred inhibition, no sense of awful limits and bounds, now stands in the way of rape, torture, murder. And what began in our time as contempt for the ancestor now widens into a contempt for posterity. Against the fatal consequence of such a change, so horrifying in its possibilities to an age that has conjured up the hydrogen bomb, the archaic culture long guarded the human race.

Archaic life, in its time-weathered, moss-covered forms, still

charms us and calls to us. When we are tired of facing the complications of civilisation, when disease has lowered our vitality
and mental conflicts have disrupted our social relations, we turn
back to some little village, almost lost to sight under the trees or
barely visible along the shore. There we feel at one both with
external nature and our own deepest selves : 'restored' as we say.
Do we ever indeed feel more fully satisfied with the passing
moment than when we go berry picking or mushroom hunting,
like dawn-man, or when we idly gather sandworn stones and
shells and driftwood along a beach? The joy of pure being : life
concentrated and consummated in the moment. Then work is
play again, and living itself no longer a problem. Jean-Jacques
Rousseau could not guess it; but the whole rationale of romanticism was an attempt to get back to the ancestral norms of Stone
Age culture.

In the midst of this satisfying milieu, so deeply harmonious
with our nature that we forget how much of it was painfully
acquired before it became natural, we ask ourselves why we
should ever leave it for a more complex, more unstable, more
anxious, certainly less harmonious existence. The answer to that
question, once we dare to ask it, is not so simple as it seems;
for it summons to the bar of rational judgment the whole development of civilisation. That is the question Herman Melville
asked himself in the midst of his Polynesian paradise among the
Typees. 'Civilisation does not engross all the virtues of humanity
. . . .' he observed. 'They flourish in greater abundance and
attain greater strength among many barbarous peoples.' Yet at
the first chance that offered Melville left this paradise behind him.
So it was with man himself, if we except those scattered tribal
communities that continued to exist in their separateness—more
than six hundred and fifty of them—down to our own era.

Civilised Man

I

At a late moment in man's emergence, he left behind the securities and intimacies and solidarities of tribal existence: what remained of archaic society served as the roadbed and right of way for the more mobile forms of civilisation. At this point an audacious minority, in a handful of specially situated communities, made a daring thrust in a new direction: the experiment of civilisation. With that step, the past ceases to be represented by dim camp-sites and scattered implements. We find buried cities, temples, all manner of works of art: presently, we come upon hieroglyphs and well-preserved records. But though all these data tell us much about what happened between the fourth millennium before Christ and the first, they do not tell why it happened. Here again we must fashion a myth to make the whole process a little more intelligible.

As we have seen, the circumscribed world of the village and the tribe did not cease to exist. All over the earth there are still little pools of humanity that did not submit to the broad collective discipline of civilisation. Even if a fresh trickle of ideas or tools slowly permeated their folkways, or sometimes revolutionised them, as the horse altered the activities of the Plains Indians, they mostly changed so slowly that when they were discovered by European explorers in the sixteenth century, they were still living the same kind of lives that civilised people had abandoned, at least in cities, from a thousand to five thousand years before. Some of these tribal groups, like the Bushmen of Australia, seem to have been shut off from the rest of mankind almost as completely as the marsupials who were isolated when the land bridge between Australia and Asia disappeared: some, like the Hottentots in Africa, have anatomical characteristics, like extra-fat buttocks, which recall stone images that date back twenty or thirty thousand years earlier.

The wide range of variations in the tribal patterns of culture has fascinated modern anthropologists: since Denis Diderot, in the eighteenth century, it has become fashionable, indeed, to hold that there are no universal culture traits, outside the bare elements of culture themselves: or at all events, that there is no common standard of values, and no line of human advance, except the doubtful one toward mere quantitative increase or complexity. In short, each culture seems a world in itself and must be taken on its own terms. This mode of judgment, in attempting to atone for the pride and ruthlessness of the conquering civilisations, overlooks the weakness of these ingrown communities: precisely the fact that they were ingrown. However harsh may be one's criticisms of civilisation, it at least moved in the direction of widening the human circle, and in time produced personalities and ideas that transcended its own limited assumptions.

In general, isolated tribal communities preferred to develop the goods in their private possession rather than to throw their gifts freely into the common stock, in which other communities might share. But they paid a price for 'keeping themselves to themselves': they limited the possibilities of a larger human growth. Gray's *Elegy Written in a Country Churchyard*, calling to mind the potential Miltons and Hampdens who had no incentive to show their mettle in their village environment, could be repeated a thousand times in every tribal culture. Even such deep life-wisdom as they may have come by rarely passed beyond the local circle until some wandering representative of civilisation opened it.

That inertia, that lethargy, that collective self-absorption, were not of course confined to tribal communities: one finds them as limiting, if not pathological, traits in all communities. On the eve of the vast changes that the new scientific method brought to Western Europe, did not Philip II of Spain class innovators and inventors with heretics: dangerous people all? Did not even Montaigne, that free mind, declare that it was better to stand any amount of injustice than to tamper with ancestral institutions that still continue to function?

2

How then did civilisation come about? What process brought scores and hundreds of dispersed villages together into the political organisation we now call the state? How did some of these villages increase in size and social complexity till they became a new kind of human settlement, the city, with its mixture of breeds, talents, and occupations, its divisions of labour, its variety of choices and its striking aesthetic forms? By what inner change did immemorial custom become written law, did the old village rituals become drama, and magical practices turn into an organised and unified religious cult, built upon cosmic myths that open up vast perspectives of time, space, power? Why, in short, has a growing portion of mankind, for the last four or five thousand years, committed itself to civilisation—or, like folk society, let itself be drawn along in its wake?

Properly, we reject the eighteenth-century myth of the social contract, in which each member of the community gave up his original autonomy and freedom for the over-all protection of life and property that came with organised government. But at the core of this myth lies a kernel of truth: the institutions of civilisation were the outcome of deliberate invention and conscious choice: indeed, they seem part of a general growth of self-consciousness, individual and collective. Behind them is no mere automatic accretion, but a mighty effort of collective will. With this new consciousness went something that seems relatively absent from the stable, well-integrated culture of simpler societies: internal struggle, competition, tension, conflict.

Civilisation brought a new kind of unity based on division and specialisation: a new uniformity imposed by deliberate repression: a new agreement that sprang out of a partial reconciliation of opposites, not, as in primitive society, out of ancestral unanimity, born of a common understanding as to the ultimate nature and purpose of life. If archaic culture rests on an internalised law and order, hardly ever consciously formulated, civilisation rests on an externalised law and order, more far-reaching than man had ever established before, binding together with explicit rules and regulations dissimilar communities and varied local customs.

Economically, the new order was based largely on the forcible exploitation of cultivators and artisans by an armed and ever-threatening minority: mobile intruders or heavily entrenched lords of the land. For civilisation brought about the equation of human life with property and power; indeed, property and power became more dear than life. Labour ceased to be a shared communal function: it became degraded into a purchasable commodity, bought and sold in the market place: even sexual 'service' could be bought. This systematic subordination of life to its mechanical and legal agents existed at the beginning of civilisation and still haunts every existing society; at bottom, the goods of civilisation have been achieved and preserved—and this is a crowning contradiction—largely by methodical compulsion and regimentation, backed by a flourish of force. In that sense, civilisation is one long affront to human dignity.

The general conditions for this transformation have now become fairly clear, though the details differ widely from region to region. Between 7000 and 2000 B.C. a series of great technical advances were made on a wide front, from Egypt to China: beginning with the domestication of plants, and furthered by the taming of cattle and beasts of burden. Above all, the cultivation of the hard grains, on fertile irrigable land, made it possible to nourish large populations in a small territory: these crops, which could be held over from the fat years to the lean years, produced security and continuity and settlement on a scale that had never been possible before. The bronze age, with its costly weapons and chariots, which gave a monopoly of power to their possessors, furthered centralised political control; while the succeeding iron age cheapened all the new facilities for conquering nature and enslaving men.

Once the ox and the plough were introduced, the rich heavy soils of the river valleys, the most open routes of communication and transport, could be cultivated. With a large supply of surplus labour available, the swift technical advances in water control— canals, irrigation, ditches, embankments, even the turning of the course of rivers, as in Mesopotamia—became possible. With these collective improvements the whole river valley became an economic and political unit. These physical changes were accompanied by comparable political and social inventions: for civilisation brought about a double transformaton of man. On one hand it developed in the pharaoh or ruler, the autonomous personality; and on the other, by the subdivision of labour and the specialisation of work, it produced the submissive, if not servile *Teilmensch*, or divided man, who has lost his primitive wholeness without yet gaining the new attribute of his ruler: autonomy.

Let us deal with the second transformation first. In the simple structure of primitive society, roles and occupational activities were largely interchangeable: apart from the biological specialisation of sex, each member, in the appropriate situation, could play any role that any other member could play. As the cycle of the year revolved, as the phases of life unfolded, so did the works and duties of the members of the community. The fact that one did a

job well did not condemn one to performing it for a whole lifetime, except perhaps in the earliest type of specialist, the shaman
or priest.

Civilisation, in contrast, created occupational groups with permanent fixed roles: soldiers, merchants, scholars, scribes, ad-
ministrators. In numbers that no earlier culture could have
supported, these specialised groups practised their callings, with
mechanical efficiency and *expertise*. From now on, right down to
our own day, '*life*' means essentially working life, withdrawn
from the general interests of the rural household—especially for
the male members of the urban community. Though until modern
times these specialised callings probably never constituted more
than a small fraction of the total population—at most possibly
ten per cent—their specialised efficiency and their conscientious
dedication to work set the mode for 'civilised' life. The gods themselves reflected the principle of specialisation: each had his prescribed sphere and role, but none, not even Atum or Marduk,
exercised all the functions of deity.

By thus building a corporate society, composed of a multitude
of castes, professions, guilds, associations, civilised man lost the
neighbourly unison of the village community, in which work and
play and family and religion were closely intermingled: above all
he lost its single-mindedness. But he gained detachment and
diversity; and the partial selves that he created revealed, long
before he invented specialised machines, the possibilities of a
limited mechanical order. Traditionally it takes nine tailors to
make a man: but Charles Fourier was not far from wrong when
he declared that it took 1,760 partial men (specialists) to make a
man. But it is only in the mind that such a gargantuan creature
could exist.

Each civilised group cultivated interests, routines, 'mysteries,'
which kept it from identifying its life with that of the whole
society. The very fact that this complex society was no longer
the visible community of the village encouraged a certain degree
of withdrawal and disaffection. In the act of entering their special
association, its members left behind—and indeed deliberately excluded—other rival organs. Each occupation had its rites of
initiation and its professional secrets. At its highest levels, it
operated as a conspiracy to pre-empt for the smaller group an
undue share of the goods of the larger community. The social
division of classes, based on private property, and the economic
division of occupations, based on technical specialisation, thus

tended to work toward the same general result: they erected a partial self that put its own specialised competence above the whole self, and a partial community (the 'insiders') that placed its own advantage above that of the whole community.

At first the gain to the prospering individual seemed indisputable. Civilised man, at an early stage, achieved a degree of autonomy, independence, self-consciousness—and therewith choice —that was unknown in primitive society. Each of the heroes in the *Iliad* was a highly individualised character in his own right, not just an undifferentiated Greek or Trojan. But as the outcome of this process, civilised man became, as we say, selfish: he no longer identified his personal concerns with the health and the prosperity of the group. In sinking into a bigger community whose membership he could never know intimately or even fully conceive in its concrete variety, civilised man took advantage of this relative anonymity. He was tempted to appropriate for himself what once belonged to the entire society. 'I and mine' now counted for more than 'We and ours.' Where the standards of civilisation remain uppermost, these generalisations still hold.

3

The other transformation of civilised man moved precisely in the opposite direction: toward the elevation of a unique personality, possessing powers uncircumscribed by the usages of society. This change at first came about through the very complexity of the new river civilisations, with their need to control the flow of water, to mark boundaries when effaced by flood, to impose communal labour and to collect taxes, to supervise trade, codify laws, guard frontiers. In this new order, the capital city was the social agent of unification; and within that city, the palace and temple were the seats of concentrated power and bureaucratic administration. Within the palace and temple one figure stood supreme: the deified ruler. In him alone man first achieved individuality.

At the top of the political and social pyramid towered the absolute monarch. He replaced the archaic council of elders, the local assembly of free—but custom-bound—men. This elevation of a single ruler took place, Henri Frankfort has told us, in times of emergency, when quick decisions had to be made. The king alone, by literally personifying society, could escape from the

fetters of local custom and routine, or proverbial wisdom that
no longer was in touch with new realities. The royal fiat gave to
the actions of society, too long fettered by precedent and collective inertia, the attributes of an integrated person : freedom,
the power of detached judgment and intelligent choice, a swift,
unified response. Herodotus long ago made the same observation :
picturing the lawlessness and confusion among the Medes, he told
how Deioces, a man of mark in his own village, rose to supreme
rulership by applying himself to the practice of justice. Such a
concentration of power and responsibility must have occurred in
many areas, as society became more complex and unexpected
crises called for new measures. At such moments the decisive
change from a dispersed village culture to centralised urban control probably took place—though historically it often relapsed,
under pressure, into a more localised feudal kind of authority.

But the point to note is that, in both government and religion,
the absolute ruler first developed an autonomous personality,
completely detached from its social envelope : for both good and
bad a law unto himself. While the subdivision of labour diffused
itself rapidly through society, the development of the complete
autonomous person has remained a rare occurrence throughout
human history. If at a relatively early date the common man
shared his divine ruler's claims to immortality, it is only after
thousands of years that other attributes of royalty have been,
reluctantly and grudgingly, passed on to the community as a
whole, and treated as a natural attribute of man.

The prime mark of civilisation, then, is the bringing together of
larger bodies of men, by means of technical agents, symbolic
abstractions, and centralised political authority, into a greater
community of purpose than had ever existed before. Written
records and the practice of record keeping, written legends and
myths, the common calendar, the common monetary unit, the
common law, the common utilities, the common meeting place,
capable of uniting tens of thousands of people into a cohesive
organisation, were all immense achievements. By these agents of a
common order and a common life mankind still continues to live.
In so far as it has made possible this enlargement of the human
circle, civilisation justifies, in no little measure, its heavy exactions.

But unfortunately this transformation of man has an ugly side :
civilised man, if more law-abiding, is likewise more calculating :
if he is more skilful and intelligent, he is more selfish. If he is
stirred by ambitions and desires that were foreign to the modest

expectations of archaic culture, he is also subject to perverse derangements and criminal insubordinations: as a result, civilisation has often brought about gigantic miscarriages of life, in bestialities and butcheries that simpler communities lack the animus as well as the power to inflict.

Something intimate and indubitably precious was lost in the transition to civilisation, or almost lost. But the decrease in depth was partly offset by a gain in breadth: under the rule of a common law and a common way of life, a much larger body of people met and mingled. Civilisation at least overcame the insularity and isolation of primitive rural society.

For all its internal contradictions, the development of civilisation brought real goods no primitive society could show. By the sheer weight of numbers, civilisation gave its members new social and intellectual advantages. If there is likely to be one person of exceptional ability in every generation, in say ten thousand people, a group of only a thousand people may have to wait many generations before it has the advantage of a superior mind; and that mind, by its very isolation, may find nothing to nourish it. But a hundred thousand people, in Sumer or Akkad, in Athens or Rome, in Peking or Benares, might produce at least fifty good minds in a single lifetime; and these minds, by the very fact of close communication in space and time, would be open to a variety of challenges and stimuli not possible if they appeared alone. So, too, specialisation in trades and occupations, and further refinement of skills, depend upon mere numbers, both to provide the demand and produce the necessary variety of services. Once these conditions obtain, greater productivity will follow, even without mechanical invention.

With exemplary symbolism, the function of the Egyptian creator god, Atum, 'was to bring the world into order and assign places and functions.' There lay the achievement of civilisation: it multiplied power and widened order: visible power in armies and work gangs, visible order in canals, storehouses, cities. The beauty of an ordered life was no small aesthetic triumph. But in this achievement, the repetitive-compulsive note was never entirely absent: regularity, formal discipline, specialised efficiency were purchased only by a willingness to exclude many of the tempting departures that life may spontaneously offer. The holiday functions of life themselves became segregated and specialised, as erotic expression itself did, in the interests of working efficiency and order. That pervasive order has stamped the 'civilised self.'

Though the whole routine of life became more elaborate, civilisation, by its mastery of physical organisation, liberated whole classes from the necessity of breadwinning and permitted them to cultivate their minds, likewise in an orderly fashion. In the city, the economic surplus was funnelled into capital investments no mere primitive culture could afford: temples, palaces, observatories, libraries, courts of justice, came into existence, along with the daily activities that went on within them. If often misused, these institutions ultimately served all men. In the dynamic interplay of social and personal functions life itself became a drama, and the drama in time typified and reflected life. Civilised man, indeed, was 'not himself' outside the city; for without this urban background he faltered in the interpretation of his roles and missed his cues.

In Chaldea and Egypt, the priesthood extended their special power and authority through observation of the skies: they studied the passage of the heavenly bodies and established the solar year. This astronomical measurement brought regularity into life: personal order conformed in some measure to this impersonal (cosmic) order. By synchronising the actions of men with predictable natural cycles and recurrent events, the calendar eventually introduced a seasonable sequence into all activities, beginning with agriculture. In turn, the discipline of astronomy refined the whole process of calculating and counting: the abstractions of number made possible a new kind of symbolism that came in with civilisation: the symbolism of money—and finally the equation of power and wealth with money.

Civilisation replaced a primitive life economy with a money economy, at least in the great urban centres: though the archaic life economy kept a hold over the rural areas, only slightly corroded by the abstract love of gain. In the new urban environment, civilised man was stirred by ambitions and emulations, by anxieties and imaginative projections that man did not know in the archaic period: the voice of Hesiod or Amos, speaking on behalf of archaic man, rose in anxious protest against this new conception of human life.

They had reason for this protest. There was doubtless a certain intensification of life in the great urban centres, among those who had mastered the new procedures of religion and trade and law and administration: but there was also—then as now—a falling off of life, a lowering of values, in the small tributary communities. As society as a whole became more powerful, through organisation, discipline, co-ordination, division of labour, each individual person became enfeebled: he was reduced to a fractional part, and no longer exercised either the understanding or control that was his in a small community: he had become a vicarious participator in the values of the great community. Certainly, the corporate power of civilisation was much greater than man could achieve within the more personal sphere of the village community: was this, perhaps, why he came to value, indeed to worship, his corporate self, in the person of the monarch, as the highest possible good: no less than a god? Both in origin and in modern times, that corporate projection seems to be a compensation for the meagreness of personal existence.

<h2 style="text-align:center">4</h2>

Some of civilisation's imputed benefits may have been challenged by archaic man; he might well have anticipated the disaffected sailor in Melville's *Redburn*, who felt that the only result of 'snivelisation' was to make men snivel. Looking back over the whole development, one may still challenge some of the institutions that have been most rigidly structured into every civilisation, without, like Rousseau, also rejecting the goods that were in fact promoted.

Note the social contradiction. For those who mastered the arts of civilisation, it brought, no doubt, an intensification of life, a heightening of consciousness, a sense of the individual ego combined with a pride in collective achievement that justified the sacrifice it demanded. But those upon whom the sacrifices were imposed formed a majority of the population, and their willingness to submit to this compulsive routine remains, even now, a little mysterious. For one thing, the division of labour closed many doors that were open in a more loosely organised society; and the habit of working day after day at the same task, without any immediate reward, deferring present goods for doubtful future benefits, with the work life itself absorbing energy that might be profitably expended in the offices of love and parenthood—all this is not self-explanatory, still less self-justifying. Though one must allow for the pride and presumption of the scribe, who put his own profession above all others, the early Egyptian *Satire on the Trades* (*circa* 2000 B.C.) utters a judgment on this general depletion of life that remains classic. Yet from the beginning civilisation rested on the depersonalisation of mechanised effort; and cheerful submission to this routine is perhaps the chief mark of civilised man. If no external master exercises this authority, civilised man will impose the pattern on himself, in pursuit of money, prestige, or power.

The repression that Sigmund Freud regarded as a necessary accompaniment of civilisation is indeed a fact: but it is not confined to sexual activities. Rather, it applies to all the autonomous functions, and still more to autonomous expressions. Sex itself has rather a compensatory role: from the orgiastic rituals of early religions to the exploitation of sex for political and commercial purposes in later societies, sexuality serves as counterweight to other forms of denial. Woman, in pursuance of her own biological goals, has always been in some measure opposed to this narrowing scheme of life: in that sense, Meredith's dictum that woman would be the last creature to be civilised by man is profoundly true. When in modern times women claimed the right to take part in all the occupations men practised, they forgot to ask how far these occupations were self-justifying, or what modifications might be made in their compulsive rituals to fit them more closely to the central needs of life. Instead of restoring men to a whole life that fully included woman's own special interests, love, sex, human nurture, the leaders of feminism were too easily content with the half-life men had allotted to themselves.

While the working life of civilised man is itself something of an aberration, in the unconditional submission it exacts, its ambivalent achievements in law and order seem even more open to criticism. By organising the police functions of the state, civilised man increased the internal security of its members, rescuing them from blood feuds, random violence, and unjust deprivation of freedom or property. But the price of peace and security and justice within the state was an extension of insecurity and violence outside the domestic realm.

From the beginning, as Plato long ago observed, war was the natural relation of civilised states to one another. The ultimate irrationality of civilisation was to invent, perfect, and incorporate into the whole structure of civilised life the art of war. For war was not a mere residue of more common primitive forms of aggression, as depicted in the myth of Leviathan. In all its typical aspects, its discipline, its drill, its handling of large masses of men as units, in its destructive assaults *en masse*, in its heroic sacrifices, its final destructions, exterminations, seizures, enslavements, war was rather the special invention of civilisation: its ultimate drama. The final negation that tragically justified all its preparatory negations. The organised army was not merely the instrument but the symbol of civilised power—the first application of technology to politics. Like the genocidal applications of nuclear energy in our time, it effectively undermined the creative achievements of civilisation.

Apart from its more obvious pretexts, the expansion of state power and the seizure of manpower, the possibility of gaining by pillage more than can be won in a short time by toil, war had still another reason for existence: it projected outside the state the internal conflicts that civilisation at once promoted and dractically repressed within the state. While every civilisation released opportunities for human development that were not possible till large groups of men were welded together into great intercommunicating organisations, it likewise compounded explosive forces that repeatedly got beyond control. If organised force brings civilisations into existence, organised force is likewise the agent of disintegration that ultimately brings them to an end.

Aside from playing this sinister part, the institution of war had other unfavourable effects in curtailing the benefits of civilisation: for in time it brought a habit of regimentation into activities that might, under the influence of more healthy human needs, have liberated themselves from routine. Under the general pressure of drill, sharpened by vocational specialisation, civilised man turned himself into a mechanical object, long before he invented any comparable complex and effective nonhuman mechanism. With the development of civilisation, its useful divisions of labour—not necessarily harmful, if kept open and interchangeable—hardened into rigid caste systems. This tendency was pushed to its logical conclusion in the hereditary social castes of India, in turn minutely divided into occupatonal castes, but no civilisation has been free from this kind of caricature of the figure of man. Men made themselves into collective machines thousands of years before they acquired sufficient technical skill to make machines into working counterparts of their collective selves.

Though no human group has yet gone so far as to make the worker caste unfit for reproduction, the actual physiological differences between classes and occupations still leaves a marked trail over their disease and death rate even in progressive countries; and even in relatively dynamic societies, caste lines and relatively small economic and social differences may not be passed over easily: status is often more important than functional capacity.

Thus man, in achieving the docilities and co-operation of civilisation, independently reinvented an institution not found in nature except among creatures who are equally divided and crippled in their nature: the social insects. Now that he must undo this radical error, in order to save himself from his own misguided inventions, it is time to re-examine with a sharper eye other related institutions he has taken too complacently for granted.

5

Slavery, compulsory labour, social regimentation, economic exploitation, and organised warfare: this is the darker side of the 'progress of civilisation.' In modified forms, these negations and repressions are still active today; indeed, while part of the curse of forced labour has been lifted, through the invention of power-driven and automatic machinery, war has taken on an infinitely more destructive form: breaking through all physical barriers and moral restraints, it has turned in our own day into unrestricted genocide, which now threatens all life on this planet.

This was a heavy price to pay for the humanising feats of civilisation: yet all over the world men once paid that price. Though from the very beginning a dominant minority took command of the agents of civilisation and appropriated its goods, the mass of mankind tamely acquiesced in that act.

This whole perversion of the universal goods of civilisation to the interests of a few seems to defy reason and baffle explanation. By what process did the mass of men come to accept it so meekly? The disciplinary rigours, the systematic sacrifices, might all be justified on a shrewd balance of gains and losses, if the resultant goods were evenly distributed over the whole society. But for thousands of years nothing like such a distribution was even thought of, much less attempted. It was only grudgingly that the principle of justice was applied even to particular wrongs, so that the judge would give the verdict, not to those who had bribed him most heavily, but to him who was entitled to it by right: it was a milestone in justice, as Breasted has pointed out, when a judge went so far as to decide a case at law against his own relatives. Slaves and poor men had no rights that their superiors would recognise; and they gain a foothold on the social ladder in one era only to lose it again.

The reason for civilisation's acceptance remains undiscoverable until we allow for the influence of the irrational and the supernatural. Civilisation was made possible by an inner transformation almost too deep for analysis: a transformation that brought into existence two magnified kinds of being, the hero and the god, and combined their functions in the office of kingship. In this change civilised man freed himself partly from his preoccupation with his inner self: he turned increasingly to external objects, detached from bodily feelings: his ideal self was the hero, the person of giant strength, capable of performing mighty feats of prowess, like the labours of Heracles, and his hero god was a Prometheus, who stole fire from heaven for the benefit of man.

The trials that the hero faces are physical trials: the slaying of giants and dragons, the moving of giant stones, the turning of the course of rivers; and it was in such feats that the godlike monarchs of ancient civilisations traditionally excelled. Such a turning toward outward reality may be a historic sign of the integration of the human ego: a prime acknowledgment of everything outside the self that resists it and independently reacts on it. This was the way to further individuation and conscious control over both the outer and the inner world. Certainly the epics of the heroes seem to flourish precisely at this moment of emergence; and in that general change of consciousness even those who were deprived and oppressed have shared—as the exploited factory workers of the nineteenth century shared the belief in mechanical improvement and social progress.

Through the hero and the king, man achieved a more exalted image of himself: a sense of capabilities for action and achievement that he had hardly dreamed of before. We may infer from the appearance of winged creatures in art that the audacious dream of human flight itself took shape at this moment: there is no evidence of it in the representations of the palaeolithic cave man. In the person of the hero, civilised man imposed on himself heavier tasks, demanding longer periods of concentrated effort, than he had ever before undertaken. Relaxation and indulgence, the normal rewards of normal toil, now seemed to him perils rather than attractions. Gilgamesh, in the early Babylonian epic, rejected the love of the goddess, Inanna, but readily slew the bull she sent against him. Odysseus, under Calypso's enchantment, lost his initiative; and Samson, by sinking into the arms of Delilah, was shorn of his physical power. Only by spurning his sexuality, pouring all his energies into work, will the hero have the power to perform these superhuman tasks. The pioneers of civilisation are not at home in woman's world; on their typical adventures they leave her behind. If, like Heracles, they boast of having intercourse with fifty women in one night, that boast itself shows that they confused the mere breaking of records with amorous delight —a further proof of their undeveloped erotic life.

Primitive man was sustained by a sense of union with his world : stones, trees, animals, spirits, people, all spoke to him and responded to him; and he was in them and of them. Civilised man throve on struggle and opposition : he must master or be mastered, and the more formidable the struggle the greater his own sense of life. Dominated by this attitude he punishes himself, as well as those who are the objects of his aggression; and it is in the negative moments of life, in flood, shipwreck, earthquake, fire, or war, that he rises to his highest achievements, while periods of prosperity leave him fat and foolish, without a worthy object that evokes his extraverted powers.

With civilisation, life became something more than a repetitive round of days and acts, however harmonious : it was an *agon*, or contest : a test of strength and skill, in which powers of endurance might be pushed to a heartbreaking point : literally an agony. By projecting the hero and emulating his acts, civilised man lengthened his span of attention and increased the pressure of effort. In his more anxious moments, he ensured beforehand the ability to perform superhuman feats by exercise, self-discipline, drill. But one cannot command these new powers without renunciation : a modicum of death is part of the daily routine : life postponed, life diminished, life denied. The fact is that civilisation, for all its immense increase in vitality, casts contempt on the life-nurturing functions as weak, sentimental, effeminate. In civilised man, sexuality and work reverse their roles : production dominates reproduction, and field and womb alike take second place.

But if the hero symbolised the new processes of civilisation, with their vehement dedication to work, it was through the cult of the gods, subjectively magnified, that civilised man evoked from his own unconscious the powers that helped offset the brutalities and deprivations of his new mode of life. For with civilisation, his animal sources of vitality had been threatened, and his sense of resentment did not quickly disappear. A consciousness of the imminence of death haunts him, perhaps because the larger life civilisation opens has quickened his expectations. Instead of taking death naturally, civilised man fights against it : indeed a good part of his life becomes a dramatisation of this struggle. Sumerian mythology plainly indicates a conviction that the ruling cosmic powers had stacked the cards against man and that death always wins the game. But the Egyptians, through the very elaborateness of their counter-measures—the mummy, the tomb, the pyramid—almost deceived themselves into believing that they had transposed death into life. The ironic price of that triumph was to make death supreme in both realms.

Civilisation accordingly expanded man's fears as well as his knowledge; and in turn the powers of the universe themselves loomed larger as his own corporate powers increased : so the gods became responsible for all the phenomena of earth and heaven, of life and death. Only by submission, indeed, blind obedience, could ordinary men hope to be the beneficiary of their powers. This sense of human inadequacy seems to have enlarged as the community itself, by its expansion and increasing complexity, grew beyond the human scale : even the absolute ruler became as circumscribed in his moves as is the king in the ancient game of chess—that admirable symbol of the chief agents and gambits of civilisation.

As reason and order began methodically to prevail in life, the irrational and the supernatural intervened in order to maintain social stability; for religion, by commanding service to the gods, restored the capacity of a community to endure through the common efforts and sacrifices of its members, at the moment when selfish rationality would have counselled each member to seek only his private good in his own limited lifetime. When the conditions of daily living pressed hard, multiplying the frustrations and self-mutilations needed to keep the civilised order together, religion opened more distant prospects and a happier destination : another world and another life. Henri Bergson's description of religion, as an offset to consciousness of the brevity of life, the certainty of death, and the disparity between our plans and our achievements, applies with particular force to the preaxial religions of early civilisations. But some of these preoccupations lingered in the higher religions that followed.

6

Civilisation, then, provided the insurgent and irrational elements in man's nature with a vast imaginative outlet through highly institutionalised religion. Here civilised man confronted the many mysterious forces that sometimes seem to further his life, yet sometimes seem quite at cross-purposes with it; here, too, by transference and identification with deity, he added to his own sense of power. Yet the transposition of life into immortality, of human ignorance into divine omniscience, was not easily effected. At his first moment of relaxation, Gilgamesh lost the fruit that gave eternal life to the serpent, while merely eating of the fruit of the knowledge of good and evil brought Adam and Eve's exile from Paradise.

Religion, as it comes before us in the early civilisations, is plainly an upsurging of unconscious forces. These divine powers seem to erupt from the hot magma of the human soul: the gods at first have nothing to do with morality or civic duty, with love and justice. So far from being moralisers, the gods are rather pure expressions of lust, ferocity, and wanton energy: the very qualities that civilisation, seemingly for man's own good, seeks to modify and soften, or at least to divert to more pragmatic purposes. Listen to what Horus says to the enemies of his father, Osiris. 'Your arms are tied to your heads, O you evil ones. You are fettered from behind, you are the evil ones to be decapitated—you shall not exist.' This same unrestrained murderous anger belches forth likewise from the mouth of Yahweh: he who unlooses every method of extermination, from sword to plague, upon those who stand in the way of his Chosen People.

One may interpret the insolent powers of these monstrous divinities, at least in part, as attempts to restore by unconscious projection the human vitalities repressed by civilisation: they were likewise a means—irrational but plausible—of creating an active superpersonal authority to make up for the absence of an archaic morality based on consensus, in a mixed urban society filled with newcomers and outsiders who had few shared values and common folkways. Finally the gods, though created independently of this need, lent countenance to social stratifications that nullified the natural harmonies and human solidarities of more primitive cultures.

In time the unconscious processes that create divinities become subject to corruption by conscious manipulation. As early as the Egyptian *Book of the Dead*, we find the priesthood supplementing faith by magic and guaranteeing immortality at so much per head, in written documents that leave a blank space for the buyer to fill in : many thousands of years before Jacob Fugger, in the sixteenth century, purchased the exclusive agency for selling holy Christian indulgences. This goes along with the identification of super-natural religious power, plainly projected from man's unconscious, with organised political power, marshalled into action by the officers of the state, whose head may be a priest or even a god. The recurrence of these debasements in all religions justifies the cynical grin of Voltaire.

If, despite these crudities and perversions, religion has played an integral part in every civilisation, it is because the mysterious forces discernible in both the cosmos and the human soul are too important to remain unacknowledged. Both for good and bad, religion magnified the realm of creative possibility. In religion, civilisation compensated for its own frustrations by creating aesthetic objects and ideal presences, deeply rooted in man's nature, and so imposing that man became more deeply attached to them than to life itself.

As long as their faith in the gods and their expectations of a life to come remained active, that is, as long as they could draw on springs of life in their unconscious to offset the aridities and rigidities of civilisation, the daily claims of the outer world could be met, with resignation if not with cheerfulness. What happens when the external exactions become heavier, and the unconscious itself becomes empty of everything except a turbid, poisonous residue of demonic life, we only now begin to realise in our own day. Such stability as civilisations achieved—and the civilisation most completely dominated by other-worldly religion, Egypt, lasted the longest—was due to the fact that an uneasy balance between the inner and the outer state was effected.

In time, as man mastered the civil arts of co-operation, his gods became more tender and beneficent. Thanks to the transcendent claims of religion, civilisation encouraged man's higher functions as never before. With power came leisure, with leisure came reflective thought. The physical exertions of the hunter and the miner and the peasant absorb all vitality in the daily round : Emerson's discovery, that a morning spent in gardening left him destitute of any ideas, bears a universal application. Too much physical exertion, like too much liquor, too heavy a meal, too much sexual intercourse, lessens the possibility of productive thought.

In setting aside a class that nourished the products of the unconscious, by solitary communion and orderly public ritual, religion likewise extended the province of conscious, directed thought : the priest, the prophet, the sage, the scholar, the scientist, the bard were all members of one family; and in time they gathered sufficient strength to break through both the compulsive routines of civilisation and the compensating irrationalities of the early religions.

7

If our myth has accounted for the general acceptance of civilisation, despite the fact that it gave so much to so few and so little to so many, we have still only partly explained its long dominance. We are left with the fact that each of the great civilisations has been self-limited and self-enclosed : so much so that in our time two voluminous philosophies of history have been written without their authors' taking into account the underlying extensions of communication and mutual aid which even the brutal conquests of an Alexander or a Jenghiz Khan in some degree served. Yet without constantly enlarging the boundaries of human intercourse, without making its powers more obedient to human intention, what justification can civilisation offer for its curtailment of life's full possibilities? Are either the gods or the goals of civilisation a worthy terminus for human effort?

The fact is that man has never wholeheartedly accepted civilisation or loved his completely civilised self. Beneath class conflicts and rebellions against the unjust economic arrangements that so long remained engrained in civilisation, one detects even more corrosive assaults, brought about by the beneficiaries of civilisation, who cure their boredom in war and recover purpose by spreading destruction.

Civilisation saved itself mainly through two devices : a constant recruitment of fresh, undisillusioned personnel, brought in every generation from the rural areas, still throbbing with unspoiled life; and, no less, a persistence of rural habits and customs, and an infiltration of homely wisdom, from one of the earliest of didactic writings, that of worldly-wise Ptah-Hotep in Egypt, to the parables of Jesus. In short, civilisation, at least up to our own time, has always been sustained by pagan vitalities, undivided and unde-pressed; and when these ceased to be sufficient, it was redeemed again, as we shall see, by the opening up of a post-civilised prospect, through the agency of the axial religions, transposing all the values of civilisation into a new mode of life, and so using even its worst features as a condition for salvation.

But note : the very extension of civilisation weakened the fabric of archaic society, whose elementary morality sustained it : what men had once done unconsciously, for the good of their visible neighbour, they found it hard to do consciously, for the good of many invisible neighbours. It was not by accident that Augustus Caesar followed up the consolidation of the Roman Empire by attempting to revive the festivals and rituals of archaic society : he seems to have grasped intuitively that the vast mechanical fabric of Roman civilisation was not self-sustaining, and he hoped, it seems, to cement it on the lower level of folk feeling and sexual renewal, if not on the upper level of conscious ethical purpose, as the Stoics had sought to do.

The heroic efforts that enabled men to take the great step toward mechanical organisation and sustained common effort far beyond the immediate needs for survival eventually give way, in every civilisation, to a dreary later stage, the unadventurous one of keeping the wheels turning. Then the will to order ceases to be self-sustaining and inherently purposeful : life becomes empty. Are not the sacrifices and burdens greater than the tangible re-wards? At a certain stage of every civilisation, accordingly, it reaches a point revealed in the early Egyptian Dialogue Between Man and His Shadow Self, or Soul, when he asks himself why he should go on living : would he not be better dead? This internal dissolution of meaning and value may be hastened by external mischances and failures, such as Arnold Toynbee has examined in great detail; but as he wisely points out, the main blows come from within. Perhaps the most serious limitation is that the effort to expand the physical shell of civilisation—as the main source of its values—leads to a thickening of its walls and a steadily diminishing amount of space for the living creature within. Civilisation begins by a magnificent materialisation of human purpose : it ends in a purposeless materialism. An empty triumph, which revolts even the self that created it.

The sudden evaporation of meaning and value in a civilisation, often at the moment when it seems at its height, has long been one of the enigmas of history: we face it again in our own time. If the values of civilisation were in fact a sufficient fulfilment of man's nature, it would be impossible to explain this inner emptiness and purposelessness. Military defeats, economic crises, political dissensions, do not account for this inner collapse: at best they are symptomatic, for the victor is equally the victim and he who becomes rich feels impoverished. The deeper cause seems to be man's self-alienation from the sources of life.

When continued frustration and despair finally produce existential nausea, only desperate courses seem to open. The mildest of these courses is that of escapism: withdrawal from society by physical adventure or by spiritual seclusion, often in the *sauve qui peut* mood of the refugee, fleeing from disaster. Lacking this avenue, the old anesthetics of strong drink and sexual promiscuity offer quick alleviation, only to deepen the original disgust that prompted their use. Still another way, even more desperate and self-defeating, is to concentrate further on the technical agents that have made life so meaningless, making the machine a fetish that serves as an object of love, otherwise thwarted. Too often this technical glorification carries out the most perverse infantile fantasies, and turns into a corrupt assault on all that is still vital and healthy.

Against this chronic miscarriage of civilisation the official religious cults offered no relief: indeed their own institutional paraphernalia, their own exorbitant material demands, only added to the economic burden without lifting the inner depression. Only one course has so far opened up the way to further development: one that challenges the axioms of civilisation and places human life on a new foundation. This was originally the moment of the axial religions.

Axial Man

I

The terms axial period and axial religions have been used by the philosopher, Karl Jaspers, to describe a fact that various observers had intermittently noted during the last century: namely, that in Europe and Asia a profound change of a religious and moral nature took place, more or less within the span of the sixth century B.C. at widely separated points. At that time, the earliest universal religions, Buddhism and Zoroastrianism, came forth, while those that appeared later, Christianity, Mithraism, Manichaeism, Islam, continued the transformations begun then. With this a new kind of person and a new kind of community took form.

The word axial, as I myself used it independently in *The Conduct of Life*, presents a double meaning. It marks, first of all, a real turning point of human history; this change of direction was noted early in the present century by J. Stuart Glennie. But axial has also another meaning, as in the discipline of axiology: it has to do with values; and one uses it to indicate the profound change in human values and goals that took place after the sixth century. Though this change was a decisive one, I would not separate it as arbitrarily as Jaspers has done from the earlier developments of religion and ethics. If the theological perceptions of Ikhnaton (Akh-en-aton) had not been resisted and forcibly overthrown by the old Memphite priesthood, Egypt would probably have produced the first viable axial religion, centred in a naturalistic monotheism, appealing to all men, seven centuries or so before Zoroaster, Buddha, or Confucius.

The individual elements that went into the axial religions had already existed in embryonic forms, sometimes indeed in a well-developed state, in earlier religions. The most fundamental early contribution was the notion that temporal events, touching finite beings, had an eternal significance: that the brief life of man does not end at death, but is continued in another sphere; and that the quality of that longer existence is the subject of an ultimate

57

judgment, which determines whether he who is judged is to participate fully in that after-life or be deprived of its benefits, perhaps even punished.

That the cosmic forces themselves make for righteousness, that there is some close connection between man's assumed role and processes that lie outside his control, shaping his life for good or bad, were well-established principles in Chaldea and Egypt before even the correlated idea, of a single divine providence, came into existence. Religion's basic premises are the unity and meaningfulness of all life, indeed, of all existence. This reached its ultimate expression in the Upanishads: Brahman and Atman are one. One may interpret this to mean that the outer world and the inner self are in origin identical, or that they become one through a dynamic process of reciprocal creation.

Even before their axial prophets, Amos and Isaiah, had given a wider province to the religion of the Jews, the Israelites had transformed their tribal deity into the single unqualified creator and ruler of the universe: indeed, they had gone farther and attributed to him an existence so different in every dimension from man's that, though intercourse was under certain conditions possible, God remained at best without name or describable attributes: the inscrutable power Moses and Job confronted, whose ways defy reasoned explanation and override human judgment. If we now see in Moses' monotheism a continuation of Ikhnaton's vision, we must call these religions preaxial, for they were based on similar intuitions and pointed in the same direction. But the Transformation of the Divine Ruler into the humble Prophet was no natural evolution: it broke with the cult of centralised power and sought a new line of development.

The axial tendency to picture life itself as a constant battle between the forces of good and evil, between Ahriman and Ormazd, as the followers of Zoroaster put it, goes back to an earlier dawn of ethical consciousness among the Egyptians. With them, the gods, who at first exacted only obedience, in time imposed honesty and justice, mercy and forbearance, in all human relations; and they applied their own cosmic time scale to all petty human operations, rescuing them from that pettiness. To exercise watchful care, not only in the rituals and sacrifices to the gods, but in one's relations to one's fellows, became a mark of civilised man's waxing religious sense. If he were violent, deceitful, unjust, brutal, reckless of consequences, he would offend the gods

no less than if he neglected to pay respect to their image or give
offerings to the priesthood.

Even the tendency to cultivate the inner life at the expense of
the outer life, and to make a complete separation between the
natural and the ideal is far from a novel contribution: that in fact
is the whole duty of the priesthood, forever dividing the sacred
from the secular. By the time of Isaiah, a new type of person,
meek, silent, unassertive—introverted, as we would now say—was
beginning to replace the proud energetic hero as an ideal type.
In what respects, then do the axial religions make a radical
departure?

2

The central change brought in by axial religion is the re-
definition—in fact the recasting—of the human personality. In
that act, values that emerge only in the personality replace those
that belonged to institutions and institutional roles. The new
feelings, emotional attachments, sentiments are now incarnated in
a living image, that of the prophet. The life that he lives, the
values he expresses, become a visible pattern for other men to
follow. The Son of Man is man in his proper person—raised to his
highest power—not a supernatural being to fear and obey, but a
true man, to love and follow. The godlike images that preaxial
man had projected were indeed remote and awful; but when
examined more closely, they only magnified human or subhuman
dispositions that were all too accessible to the mean sensual man.
One might envy the gods their supernatural powers; but men who
lived in communities could not imitate the gods without running
into trouble: on the human level these qualities expressed paranoia
and produced crime.

The axial prophet both remakes the concept of God and re-
mints the human image. The personal takes precedence over the
social. In the case of Buddhism, Buddha's original presentation of
the cosmic process divested it of all organic images, animal or
human. Though his analysis denied the reality of 'self,' his own
self became, ironically, a pattern for his followers to imitate. He
could not by rational means do away with the deepest source of
his own appeal. Even where, as in most of the other axial
religions, God is attached not only to process and power, but to
love and fulfilment, the emphasis falls on the great mediator,

seemingly almost God himself in human form, who initiates the axial change: a Confucius, a Jesus, a Mahomet, or their successors who, in their own persons, renew the original image through their faithful reincarnation. Was there not some singular power in a Buddha who could create generation upon generation of Buddhists, transforming the idea into flesh? Upon the organic tissue and social skin of man, the axial prophet superimposes a new self, an impalpable envelope, the platonic form of axial man.

What is this new self? In the first place it is a self that is purified, as those conceived in the image of older deities were not, from too close attachment to man's animal nature. The ritual of the baptismal bath, threading through the axial religions, gives a symbolic emphasis to this inner cleansing. It is not merely that the prophet rejects the animal role of eating and sleeping and feeding and mating as a sufficient occupation for men: he seeks to subdue every kind of animal craving and desire, to loosen all the bonds that tie him too closely to bare survival, to turn all organic and social activities into mere preparations for an existence of greater significance and beatitude. To live in the highest sense is to be released from the pressure to survive.

This curbing of man's biological nature imposes a whole regimen of self-denial and bodily starvation: the eye must not be tempted by beautiful images; the palate must not be delighted with tastes nor the skin with sleek clothing nor the body bedizened with ornament; nor yet must the muscles be encouraged by dances or gymnastic exercises. In short, every sort of bodily activity must be repressed or starved; and above all, the sexual impulses. The ideal life for the axial prophet—there are exceptions like Confucius and Mahomet—is one released from sexual excitation and domestic responsibility: chaste, self-contained, subdued, conducted as far as possible away from the temptations that the mere presence of a member of the other sex may arouse. By all these means, the soul is to be quickened, and freed from the sordid cares and delusive pleasures that lower its powers.

With this emancipation from man's bodily appetites and cravings goes another kind of emancipation, almost equally hard to achieve: an emancipation from social attachments. The goods of civilisation, too, are rejected or treated as threats to the soul's integrity. As Socrates, most influential of the Western axial philosophers, said: 'All I do is go round and persuade young and old among you not to give so much attention to your bodies and your money as to the perfection of your souls.' In preferring bachelorhood to wedlock, the prophet may, like Buddha, Jesus, and Mani, turn his back on the family: the obligations of the household become obstacles to self-perfection; for he who strives to please his wife forgets to please God, as Paul of Tarsus observed. As far as possible this new self is detached, too, from the responsibilities of an organised community: its law, government, military obligations, economic operations, social duties, sacred rituals and symbols seem both hateful and harmful to the new self. What are they but a mass of vain repetitions and empty observances that, in the very act of ensuring a society's existence, hamper the soul's development?

By rejection of tribal and civilised institutions the believer dismantles a great part of the apparatus of civilised life. In this new attitude toward one's fellow, in this emphasis on personal values that challenge the customs of society, the prophet seeks indeed to bring about a new kind of community: the community of the 'saved.' Herein lies the great appeal of these axial religions to those who are disoriented or depressed by the hollowness of civilisation's achievements. In forfeiting the goods of this world those who have found 'salvation' seek to gain dominion over death itself: in giving up the goods of life they hope to achieve a greater good in eternity.

This image of a new man does not at first seek to impose itself by force or command: it relies upon the persuasiveness, or say rather the infectiousness, of the prophet's example. And the fact that men rally about him and seek in astonishing numbers to understand his precepts, to follow his way, and to refashion themselves in his very image shows that he represents a part of the human self that had not hitherto been adequately represented either by archaic or civilised society. In some measure, he makes them conscious of their secret aspirations, as he reinforces their dissatisfaction with animal complacency, technical proficiency, social routine, in short, with what William James called the Bitch Goddess, Success. The wonders and miracles that the prophet works awaken them truly to the undisclosed inner resources of life. As once the hero had stirred his fellows to conscious collective deeds that transformed the external world, so the saint rouses them to spiritual efforts that had heretofore been equally unimaginable. These new spiritual attributes often prove evanescent, like those products of nuclear fission that have but a brief half life; but, like them, they show potentialities that go far beyond the familiar organic and social stabilities.

This heightening of the human potential may itself indicate from within something about the nature of the universe. An underlying urge to self-transformation possibly lies at the basis of all existence, finding expression in the process of growth, development, renewal, directed change, perfection. This impulse to self-transformation may be structured in the whole organic world; in fact, it may have its origins in the whole self-constituting cosmic process that built up the elements; for the farther back one pushes the tendency toward self-transformation, the more basic it seems— and the more utterly unexplainable, except in mythical terms that derive from conscious human purpose.

Living forms transcended the limited possibilities of 'matter' by arriving, through the complex protein molecule, at a succession of unstable combinations that were self-sustaining—transient but capable of development. The process of self-transformation, finding wider scope in living organisms, resulted in one species after another, in a staggering diversity of forms, moving slowly upward toward mind, consciousness, widened opportunities for expression and self-direction. When the energy of this formative movement was exhausted, each species showed a tendency to level off at its own grade and remain there indefinitely, until either external pressure or some irresistible internal impulse resulted in a further transformation. This has its parallels in man's own self-transformation.

Archaic man had gone so far and had halted: civilised man had gone so far and had halted again. Now axial man came forward to attempt by faith and watchful discipline a further transformation, lessening his bodily needs, his physical apparatus, his institutional supports, in order to concentrate upon inner growth. He demanded a great change in the human form: but in a more restricted area, for his province is the individual soul. At the beginning of Egyptian civilisation, only the Pharaoh dared to lay claim to a soul. With the axial religions, the democratisation of heaven, which had already begun in Babylonia and in Egypt, became universal. At this point the soul seems to 'step forth' from the body, to use a term known to the Dionysiac cult.

Through axial man there rise to consciousness perceptions, feelings, and aspirations of a transcendent order, probably long buried in the unconscious. These stirrings now become objects of mediation and deliberate search. To achieve his new self, axial man at first forgoes the whole man, and is indifferent to the natural question as to what would happen if the new principles of his religion, with their detachment and disembodiment, were widely adopted. Would not the birth rate be perilously lowered if the prophet's following took his injunctions seriously? Would the axial religion itself not be overwhelmed by numbers, if not by force, on the part of non-believers? The fact that these vexatious questions did not keep the axial religions from spreading widely shows that other pressures were powerfully at work.

3

With axial religion came a new challenge and a new possibility. Unlike earlier cults, the axial religions were not confined to a territory or society; their members did not enter them by birth. One inherited the gods of Egypt or Babylonia, just as one inherited the other elements of their culture; but one did not, in their formative period, inherit the axial God or his prophet: one rather embraced them by a conscious act of choice, by an expression of faith that accompanied an effort at inner transformation. The new self was to be achieved, not primarily by indoctrination and habituation, though that would come later, but by conversion: an act of grace. This universal self was, fundamentally, the product of a revulsion against the accepted forms of life, fortified by a sense of unfathomed possibilities that remained to be explored.

The axial religions often took form during a period of social disintegration, when the normal satisfactions and the normal securities of civilised life no longer seemed possible: they sought to give a positive content to these negative moments. But a time of troubles does not inevitably lead to this particular remedy: if it did, it would be hard to explain the absorption in worldly enterprise after the disruptions of the fourteenth century, when Europe experienced the most catastrophic loss of population it had known since the sixth century A.D. Similarly, but in reverse, the first appearance of the mystery religions came in the sixth century B.C. before the full flowering of Hellenic culture, and antedated by more than a century the wars and devastations that followed. Probably it would be closer to truth to say that the heat of events often hastened a slow process of inner ripening, which was going on under widely different circumstances, to produce the same ultimate fruit.

Through the axial religions, a new kind of society was formed which overpassed all existing boundaries: a society of believers, united by a supernatural faith and a vision of perfection. The axial religions broke down the ancient isolation of tribe and village, city, state and even of empire: they marched across frontiers and summoned all men to a new life. The dividing lines between the in-group and the out-group, between Jew and Gentile, between Greek and barbarian, between neighbour and foreigner, were effaced. All men could become part of this new society, no matter what their social rank, their economic status, their political obligations, their colour or their sex: they were children of one god, brothers and sisters in a single family.

This fact gave to each of the axial religions a far wider potential territory than the greatest of empires had ever achieved by force of arms. In that widening of the area of communication and co-operation they carried further the great advance made by civilisation. True: no axial religion has up to now ever achieved anything like effective world-wide distribution; and that limitation should awaken pertinent questions. But the belief in universality was part of this new orientation; for the soul came from God and all men were subject equally to his providence, and had a share in the heavenly promise.

In this respect, no less than in its sense of the unplumbed resources of the inner life, when freed from external compulsions, axial religion was in the line of growth: it projected a destination far beyond that of archaic or civilised man, and conceived a new kind of person, capable of imagining and preparing for a universal community, if not capable on its own one-sided terms of achieving such a society. While this capacity for ignoring boundaries was one of the distinguishing marks of the axial religions, they broke down another great division equally characteristic of civilised man: they broke down, at least in relation to God and eternity, the division between classes. In times when the cult of arbitrary power and luxurious indulgence had increased the oppressions of the rich and powerful and aroused the resentments of the poor, the axial religions intervened with a temporary solution. In the sight of God, even the rich and poor were brothers. That again was not a new perception: one finds it already in the Egyptian texts. But it now became a principle of organisation within a new institution: the church, or congregation of believers. To be saved was to be accepted as a member of this new community, in an unfettered fellowship that transcended all other ties, even that of the family.

From this time on the human personality can be formally

divided into three parts, lately detected and described by Sigmund Freud, but always more or less acknowledged since the time of Aristotle. First: a basic biological self (the Old Adam), connected with man's animal past, stable, durable, requiring tens of thousands of years to produce any fundamental organic changes. This primeval self is the seat of all the vital processes: it holds, in its organs and tissues, the ultimate potentialities of mind and spirit; but it is to the more developed self as the quarry is to the carved statue. Second: a derivative social self, shaped by man's transmitted culture, by nurture, discipline, education, externalised in institutions and structures that create a common recognisable form for all its members. This self shows the beginnings of a differentiated ego; but it is largely a creature of habit and tradition; and in civilised regimes it splits up into an occupational self, a domestic self, a political self, as various situations impose their appropriate roles and dramas. In its most inclusive form it becomes the corporate 'national self,' on its way to a common human goal, but unable on its own terms to reach it. These civilised fragments are the relatively uniform blocks of stone, far removed from the quarry, but still to be shaped into individualised statues.

Finally, there is an ideal self, the super ego, the latest layer of the self, though dimly visible from the moment of man's emergence: the most frail, the most unstable, the most easily overthrown part of the human psyche, perhaps also the most subject to debasement. Yet this ideal self seeks a position of dominance, for it represents the path of continued growth and development.

One is born *with* the first self, the biological substratum or id: one is born *into* the second self, the social self, which makes the animal over into a modified human image, and directs its purely animal propensities into useful social channels, carved by a particular group. But one must be reborn if one is to achieve the third self. In that rebirth, the latest part of the self, assuming leadership, projects a destination that neither man's animal nature nor his social achievements have so far more than faintly indicated. In this detachment lies the promise of further growth.

The belief in the possibility of this rebirth is one of the identifying marks of the axial religions, indeed their chief contribution to the human condition. But in the act of defining these new possibilities for development, they failed, to their eventual embarrassment, to allow for the natural history of man. In the hope of speeding conversion, they rejected the lower elements and broke up the unity of the living organism, instead of putting man's vitalities more fully at the service of the higher self.

4

In the beginning, the axial development does not rest on an institutional change. So far from consisting in a series of proposals for modifying the usages of the community, it seeks rather to set them aside, or at least to by-pass them, in the effort to establish a more immediate connection with the values it deems central to man. In that lies both its attraction and its peril. By making the transformation rest on the inner response of an individual, immediately effected by the individual's surrender to a higher power that commands him, it avoids the effort to penetrate the tough hide of the corporate self. By taking wings instead of trudging along the paved road of civilisation the axial prophet seems able, at least at the beginning, to leap over centuries of collective effort in a single generation. At the moment of alienation and disillusion, the heartfelt demand for speedy salvation underwrites this short cut. Under the prophet's hypnotic influence—of old it was called *charisma*—the blind see, the lame throw away their crutches and walk, the dead rise up and throw off their shrouds. Influenced by the new vision the rich may even sell all their goods and give the proceeds to the poor; or the proud may wash the feet and bathe the sores of the humble.

As long as one accepts the social order in its historic form, it seems as difficult to change as a confused and congested metropolis: too solid, above all too complex, to permit anyone to carve a straight avenue of ideal dimensions through its tangle of buildings and streets, monuments and property rights. So various are the needs and interests of even a simple society, so many groups and so many institutions must be brought into line, so difficult is it to foresee what a change in one portion of the fabric will do in a remote part of it, that one is tempted to leave it alone, until its further breakdown simplifies the problem. Certainly it seems impossible for even the wisest ruler, a Solon or an Asoka, to carry through any proposals sufficiently comprehensive to change the texture of life in the community: they must be content with partial measures and even more partial successes.

If piecemeal reform leaves too much of the old structure standing, a revolutionary transformation by attempting to destroy the old structure and start again on new foundations promises only impoverishment: the operation that extirpates the disease may also kill the organism. Plato, for example, contemplated a radical change in the social order during the early axial period: he gave earnest attention both to its underlying principles, in the *Republic*, and to its detailed regulation, in the *Laws*. But his own experience as a revolutionary innovator in Syracuse should have disillusioned him: he met with equal resistance from the tyrant who invited him there and from the populace for whose good he sought to legislate.

So the utopian method of change, though Plato was neither the first nor the last to advocate it, was never the favoured way of the axial religions. These new prophets left society, generally, as they found it; they might mildly rebuke its institutions, but they left them alone. They turned their attention rather to the individual soul, in whose depths they thought the essential work could be done. Individual men, once deeply stirred, might bring about a complete self-transformation. As their numbers increased, society would be changed, too.

In putting their emphasis on the individual soul, the axial prophets were of course generalising their own experience: by withdrawal and solitary communion, they had invited an influx of spiritual energy that miraculously changed human relations. After a period of frustration, disappointment, and despair, often after a period of intense spiritual desolation, they had found. themselves filled with an illumination: they were in possession of a new law governing human relations, which detached them from their past, from all corporate limitations, and made them part of a larger society, where they could pursue remoter goals. In so far as their experience was open to other men, they seemed to have a basis for their wider hopes.

When put into mere words, the typical axial insights too often may seem a little meagre. One must shut every avenue of desire and passion, and view the lives of all living creatures with detachment and pity, seeking an ultimate release from the cycle of births: Buddha. One must renounce the effort to achieve power over other men or over the forces of nature, in order to seek the kingdom of heaven, where the law of love prevails, and the good of one's neighbour is one's own good: Jesus. One must follow the Way, aligning one's own forces with the forces of nature, casting off customs, laws, values, symbols that blind one to the reality that underlies them: Lao-tse. These are thin substitutes for those overpowering flashes of prophetic illumination that could not be translated into words. Plainly the precepts and doctrines of axial religions are not by themselves sufficient to account for the dynamics of their appeal—or the positive transformations that issue from it.

The fact is that the axial transformation was not primarily an achievement of the conscious mind, still less a product of rational thought alone: it actually took place at far deeper levels and involved the whole personality.

At a singular moment all the forces of the prophet's own life are suddenly polarised and form a new constellation, in harmony with a fuller order of being, pointing toward a divine consummation. From that time on, he acts with an absolute sense of certitude and well-being: he has a mission, and in the performance of that mission every act bears the stamp of the new personality. This is the miracle of the second birth. As a result, the new self becomes the 'real' one, and the second mode of life alone satisfies his demands.

Doubtless this inner change had, in incomplete, shadowy forms, transpired at many points in history, long before the axial religions took form. In some degree, it takes place every day in lesser personalities, suddenly upsetting the observations of teachers, the hopes of parents, the predictions of psychological tests, the narrow requirements of employers. Those who suppose that the first birth alone counts, or that the conforming social imprint is the final one, may be disposed, like one of Walt Whitman's biographers, to regard the second birth as a species of charlatanism, an ostentatious make-believe, close to fraud. (The constant possibility of this very perversion, indeed, makes hypocrisy the characteristic vice of axial religions.) But it is by their results that the axial transformations may be measured. When the change was real, it brought a new sense of freedom. For him who was reborn neither bodily survival nor social conformity served as guides to his daily conduct. The old commitments and compulsions ceased to operate. New possibilities, beyond rational definition, appeared: man's case was no longer fixed, predictable, ultimately hopeless. Religion promised a joyful release: an alternative way to that of civilisation.

At the moment of incarnation, the new redeemer seems to have found a way of life that will supersede civilisation, curbing its violences and releasing man from its fixations. Those who follow him will be saved from the living death of conforming to institutions that, in the very effort to escape the threat of disintegration, tend to become ever more rigid, more arbitrary, more tyrannical and life-denying.

Axial religion achieves authority not only by reversing the dominance of body over soul, animal urges over spiritual aspirations, but by reversing the roles of life and death: it accepts the negations of life, pain, sin, sorrow, misfortune, as fortifying preparations for an inner transformation which will alter man's final destiny. In times of general social disintegration axial religion thus turns every threat to life into an opportunity; and by that fact it gives its believers the courage to face the worst.

With this direct connection between the individual and the deeper powers within the self of which he becomes acutely conscious, all the crises of life take on a new meaning. Birth, adolescence, maturity, marriage, vocational choice, withdrawal become valued primarily for their symbolic meanings and their spiritual consequences. 'Whatever be thy work, thine eating, thy sacrifice, thy gift, thy mortification, make thou it an offering to me,' says Krishna in the *Bhagavad-Gita*. Those who went through a second birth were born into a wider community, the church, which guarded and sanctified these symbols. The axial small community, unlike the more primitive archaic one, did not rest on the immediate basis of neighbourhood and family custom: it rested on a shared belief in man's ultimate destination. But in the congregation the intimate I-and-thou relation, which had been undermined by the more mechanical usages of civilisation, was restored: thus the synagogue and the church bound the remotest village, for the first time, to a universal community. Here was a new method of association that transcended the chaotic intermixture of the metropolis and the tyrannous uniformity of the empire. This was the great social contribution of axial religion.

The new mask or *persona* that axial religion created was designed to fit every human face and to bring out its common human quality. A certain kind of mobility and adaptability, indeed a spirit of adventure, marked this new self: men felt at home over a much wider area of the planet, because wherever they went they would find others who had undergone the same change and formed a new kind of social grouping: the twice-born, the saved, the redeemed, the transformed: imitators of a new self and followers of a new divinity. In addition, these axial

religions by their very meekness and yieldingness imposed constraints upon the violent and offered the gifts of tenderness and
mercy to the weak, the sick, the helpless, the dying.

Though the direct expressions of sexuality were subdued, often
beyond the point of endurance, sexuality in sublimated form was
widened in scope and sent forth tendrils that covered every part
of life, flowering in works of love, in smiling acts of sacrifice.
Just as civilised man, through heroic exertions and collective
discipline, left a deeper mark on the environment than man had
hitherto made, so axial man left a deeper mark on the human
soul. By his power to subordinate physical and social demands to
spiritual purposes, he achieved a sense of fresh possibilities man
had never before possessed. He showed that an imaginable ideal
self, which did not closely conform to his biological nature, could
nevertheless take form and create around it a whole society that
in some degree mirrored this new image.

5

So far I have been describing one kind of axial prophet, one
kind of axial religion: mainly that represented by Buddha,
Zoroaster, the author of the *Bhagavad-Gita*, Jesus, Mahomet, whose
images are graven, however faintly, over the natural features of
a great portion of the earth's population. These are the survivors
of many other spirits, audacious but not so successful, who
claimed equal authority, from Apollonius of Tyana, Marcion, and
Mani, down to Joseph Smith and Mary Baker Eddy in our own
day. Such leaders sought to bring about a far-reaching transformation in men's lives; and to a remarkable extent, as long as
the original impact of the founder and his immediate disciples
was vividly felt, great changes actually took place. But the results
of this new method are not cumulative, like technical improvements. In each generation, there must be a fresh incarnation, and
to carry out its founder's insights each member must be converted, renewed, reborn. I remember the mournful words of an
elder in the Amana Colony to explain the falling away from their
admirable Christian communism: 'None of us has been visited by
the spirit for more than a generation.' In the long run, what
seemed a short-cut required a persistent exertion of effort greater
than that needed to maintain the sluggish processes of civilisation.

But there is another stream of development, paralleling the

movement of the axial religions, that one must not neglect. For a long time it seemed an alternative way, sanctioned by reason and less dependent upon the uncontrollable impulses of the unconscious or the uncertainties of faith. This development is that of the axial philosophies. These philosophies rest on intuitions and proposals similar to those of axial religion: they likewise invoke man's higher nature and set goals that demand a break with the instinctual, the habitual, the conventional. Though axial philosophy does not neglect nonrational forces in the personality—did not Socrates listen to his daimon? Did not Plato reserve his highest doctrine for direct oral communication?—it emphasises the rational and the humanly controllable. These new leaders cling to the method of intellectual criticism and clarification, orderly knowledge, pedagogical discipline: whether they are quickened by mystical illumination or prophetic anxiety or intellectual curiosity, they are above all teachers.

In the West, the axial philosophies for long seemed to vie with the axial religions. Beginning in Greece with Solon and his more influential successor, Socrates, the axial philosophers branch off into a score of different schools, each with its theory of the universe, its view of the gods, its doctrines as to the nature of man; each with its emphasis on particular sets of values and particular goals. The emergent personality, highly individualised, leaves its fresh stamp on each of the axial philosophies: from that comes its characteristic discipline for the daily life and its system of education, passed on from master to disciple.

If axial religion takes form in the ecclesia or congregation, philosophy takes form in the school. Plato founded the first academy in the West, and in its symbolic shadow a succession of philosophers held forth for a thousand years from Epicurus and Zeno to Plotinus and Boëthius, each wrestling with the problem of forming the personality and mastering the forces of society— or seeking, by intellectual concentration, to find a means of guarding the spirit by withdrawal from 'all the noisy crowding up of things and whatsoever wars on the divine.'

In the East, a similar development took place. Judged by his durable influence, the most effective of these axial philosophers was Confucius. To remember his example is to emphasise how much that was similar to the work of the axial religions could be accomplished without a theology. For philosophy works by a different process, which relies on studious exercises and rationally validated customs, rather than on conversion and faith. Reluctant

to speak about God or to summon up the forces of the unconscious, not even giving himself the Socratic licence to listen to his
inner voice, Confucius nevertheless brought about a change of
the greatest magnitude. Mixing archaic ritual and music with
natural animal piety, he re-created the old fellowship between the
living family and its dead ancestors: thus he strengthened a bond
that each developing civilisation tended to weaken. By attending
to the details of etiquette, and attaching them to the forms of art,
he made politeness a moralising influence; while by concentrating
upon the reflective study of books, he trusted to the power of
thought to subdue, in the end, mere thoughtless power.

Not least, Confucius brought into existence a universal personality, the archetypal Scholar and Gentleman: perhaps the first
rounded incarnation of this type. None of man's biological or
social character was wholly renounced in this new incarnation:
but every part of his nature was watchfully tempered and controlled as he sought to achieve the golden mean. Generation after
generation of Chinese imitated this new ideal, in its detachment,
its studiousness, its courteous modulation, its sweet reasonableness.
Wherever the muses are invoked, where knowledge and natural
piety and decorum are placed above power, where the mind
governs with a humorous compassion for all that opposes it, the
living spirit of Confucius prevails: in one generation it is called
Aristotle, in another Erasmus, and in a third Goethe.

Though in outline this transformation follows closely that of
the axial religions, in one essential way it represents a departure
and is under a special handicap. Because the method is pedagogic
and calls for disciplined application, it is necessarily slow. So it
is not to the many, but to a leisured minority, capable of pursuing
their education without the embarrassment of earning a living,
that these philosophers appeal. At best, the way of life they develop can only filter down slowly from the top strata of society,
and by the time it reaches the lowest layers, much has evaporated.
The axial prophet, by contrast, touches the mass of mankind
directly by a sudden quickening of desire and dream. 'I and mine
do not convince by arguments,' as Whitman said, 'we convince
by our presence.'

Since the learning process operates slowly, the self achieved
by axial pedagogy restricts the philosopher's influence to the
small band of pupils around him: he can bring about no sudden
change, no wholesale transformation. The leisure he commands,
the detachment he seeks, belong to the upper classes, or to the

minority of promising youths who may be supported by the upper classes. For the same reason, the influence of axial philosophy has largely been confined to its own language group: indeed, each philosopher, by tending to create a private vocabulary, creates a second barrier; so philosophies do not leap easily over cultural boundaries.

In the end the main influence of axial philosophy has been through its contribution to religion and higher education. But the appeal to reason and measure in man, if less soul-shaking than that of the axial religions, had the merit of reinforcing practices that had already achieved a degree of social sanction and practical application. So there was a continuity in the working of the axial philosophies that was lacking in the axial religions—until they, too, had acquired a philosophy and a pedagogy to supplement the immediate effect of their original illumination.

In another respect, both axial philosophy and axial religion show a similar weakness. Since they have their origin, to begin with, in an impressive personality, they have an inherent tendency toward fission and schism, as one new personality succeeds another and seeks to project his own unique vision. Almost in the Buddha's lifetime, there were a score of different Buddhist sects. The same tendency, visible from the earliest moments of Christianity, crystallised in dogma and counter-dogma that drove out heretics, or, in the case of the Albigenses, exterminated them. Because of their basic likenesses in method and outlook, the lesser differences between axial religious creeds became obstacles to the universalism they all profess.

If the weakness of civilisation is corporate conformity, the weakness of axial society is sectarianism. This stems from a failure to allow in its incarnation for other types of personality than that of the founding prophet, or to include in its system of truths the saving opposites that would qualify it and make it fully inclusive. As a result each universal religion resists amalgamation with any other universal religion. Such a humble soul as Ramakrishna, who sought by devotion and exercise to experience other religions than his own Hinduism, is an exception.

These weaknesses limited the province of the whole axial transformation. Yet the fact of their partial success cannot be disputed; nor was it small. By transferring social values and loyalties to the inner world, axial religion gave freedom and initiative to the emergent person: as never before all men's actions became self-conscious and subject to independent evaluation. Civilisation now became a vehicle, not the goal toward which the vehicle travelled. But to prompt men to extraordinary efforts that often demanded a denial or reversal of ancient biological processes, the axial religions needed the spur of disaster and suffering. They prospered in adversity, when the pomps and vanities of the world became shadows, but by the same token they suffered in prosperity, when the Church, seized by worldly men, drew to itself the wealth and powers and prerogatives of the state : likewise the rivalries and coercions. For this reason, the axial saints often overvalued life's negative moments and even spurned health because it offered fewer opportunities for their drastic system of medicine. This attitude has been pushed to the point of caricature by those who hold that, since man learns only by suffering, conquerors and tyrants who promote suffering are divine instruments of man's salvation.

Great as the achievements of axial religion were, lasting as their influence remains, they rested in some degree on an illusion. The type of personality they sought to impress on mankind as a whole is not, in fact, a universal one. The axial mask did not fit easily over every face. In its overemphasis of the 'cerebral' and spiritual, the axial personality is a valuable corrective to the extroversion and shallowness of more common types : but it is not, in its isolated perfection, a sufficiently representative ideal of human potentiality, for it rejects too much that is needed for full human growth. Moreover, the inner life, which became the exclusive centre of axial attention, is not self-sufficient; and the morality that holds together in isolation may crumble when submitted to social pressure. If that inner life is, in fact, to last beyond its first moments of intense illumination, it needs an outer life, built in conformity to its perceptions, to sustain and support it. What if the new doctrine commands one to visit the sick and comfort the imprisoned, if it has no principles that apply to the transactions of the market place? Because of their original indifference to social institutions, the axial religions, preaching brotherhood, love, and peace, left untouched, or almost untouched, the practices of slavery, economic exploitation, and war : in short, the grossest evils of civilisation.

As long as men are threatened by a common crisis or drowned in a common misery, this dualism between the standards of heavenly and earthly society may not make much difference. But in the end, under more normal social conditions, the disparity between profession and practice will become an offence to all decent men. An ideal too pure to be accepted by the world may leave a deeper corruption behind than a more pedestrian morality, as non-Christian peoples often noted in the nineteenth century when they compared the practices of the trader and soldier with the professions of the missionary. The radical division between community and individual soul, between earthly attachments and heavenly aspirations, between 'this world' and 'the other world,' was one of the great flaws of most axial theologies. By his exclusively inward orientation 'Moral Man' gave scope, if not sanction, to 'Immoral Society.'

By treating the soul alone axial religion failed to do justice to man's whole nature; and its exaggerated expectations led to disappointment, frustration, and guilt.

The other great weakness of the axial religions was complementary to this. Once the new person and the new doctrines took form in the Church, the new leaders brought back into the heart of their religion, in an effort to ensure its survival, the very elements from which they had sought sudden deliverance: the routines of civilisation. In time, the Church, as an organised body, takes the place held by the living person who founded it. By ritual and drill, by symbolic 'works', by busy corporate activities, directing economic enterprises and building vast physical structures, the Church as an organisation carries the original intuition into every part of the community: yet to the extent that it is successful, it partly obscures the original impulse and diverts the new currents of life back into the well-worn channels of use and wont. This contradiction must be faced, for in their innocence the axial prophets did not foresee its workings or take precautions against it. In spite of his patent doctrine, Buddha became a god: in spite of Jesus' deliberate warning, a large part of Christian worship consists in those vain repetitions, such as the heathen use, which he forbade.

6

In reckoning with the historic weaknesses exhibited by the axial religions, we are not dealing with a perversion peculiar to supernatural religion, but with the natural history of ideas and institutions. About this history the early prophets knew too little to avert a miscarriage of their intentions; and those who have cynically criticised the frequent falling off of the axial way of life from its original purity show, by their very cynicism, that they are equally ignorant.

Elsewhere (in *The Condition of Man*) I have sought to draw a generalised picture of the fashion in which an idea of sufficient magnitude to transform the person and the community actually comes into existence and operates. This process can be divided roughly into four stages, usually successive, though aspects of the later stages may be present at the beginning.

Formulation is the first stage. Then a new idea takes shape in various minds, as a fresh mutation : an image of new possibilities, intuitively apprehended, sometimes rationally formalised, but by its very nature frail and perishable, since it as yet has no organs. The next stage toward realisation is the *Incarnation* : the translation of the idea into the living form of a human being and the acts and deeds and proposals of his life. If only a few understand the potentialities of the pure idea, many are able to take hold of the living example; and in the very act of incarnation, the nature of the idea is explored and carried further.

Once the incarnation has taken place, the next step is that of *Incorporation* within the community : the detailed working out of precept and belief in the habits of daily life, costume, hygiene, and medicine; ceremonial, manners, and laws. Finally comes the *Embodiment* : the structural organisation of the original idea into works of art and technics : buildings, monuments, landscape forms, cities, a process that may take place as swiftly, once the groundwork is laid, as the development of the stone architecture of the Pyramids.

Note that the first two stages mainly centre in the individual person : they represent the introversion of interest that leads to an exploration of modes of self-development not offered by any existing society. At this moment the self, by detachment, seeks to tap its deepest sources of creativity, and by that very fact must work mainly alone : this is the phase to which Toynbee has given the name etherialisation. But the final stages reverse this process and change its field : the inner forces turn outward and centre on the community; incorporation and embodiment seek to confirm the personal effort through the reformation of society. In axial religion materialisation, as I call this stage, is an effort to find a social method to carry on the process of self-transformation, when the first prophetic illumination has dimmed, and the singular point has passed.

This alternation of introversion and extroversion, of ethe-

rialisation and materialisation, is, on my interpretation, a fundamental process that unites the person and the community; and
one is not less necessary than the other. For without the social
process the individual effort would be lost, and without the individual bid for freedom society would be curbed and confined,
as most historic civilisations have in fact been confined, by its
very success. Those who disparage the role of ideas underestimate
the daily impact of human proposals and human choices and
imply that the whole process of social development is external
and automatic, if not accidental. The changes that take place in
man are thus supposed to be functions of forces and institutions
outside him. While those who find in the stage of materialisation
nothing but a debasement of the original idea deny the enrichment of meaning and the enlargement of possibility that this
materialisation in fact brings with it. It is only within the great
cathedrals, Chartres, Durham, Notre Dame, that one achieves in
fact an exalted glimpse of the Christian Heaven.

In one sense, the hopes of the axial prophet are cheated, because the spiritual alteration he seeks to effect so quickly does
not become operative on a collective scale until it has remoulded
social institutions. In terms of his original intuition, the hope for
a decisive transformation grows dim : the process is not as quick
and thorough with other men as it had been with the prophet :
the sinners, the backsliders, above all the routineers, impair the
whole effort. The mass of men at first turn to him, because he
shows them a path of development that seems to redeem their
usual life from its frustrations : they are sufficiently men to wish
to pass beyond their own limitations and to choose more significant goals than their society has yet offered them. But when they
make the experiment they meet with many unforeseeable disappointments : they are like the little boy who earnestly wanted
to know how to read, but complained, after his first lesson, that
he didn't want to *learn* how to read. The axial way, which leaves
all to the individual soul, is not so easy as it looks. Even success
brings a certain alienation and loneliness.

From the beginning, the axial prophets sought to keep their
vision high and pure by withdrawal from the political responsibilities and social complexities of their own community. Their
method was to form a band or brotherhood, eventually to found
a colony, of like-minded people, seeking in physical isolation to
live wholly in accord with the precepts of the prophet. These new
establishments, the Buddhist monks, the Pythagoreans, the Epicu-

reans, the Essenes, the Manichees, the Augustinians and Benedictines, often outlasted the bigger community of which they were a part. But such institutions could not hope to achieve the greater human brotherhood of which the axial prophets dreamed. In seeking purity by withdrawal their members left the wicked world unregenerate: indeed, their own salvation was open to vices peculiar to the monastic regimen, self-absorption and spiritual lethargy, brought out by a routine freed from life's constant challenges.

Now in fact axial culture produced a self far more capable of running a complex political organisation covering a wide domain than was the civilised self, with its limiting tribal and national underlayer. For the axial self, disciplined by its monastic abstensions—like those of a soldier trained for battle, as Tertullian noted —had persistence, vision, self-awareness and self-criticism, all fortified by great powers of self-sacrifice, attached to a distant goal. All these were valuable traits far beyond those normal to the soldier and the bureaucrat, inured only to mechanical repetition, and buoyed up by the prospect of necessarily limited earthly rewards. It is no accident, perhaps, that the oldest effective transnational political organisation so far recorded is that of the Church of Rome. But the very superiority of the axial self in carrying out more competently the functions of civilisation produced a new danger: axial man took on the vices of the civilisation he had become so adept at controlling and extending, and in that very triumph forfeited axial culture's chief reason for existence.

In their own development, then, each higher religion has at some point become arrested and has lapsed from its aims in the same fashion as the civilisation from which it sought to deliver man. At the very centre of the existing axial religions, we find, not a little to our dismay, the limitations of tribal societies and national aggregates. Despite the pretence of choice, one is born a Buddhist or a Christian, almost as one might be born a Kaffir or an Eskimo. Instead of mingling freely with other men, exchanging the gifts of the spirit, a stubborn pride in their own spiritual possessions, yes, and a desire for domination, has often set one axial religion at odds with every other: Mahomet's tolerance of Moses and Jesus was a happy exception—though it did not create a warm brotherhood with Christians and Jews. In the long history of human cruelty, the treatment of heretics and nonbelievers by the axial religions ranks among its blackest pages: multiplied by desolate chapters devoted to ferocious wars of religion.

Once the process of materialisation hardens sufficiently to break the organic rhythm between inner and outer, only one hope remains: the axial religion must go through a process that reverses its natural order of growth—through disembodiment and alienation to etherialisation and illumination. Characteristically, such religious reforms often begin with acts of iconoclasm: the destruction of sacred images, the denudation of sacred buildings, the abstention from traditional ceremonies. But the success of this movement rests on the possibility of bringing about a commanding reincarnation of the prophet, and in joining to the original body of ideas the insight and knowledge that further human experience has disclosed. That rebirth is not easy. Today, at the very moment when universal man clamours as never before to be born, the axial religions are almost as great an impediment to this birth as are self-enclosed tribal and national societies. What axial religion has yet embodied, in charity and humility, the universality that its founder professed?

7

The passage of civilised man into axial man was an advance, for it broadened the province of morality and heightened those dispositions toward self-direction and self-perfection that had been least valued in 'other-directed' traditional society. The gods came back into the human soul as friends, as helpers, as mid-wives of a higher birth. Within the context of eternity possibilities larger than any disclosed by man's past had come into existence.

But this transformation remained incomplete: except in isolated souls, axial man never fully supplanted civilised man or reconciled the inherent contradiction between their roles; indeed, the hope of doing so, on purely axial terms, was an illusory one. Though the introverted saint sought to replace the hero as the leader and exemplar of the new community, he was no more capable than the extroverted hero of doing justice to the whole man; nor yet was the axial philosopher.

But at least this had been accomplished: in their search for values proper to man's estate, universally human, the axial religions and philosophies had broadened the basis of human association. The basic similarities between the values and purposes of the axial ideologies outweigh their differences: they converge toward a common conception of man's nature and destiny with a kind of unanimity that contrasts with the thousand oddities and solecisms that have characterised more primitive cultures, even after they had achieved the forms of civilisation. In this the axial ideologies carried forward, to a marked degree, an underlying tendency toward diffusion, universalisation, spiritual unity and communion, which has, in time, become an increasingly important sign of human development. The elevated superego of the axial religions is still a precious contribution to—indeed an indispensable preparation for—an even more effective universalism, one still to emerge.

Old World Man

1

In following the series of transformations that lifted man out of his original animal self and brought him to his present state, we have now climbed to a watershed and face the other side. Looking back, one sees the long foreground of animal and primitive life, the muddy bottoms of tribal culture, the cultivated foothills of the archaic communities, the serried mountains of civilisation, terraced part way up, finally the glacial icefields of the axial religions, at whose summits the blue sky darkens and the air becomes too rarefied to sustain life without undue strain on lungs and heart. But on the reverse slope the contours of the landscape become sharply different: in a few short steps downward, one loses sight of the rugged heights man has been so strenuously climbing: after a sudden drop one finds oneself on a plateau whose sharp geometrical features, interlaced with concrete highways, show no evidences of geological erosion; indeed, all the natural features have been refabricated by the machine.

We are on the point of exploring a new world; and the habits acquired in the Old World are almost useless there. Yet we should not, perhaps, be surprised to find that those who have been struggling, with growing dismay, over the axial ice fields, falling into crevasses and frequently losing their direction, tempted constantly to retreat to lower levels more kind to every form of life, do not hesitate when they find themselves atop the divide. On the contrary, they plunge swiftly down to the arid plateau, destitute of woodland and ploughed field and orchard, as if they had at last found the promised land.

Yes: precisely those who have been most rigorously disciplined in axial culture, those who have acclimatised themselves best to its chilly, rarefied air, take the lead in exploring this plateau, triangulating its surface, measuring its distances, boring into the seams of rock along its surface, and abandoning the very thought of any return to the more familiar landscape on the other side of the watershed.

Before we follow this movement into the New World and appraise the new species of man who grew to enormous stature in this environment, we would do well, perhaps, to take a last backward glance and form a clear picture of him whom we may, at this point, call Old World man. Until the nineteenth century, Old World man was the chief representative of the human species on the planet: in numbers, in power, in cultural achievement he dominated the earth. No matter how far Old World societies were separated in space and time, the likenesses between them are more frequent, and more astonishing, than their differences. This applies not merely to their structure, but to their whole process of development.

Not merely do Old World societies begin at the same common starting point; but in the course of their history, seemingly so self-enclosed, they parallel each other's efforts in detail, as if a social species were as well defined, at every stage of its life, as a biological species and passed through the same cycle of maturation. Thus the economic changes that transform a primitive manorial economy, whose properties largely belong to the ruling deity, into a mercantile town economy with the beginning of craft specialisation and a market are roughly the same in Mesopotamia, two or three thousand years before Christ, as in Western Europe in the Middle Ages, between the tenth and the thirteenth centuries, when the feudal system was partly replaced by the free towns.

So, too, the clashes between local autarchy and a centralised national economy in Egypt parallel the conflicts that occurred in France and England when they became national states; while the alliance of the absolute monarch with the masses against the landed proprietors and the priesthood seems the same in China as in Egypt, and accounts for the persistent misalliance, noted by Aristotle, between democracy and tyranny.

What applies at so many points to the economic and political existence of Old World civilisations applies, in an equally remarkable degree, to their spiritual life. Hindu and Chinese philosophy run through all the variations from naturalism to Platonism, from scepticism to Stoicism, that one finds in Western Europe. When I asked Ananda Coomaraswamy to define the three gunas (qualities) described in the *Bhagavad-Gita*, he replied with illustrative passages from Dante's *Divine Comedy*. The Chinese mother image of

Kwannon carried the same benign message as that of the Virgin Mary; and Buddhism preserved the holy life in monasteries that anticipated in detail the orders of the West—and in time disclosed the same kind of inner corruption, too. The sophisticated *Tale of the Genji* from eleventh-century Japan reads like a modern French novel in its delicately amoral eroticism.

Old World man did not produce a single world culture; indeed, it was part of the nature of this Old World scheme to accentuate its variety and its inviolable individuality. But there is essentially no idea or ideal familiar to one Old World society that cannot be translated more or less fully into every other. The life they produced had the same texture: their minds operated within the same frame.

At long intervals before the fifteenth century A.D. this Old World culture may have overpassed the limits of its natural habitat in Europe, Asia, and North Africa. But though similar transformations seem to have taken place in Andean and Mayan societies, whatever their origins, they lacked, as far as we know, an essential ingredient, that contributed by the axial religions. At all events, in the course of five thousand years, Old World culture spread over the larger part of the Northern Hemisphere; and because of its characteristic innovations, it tended to supplant —or what is almost the same thing, absorb—the unadventurous, repetitive cultures of the tribe. On the fringes of the Old World culture, these earlier forms, sparse in numbers, but with the tenacity of lower organisms, could only hold their own, like molluscs clinging to a rock.

2

Though the Old World culture is readily definable, it does not at any moment compose into a uniform whole; for it represents a long historic accumulation. The three layers of Old World culture, the archaic layer, the civilised layer, and the axial layer, lie one upon the other, above the even more primitive layer that it shares with other forms of human society. In some places, one layer will be heavier than another: here the rock will be of the same even grain, deposited in the same period of sedimentation: in other places, it may be a composite formation, made up of the debris of other cultural forms, with pockets of gold that have formed in the vein of quartz, or mica that has been washed down from the hills. But it is the active presence of these three layers of culture that characterise Old World society. When the two top layers are partly eroded, the deep archaic layer still remains.

One of the most characteristic features of the Old World culture, indeed, is that it preserves its archaic ways and has in turn been preserved by them : its art was as precious to it as its technics, for it cherished every artifact and ritual that bore the imprint of the human imagination. The revolutions of civilisations do not touch this stratum. When this culture is too depleted to meet a difficult situation by fresh invention, it will fall back on memory : its faith in its own survival is due to its recollection of the way that its ancestors went through situations equally formidable and lived to tell the tale.

The Old World culture made history and remembered history; but the very qualities that so long preserved it, its tenacious memory, its delight in its accumulated treasures, also limited its achievements. Its priests and scholars spent so much time in the mere preservation of their possessions, cataloguing, ordering, dusting them, that too often they lacked the energy to add to them, or to venture forth over territory where no ancestral roads had been built. In Old World culture no one can entertain a fresh thought without being chilled by the reminder that some long-dead mind once harboured it too : vanity of vanities! Through ages of sedulous repetition what was once active drama slumped back into stale ritual; and by sheer over-elaboration the original meaning of its forms of life often became obscured, and the living impulse within stifled.

Old World culture throve, and dominated the earth, probably, because of its early technical superiority in domesticating plants, in working up metals and manufacturing simple machines and utilities, and in creating cultural artifacts like writing and record keeping, which organised and unified the actions of men. But in the end, this culture prevailed because at its best it carried with it a richness of life, an exhilarating inventiveness, and a capacity for self-renewal that no cruder kind of society possessed : it demanded more of man's innate capabilities, and in turn it represented more of him.

The highest achievements of human self-cultivation, the hero, the saint, the sage, the lover, were primarily, as ideal types, the work of Old World man. But even the humbler types, those of the craftsman, the peasant, the simple householder, with their faithfulness to life's demands, through all trials and defeats, had their place and contributed to the whole: each a necessary block in the social pyramid. Religion and government, by means of art, deepened the human imprint: in the city Old World man plumbed every variety of social experience. This teeming vitality of Old World culture offsets in no small degree its residual weaknesses. Yet those weaknesses, often accumulating into a solid mass of corruption, must be appraised if we are to understand why New World man so readily left the whole fabric behind him; nay, took pleasure in actively demolishing much of it.

In the course of purely biological evolution, aberrations and deformations of a serious kind tend to be eliminated. Even in nature, however, the existence of parasites reminds us that natural selection may not get rid of deteriorated stocks, incapable of living by their own efforts; for mutual accommodation may overcome such defects. The capacity for coexistence and co-adaptation, rather than domination through individual excellence, seems often the ecological reason for survival. In the case of the social heritage natural selection operates even less drastically: the burdens of the past seem to be conserved almost as carefully as the benefits, and even radical human errors, like the institution of war, seem often to be self-perpetuating.

Though human culture is by nature a symbiosis, a mutually helpful living together of many different kinds of social partners within a common milieu, predatory and parasitic practices often prevail over co-operative ones. This fact is markedly true in Old World culture; for it never purged itself of its inherited, if not its inherent, defects. Perhaps the worst of these was the pursuit and ruthless exploitation of power, by means of organised armies, specially trained for slaughter and destruction. Old World society conserved this fatal invention; despite the precepts of the axial religions, war remained a respected institution, embedded in the Old World political structure. What is worse, Old World man handed over this invention to New World man, without adding those prudent limitations, those moral misgivings, those salutary ineptitudes and inertias which had, over the years, slowed down the rate of destruction and limited the area of violence to those professionally implicated.

But other evils also dogged Old World man. This culture did not diffuse its higher values as effectively as it spread the technology of the wheel, the plough, and the water mill. Not merely did the largest share of the income of these societies go to the small minority at the top, so that most of its members lived at the margin of subsistence, a grim, necessitous life, full of physical anxieties: this same distribution held for nonmaterial goods as well. A small group preserved for themselves a monopoly of knowledge, which set them apart from their fellows and gave them extra power to rule over them, artfully supplementing their monopoly of property and hired man power. In short, by both caste organisation and political skill, the dominant minority perpetuated and promoted their own kind, at the expense of the rest of the race.

In addition, these Old World upper castes reserved for their own initiates and clients the most valuable kinds of knowledge, beginning with the sacred forms and rites, and extending to technical inventions such as the early steam engines, contraceptives, and anaesthetics—all of which might have contributed to the common stock, at a far earlier date, if they had not been restricted. By their command of weapons, by their display of physical prowess, and often by cool brazen arrogance, the dominant minority achieved their position: then they sealed their claims by pre-empting land and property, often held in common in archaic society, for their own private uses.

The legal resources of government and the moral homilies of religion in time gave the sanction of a higher authority to these low practices. That the larger part of society should remain illiterate and unlearned, saddled with brute toil pushed to a point that would produce a surplus for the minority to enjoy, supplied with just sufficient food to keep them in working condition, with no hope of rising above this miserable state—all this was almost an axiom of Old World culture: the unstated major premise. Where this culture is intact, these characterisations still largely hold.

There were loopholes in this scheme, it goes without saying. Occasionally, sexual passion broke down the barriers erected between the ruling minorities and the common folk: the princess might marry a swineherd, or at least he might fall in love with her: a slave might be permitted, not without the friendly aid of his master, to accumulate sufficient property to purchase his own freedom. The great and powerful, by over-reaching themselves like Solon's proud contemporary, Croesus, might bring about their own downfall. And in times of plague or famine, the more able or the more crafty in the lower ranks might push their way into the seats of their one-time masters, even as a common soldier sometimes earns an officership on the battlefield. Sometimes, too, by strenuous effort, the son of a serf or a peasant, through exceptional ability, might acquire the letters and learning necessary to become one of the ruling group. The Chinese, with their imperial examination system, deliberately opened a place for this kind of talent; and the papacy of Rome, in the administrative and sacred offices of the Church, did likewise.

In Old World culture there was, in fact, just a sufficient amount of intermarriage, a sufficient loosening of the bonds of social status, a sufficient infiltration of able and intelligent spirits into the ranks above, to ensure the health and intellectual leadership of the upper classes themselves. Without this recruitment, they would have lacked the biological advantages of wide hybridisation or the social challenge of competition.

3

The main outlines of Old World culture have remained firm for some twenty-five hundred years: a dominant minority, seeking to monopolise the goods of civilisation for itself and a more or less oppressed, or at least circumscribed, majority, the 'internal or external proletariat,' as Toynbee calls them, who are allowed only a vicarious participation in the culture that they have helped to create and that, by their daily efforts and sacrifices, they keep going. This relationship never entirely solidified, not even in ancient Egypt or in India; for the privileges of the minority fostered insolence, and insolence hardened into a brutality that brought on resentment and protest: when these underlying tensions grew too formidable, they could be put down only by torturing, persecuting, and wiping out the rebels. Either by positive or negative means the result was disintegration.

But other means of diverting these protests from their natural objects became ingrained in Old World society: hatred of the ruling classes, for example, could be turned into hatred of the foreigner; and the desire to have some active share in the goods and creative activities of the fatherland could be turned into assault and destruction, pillage and rape, performed on some neighbouring community. When this did not avail, other devices would keep the shaky social pyramid stable—bread and circuses in all their many forms: occasional feasts, if not daily distribution of food, great civic and religious festivals, dances and games, carnival and saturnalia. When the sting of penury and toil grew too sharp, spirituous liquors, as old as civilisation itself, would serve as anesthetic. By these devices, Old World culture was kept alive, in spite of its errors and sins, through the centuries.

Perhaps the term 'vicarious participation' explains the strange submissiveness of the common man. Despite their social distance from the seats of power and glory, the masses of men, shining by the reflected light from their betters, felt their whole life illuminated by the power and glory of Old World culture. They had a sense of active involvement in an adventure that went far beyond their own capacity to dream and demand and yet was, in some odd way, deeply their own, pointing toward a future in which they would have a greater part. Without these symbols of glory, no amount of physical oppression would probably have availed.

For all their arrests and perversions, the Old World cultures produced in time a common background of meaning, value, and form, and with that an incentive toward greater efforts of creativity. The total achievement of Old World man, when taken as the basis for man's further self-transformation, deservedly ranks far higher than that of the isolated tribal cultures outside its orbit; for it contained a richer past and opened a more abundant promise for the future. The myths and fables and dramas of Old World man captivated and cultivated the mind: his monuments and cities, not least his cultivated landscapes, served as visible reminders of even greater invisible aspirations. In the service of his gods—sometimes, like Michelangelo, only in the service of those who professed to represent his gods—Old World man had evoked his own highest powers, with deeds of sustained physical exertion and spiritual daring.

Yet the essence of this achievement, the source of its inner tranquility and indeed its sleepy complacency, was the Old World sense of limits. If one excepts perhaps the great cosmic visions of the Hindus, Old World man inhabited a limited universe: the acceptance of these limits in time and space was part of his wisdom. Even the concepts of infinity or immortality, of divine omniscience and omnipotence, did not disturb his sense of his own boundaries. He dwelt within a circle whereof he was the centre, as his earth was the centre of the planets and the stars. Those who dwelt in the dim space beyond these boundaries were as if invisible: they were gentiles, barbarians, monkeys, savages, natives.

Even in relation to other cultures on the same level as its own, each group tended to regard only its own forms as truly human, and to deny, except under pressure of conquest, any merging of cultural differences. What Bergson said of biological species, in *Creative Evolution*, might be said of each of the Old World cultures, and of Old World culture itself, considered as an entity: 'It thinks only for itself, it lives only for itself.' Truth, beauty, goodness were conceived as proprietary products of the Old World mind: other forms and values, as the Hyberborean or the Hottentot might find them, did not fall within the canon of culture. By the same token any radical departure in a new direction which could not easily be reconciled with the existing body of customary thought was equally suspect. What could not be found in the Analects, in the Bible, in the Koran, or in Aristotle, or somehow attached to such central landmarks, was suspect.

As long as Old World economy enabled the dominant minority to flourish without driving the majority to vengeful violence or hopeless despair, this culture remained stable: indeed, the older it grew, the more adequate it was, through the very mixture of archaic, civilised, and axial forms, to meet any new challenge by a process of artful adjustment that drew on one or another part of its heritage, and brought the whole back into a state of balance. Predatory and profligate ways, on the part of the rulers, often upset this balance: violent assaults on the very mechanism of social memory, as in the burning of books under the First Emperor in China, the destruction of the Library at Alexandria, might imperil the superstructure; but the foundations in archaic culture remained sound. Olive trees might be cut down in war, or dams and aqueducts destroyed; but the essential sustenance for a life rich in human values, retrospective and prospective, remained.

In this scheme, the useful and the practical played only a subordinate part. So far was this accepted that the ruling castes paid little attention, even for selfish reasons, to improving the physical basis of their existence: they merely demanded a lion's portion of income from the utilities that were already employed. If an appetite for luxuries prompted them to predatory activities that demanded a larger field of operations, their conception of physical goods nevertheless remained primitive: an endless succession of gluttonous feasts and drinking bouts, or a galaxy of concubines to sate their sexual appetites.

Mark the stability and mediocrity of Old World technics, once the great early advances had been made. For all their experience with draught animals, the Romans, for example, never learned efficiently to harness a horse to a wagon. The strength of Old World achievement lay in its patient application of modest technical agents, backed by organised manpower, to great imaginative constructions: even when Old World man produced cunning technical devices, like gunpowder or steam, he would apply them at first merely to playful ends. Until the second millennium A.D. there had been, relatively, only a handful of serious technical advances in three thousand years. Perhaps the highest technical achievement of Old World culture, the casting of the great iron lions of China or the bronze sculptures of the Greeks—difficult tasks that would tax even present-day facilities— was devoted to works of art, not practical necessity. Though a great column of iron, of a chemical purity no present method of smelting achieves, was produced in ancient India, that achievement brought no further technical changes: it remained sterile. While iron cutting tools and mechanical devices made work easier, little was done with them that had not already been achieved with stone and copper implements.

In short, the acceptance of technical boundaries, too, remained a mark of Old World culture; and it was reinforced by similar moral restraints. Did not Leonardo da Vinci, himself a harbinger of New World interests, suppress his invention of the submarine for fear of putting such a destructive agent in human hands? In that inhibition, Old World wisdom, even when untempered by fear of the gods, still dominated.

This brings us to the core of Old World culture. From the beginning, it was to the gods that Old World man was dedicated. The discovery of the gods, the increasing definition and clarification of these possessive images, with their commanding visions of perfection, was perhaps the central contribution of Old World culture. The goods of life, as the Old World sages viewed them, were not set in the visible material world, for that world was increasingly viewed as an illusion of the senses, a counterfeit of reality: they existed rather in invisible presences and forces that manifested themselves in all the occasions of life. To approach the gods and understand them, one must withdraw from practical duties and household cares: one must listen to the admonitions of dream, the voice of reason, the commands of the spirit. In the axial religions the multitudinous images of godhood united into a single generalised figure of power and love, largely purified of the perverse, neurotic, and demonic projections of a more primordial unconscious.

The knowledge of this divine possibility became the key to every other form of knowledge. To understand reality, one did not look at or manipulate visible things: one sought to penetrate God's mind and imitate its perfection. In that purity of abstraction mathematics flourished: a world of ideal forms and self-defined possibilities. As late as the seventeenth century, an able young French physicist, Mersenne, could say: 'If I could be convinced that God always did things in the shortest and easiest way, then I should certainly have to recognise that the world does move.'

On this basis, only those who held aloof in some degree from servile tasks and utilitarian chores were capable of living a truly human life: that dedicated to the contemplation of God and the pursuit of wisdom. The Biblical author of Ecclesiasticus had uttered that Old World conviction long ago. By these standards the priest and the prophet, the poet and the philosopher and the saint, were fulfilling man's highest possible destiny: their activities were sacred, and the support of them was thus the most pressing obligation of society. To serve man one must first serve God; to achieve even the level of the human one must reach for the divine. That belief unites the Bible of Moses and the Koran of Mahomet: the *Bhagavad-Gita* and the New Testament. Life at its fullest and best is divine service, and nothing less than that service will lift the soul of Old World man. When he falls short of this ideal, as he so often does, he is cast down by feelings of guilt and self-reproach: when he thrusts it behind him altogether, he is lost. Lacking faith in the divine essence, Old World man could not without dismay confront existence.

At the beginning, in Egypt or Babylonia, there was no such clear sense of a divine destination: the cosmic and the human interpenetrated, somewhat to the debasement of the gods. Though the divine powers might seem terrible, yet, if one knew their true name or otherwise could bring some effective magic to bear, one might cheat them or deceive them. If they disobeyed one's prayers one might curse them: under certain conditions one might even capture them and seize some of their attributes. But in the development of Old World man, the axial religions and philosophies had finally succeeded in erecting a graded hierarchy of meanings and values. At the bottom was the visible, the tangible, the knowable, the urgent, the practical: at the top were the mysterious, the ideal, the transcendent, the divine. Even those who were most active in the lower stories of this edifice admitted the primacy of the upper floors and paid special reverence to those who concerned themselves with the expression of ultimate values. People with technical skill or political power never presumed to take precedence over those who dreamed dreams or interpreted meanings. If they did, as Alexander the Great did when he summoned Hindu sages to his presence, they were swiftly rebuked.

But the purity of this effort at divine transcendence was debased in all the Old World cultures by the temporal rewards that frequently accompanied or, sometimes inadvertently, flowed from it. Thus the beautiful life of the Benedictine abbeys, dedicated to divine service by prayer and manual toil and reflection, produced, by the very success of the system, the temptations of worldly wealth and power. Each attempt to find a new form for the divine vision—since only by renewal could it be preserved—was limited, furthermore, by the impulse to fit it into a serviceable traditional mould: witness the all-too-swift materialisation of the Franciscan order, in opposition to Francis' own deepest intuitions. Thus, too, each axial religion, despite its professed universality, became infected with national or racial particularity. The guardians of this society, in fact, never understood the causal processes that conditioned their higher achievements; not understanding them, they repeated, in epoch after epoch, the same fatal mistakes. The knowledge and detachment needed to overcome this tendency toward fixation at a lower level were lacking: even more lacking, perhaps, was the consciousness that such knowledge might be of service in finding a way out.

4

The cyclic frustration of every Old World culture is significant. Civilisation in itself is not good enough to justify the sacrifices it exacts: there must be a 'beyond.' That beyond was presented by religion as Heaven: at first only in an image and a myth that carried no viable promise of realisation, except in so far as its illusory presence made itself felt in every daily act. By the association of the beyond with life's negative moments, culminating in death, all the positive goods of life became frivolous and senseless. Religion, to preserve itself from undercutting its own foundations, was drawn back repeatedly into making the institutional form a substitute for the original vision, since it failed to find a beyond that was attainable on earth, and yet would be lifted to a higher plane and get sight of a more impelling ideal with every successive fulfilment. No final revelation was capable of creating such an ever-enlarging, ever-receding goal.

The cyclic nature of civilisation has been the subject of examination over a long period; and in our own time, a series of acute observers, beginning with Jakob Burckhardt, Patrick Geddes, and Henry Adams, have come forward with their partial explanations. Oswald Spengler's effort to interpret this cyclic process, through the use of metaphors deriving from seasonal changes and plant growth, was plausible but meretricious: for it wilfully hid all evidences of a later manifestation when present in an earlier stage—such as the gridiron plan of 'sterile mechanical civilisation' in medieval frontier towns. So, too, it misinterpreted or ignored all the continuities, the interchanges; and it failed to account for early disintegrations and belated renewals—end products at the beginning as the result of injury, or fresh flowerings in autumn when one looks only for seeds.

Arnold Toynbee's more exhaustive inquiry, which exchanged Spengler's crude biological figure for a detailed study of causes and reasons, is itself so much the product of Old World ideology that it never confronts its own unexamined premises: hence, in the very definition of society as an intelligible field for study, it bestows on the actual nature of the community, which may require knowledge of much that happened outside this field, its own self-limiting assumptions. Toynbee's final conclusion is that the disintegration of civilisations, which comes sooner or later, has meaning as the prelude of a new kind of society, founded by a new kind of organisation, the universal church, whose province is 'outside history.' Such a heavenly form of salvation is achieved only by the individual soul. That such a destiny should seem to either explain or justify history seems incredible to one not involved at the outset in Toynbee's theological premises. But there is a hardly less drastic criticism to be made in terms of history itself: namely, that each universal church has turned out to be far from universal. Even more damaging to Toynbee's conclusions is the fact that the universal religions are obviously subject to the same cyclic frustration as secular civilisations themselves.

On the evidence, some fundamental elements, some growth hormones, seem lacking in the Old World cultures; and this has kept them from developing beyond a certain point. No one can pretend to have discovered these elements as yet: but perhaps what has been absent has been overlooked only because it is so obvious, like the cell door in the Scots village jail that Houdini struggled in vain to break open by his usual methods, because it was actually unlocked. What perhaps has been needed is a system of intercommunication and co-operation that would enable all the elements of the Old World cultures to coalesce into a larger unity. In short, it is perhaps the very self-enclosure of the Old World pattern that made it, not merely a dominant on the planet, but also made it seem an ecological 'climax.' That cyclic existence condemned it to terminate in frustration, corruption, schism, and mortal disintegration : only to repeat, with each succeeding civilisation and religion, the same dismal round.

This would be a difficult point to establish, even provisionally, were it not for a change that has taken place during the last four centuries: the first radical breakthrough in this cyclic scheme. That singular transformation—which I shall call for contrast New World culture—has already displaced the archaic and axial components of Old World culture as ruthlessly as the cities of the ancient river civilisations displaced the village culture of the neolithic period. The materials for this new culture, with its world-wide provenance, had long been present in many other societies; but they had hardly done more than colour the surface in a few scattered places. Now this New World culture has formed a pattern of its own. Because of its methodical efficiency and mechanical universality it plainly threatens to wreck what is left of Old World culture.

Thus the emergency of New World culture, in completed form, in our time has produced of itself a world crisis. As far as the records tell, this is the first planet-wide crisis that has taken place since the last glacial period. But the menace that then came from nature now comes from the busy hands and minds of men.

6

New World Man

I

Even contemporaries of Columbus, like the Florentine humanist, Poliziano, recognised that the discovery of the New World was an event of the greatest significance. But the New World that Columbus daringly stumbled upon was a fact of geography, a part of the planet that had long remained out of association with Europe and Asia; whereas New World culture, as I shall here define it, is a larger conception, a new territory of the mind, a new province of human activity, in whose development the geographic area played an important but subordinate part. The leaders in this broader movement understood its promise no less than Poliziano. 'The novelties of ancient truths,' Campanella wrote to Galileo, 'of new worlds, new systems, new nations, are the beginning of a new era.'

By New World culture I refer to two radically different ideologies, from which sprang two equally different ideal human types: almost opposite poles of the human personality. One may call them, with a general extension of meaning, the romantic and the mechanical. The first accompanied a general resurgence of vitality and sexuality in Europe. This became visible in early baroque architecture and painting, and reached its apex, symbolically, in Michelangelo's paintings in the Sistine Chapel. To the conquest of new lands, the explorer, the conquistador, the pioneer brought an Homeric courage and daring, and a readiness to face the untried and the unknown with unshakable self-reliance. The second traded vitality for power: by a process of systematic regimentation in pursuit of gain, he carried further the material triumphs—likewise the restrictive uniformities—of civilisation.

During the last two centuries, these modes flourished side by side, attracting and producing contrasting types of human character, one dominant, the other recessive. For one ideal moment, they were united in Defoe's myth of Robinson Crusoe. What bound them together and made them temporarily allies was the fact that they were both in revolt against Old World culture. But as the geographic New World filled with immigrants, indeed as population generally began to increase, the mechanical New World almost automatically became dominant. The unfettered vitalities of romantic man, wedded only to nature, soon became decorative activities that graced a purely mechanical routine, like a picnic with an open fire in a paved urban back yard.

Both types of New World man sought to leave the Old World culture behind : they wanted to make precedents instead of following them. Romantic man went back to nature and sought a new start on cultural territory that antedated the historical development of civilisation : mechanical man went forward to the machine. These two efforts intersected, as it were, on the island of Utopia. But I shall first deal with that part of New World culture whose uniform institutions encompass the whole planet, and now threaten to wipe out or absorb every other culture.

Philosophically speaking, this New World was a product of rationalism, utilitarianism, scientific positivism. Objectivity and causality were the dominating principles of the new ideology : only those aspects of human experience that were external and repeatable, open to the inspection of other men, verifiable either by experiment or strictly controlled induction and deduction, were treated as real. By the same token, subjectivity and teleology had no place in this new framework of ideas : whatever was self-developed, inwardly conditioned, nonrepeatable, unique, or purposeful was excluded as unreal. New World culture meant organisation, standardisation, regularity, control, applied to every manifestation of life. Purpose, ejected from its more organic and human context, became embodied in the machine and the mechanical collective.

When defined in these terms it is plain that the materials for a New World ideology and a New World economy had been lying about, ready for use, for many millennia. In one sense, the New World merely resumed and widened the process of regimentation that had come in with civilisation itself. With the invention of money, the foundations of capitalism had long ago been laid. In the order and tactics of the Sumerian phalanx, the conception of the army as a machine, composed of specialised, interlocking parts, responsive to a single centre of command, laid a pattern that could be applied to other organisations. Concern with the measurement of space and time was not unknown in the ancient world: Roman carriages were sometimes equipped with taxi-meters; and water clocks, clepsydra, were widely used.

So, too, the regular, orderly life, free from sensuous distractions, inured to a repetitive daily round, had taken form in the monas-tery: the desire for regularity there spurred the archetypal in-vention of New World culture, the mechanical clock. The scientific basis of this culture was equally old: Thales and Democritus, Pythagoras and Euclid, Archimedes and Hero of Alexandria, had freed the observation of nature from mythic explanation and wilful subjectivity: indeed, the recovery of their texts played a critical part in the exploration of the New World: Archimedes' statics actually prompted Galileo's mechanics. In their very faith in the possibility of establishing universal scientific laws, the new scientist was sustained by the Christian theologian's vision of an all-embracing divine order: in contenting himself with piecemeal truths he still assumed an intelligible whole.

In short, at one point or another, the scattered artifacts of the mechanical New World had come into existence and served their specific uses within the general context of Old World culture. But these separate inventions and ways of thought had never coalesced into a single system, still less did they overwhelm human consciousness. When the Macedonian phalanx conquered the Near East and India, it brought Greek art and Greek philosophy to other people, not a further extension of the idea of regimentation to other departments of life.

So sedulously was the garden of Old World culture dedicated to its own chosen flowers that the seeds of rationalisation and mechanisation, even when they sprouted in its soil, were ex-tirpated as weeds: they could only take root in occasional cracks in the surrounding wall, with never enough soil to nourish their full growth. Even such an obvious invention as printing—already in existence, potentially, with the moulding and stamping of clay seals in ancient Mesopotamia, to say nothing of later coins—re-mained dormant for thousands of years. While Old World culture held together, no such gross changes as took place after the seventeenth century were possible.

That the New World culture got its start during a period of grave social and ideological disruption should not, accordingly, surprise us. In the West the beginnings of the new culture date back to the great catastrophe of the fourteenth century, the Black Death: a plague that wiped out between one-third and one-half of the population of Western Europe. This was the century that witnessed the schism in the Christian Church, with two rival popes contending for power, while the repeated efforts of Protestantism (Waldo, Wycliffe, Fox) to return to a simpler Christianity deepened that fissure. Within the span of a few centuries the focus of interest shifted from the inner world to the outer world: from a disordered and contentious subjectivity to a rigorously ordered objectivity, whose very method guaranteed agreement.

To torn, divided souls, this new order came as a blessing: and the new goods and powers brought forth by the machine briskly offset the dwindling energies of the spirit. The measurement of time and space, the multiplication of nonorganic sources of energy, the reduction of distances by speeding transportation, the quickening of the processes of production—all these acts of the New World economy advanced together, at first slowly, but presently with increasing momentum.

As early as the thirteenth century, Roger Bacon and Albertus Magnus had in their imaginations sighted this new continent and staked out claims there. Roger Bacon foretold the coming of self-propelled vehicles of locomotion, of instantaneous long-distance communication, as possibilities already visible in the further exploitation of scientific knowledge. In the iron mines of Saxony, by the beginning of the sixteenth century, Dr. Georg Bauer (Agricola) demonstrated that the embryonic environment of the machine had already come into existence: the railroad, the elevator, the artificial ventilation of mine shafts, power-driven machinery.

By the beginning of the seventeenth century, the final steps in charting this New World were taken: Francis Bacon described the role of further mechanical invention and Galileo perfected a method which equated knowledge with quantitative measurement, eliminating both subjective qualities and organic human purposes. The New World methodology progressively displaced the Old World ideology. Knowledge no longer merely served power: it produced power.

This concern with punctuality and regularity, with the impersonal and the automatic, bound together the inventor, the scientist, the businessman, the soldier, the bureaucrat. 'As regular as clockwork' became a term of eulogy: the new man regulated his bowels and even his orgasms by clock and calendar, with no respect to more organic rhythms. Different though their vocations were, these men of the New World understood each other. Within the new mechanical organisations they created—the army, the countinghouse, the factory—their success depended upon skill in fabricating uniform, interchangeable parts, assembled in an efficient machine. Their universe was one of matter and motion, of measurement and calculation : it was composed of elements that could be extracted from their organic whole, broken down into discrete atomic parts, and reassembled in a machine. The secondary qualities of matter, so real in the world of life—colour, form, rhythm, pattern, design—were rejected as irrelevant if not a mere subjective illusion.

In short, nothing in life counted except what was countable : units of weight, measure, time, space, energy, money. These were the building stones of the New World : a habitat where in the end men were acceptable only when they took on the attributes of machines, where in the foreseeable future machines would be developed to surpass and replace men.

Science was the great tool refashioned by the New World mind : the systematisation of inquiry into the forces of nature, and eventually into man himself considered merely as a product of nature. By systematic experiment and accurate observation, by logical and mathematical analysis, the sciences gave New World man a means of overcoming unguarded subjectivity. This was the durable New World contribution to man's development—apart from its progressive revelation of an immense, teeming world, a microcosm and a macrocosm, increasingly open to prediction and control. Both were superb achievements, essential for man's further growth.

But the process of methodically isolating nature from human nature, physical forces from human purposes, was not for early scientists like Galileo an end in itself : it was, at the beginning, only a beneficent enlargement of the Aristotelian and Christian cosmos, to which, as de Santillana reminds us, Galileo still piously clung. None of the early scientists could anticipate the full force of their own revolutionary system, once the containing envelope of Old World culture had dropped away, and the expansion of knowledge and power became its own supposedly self-justifying goal.

Though pure science was often pursued in relative independence from the needs of technics and industry, the new scientists submitted to the same canons of economy and efficiency : the continued subdivision of labour and specialisation of the product, in the interest of greater quantitative output. By ignoring organic complexities, inter-relationships, and integrated wholes, the new investigators gained speed and accuracy in dealing with the data so isolated. But unfortunately, in accepting a strict division of labour as a necessity for accurate, objective thought, the scientists uncritically carried into their new calling the typical vocational restrictions—and some of the defects of life and character—exhibited by Civilised Man.

In return for absolute authority within his narrowed field, the scientist progressively forfeited contact with the whole, even in related departments of science, and still more within the general sphere of life. This furnished an excuse for his ignorance outside his specialism, and a justification of his claim to social irresponsibility: above all, it provided the ideal conditions for untrammelled productivity, released from any other ends except the systematic pursuit of scientific truths. The ultimate goal of New World expansion in this department—if one may speak thus of a method that boasted its non-concern for ultimate goals—was invisible to the great minds that originally shaped the New World ideology. Even now, the anti-rational results of its rational procedures and the intellectual disorder produced by its partial concept of order, have hardly been adequately appraised. As long as expansion itself remained the dominant value, no criterion for appraisal in non-quantitative terms existed: at least none that scientists felt obliged to accept. As with the productivity of an expanding economy, such an inquiry might lead to deflation and even bring an admission of bankruptcy that would make necessary a general reorganisation.

2

The New World economy, it goes without saying, did not come into existence overnight: it is only in the twentieth century that it finally reached a point of development that clearly revealed its characteristics as a complete system. But wherever it penetrated, New World culture swiftly created its own environment: dehumanised, depersonalised, mechanically ordered, uniform. Where the Old World culture held firm, as in Italy, Spain, and France, the New World culture had only a weak foothold: the strength of Catholic civilisation deprived Latin America, too, of many typical New World characteristics. The machine-centred way of life throve best, in fact, in culturally backward areas, sparsely settled and isolated; and the new towns it created were urban wildernesses, rampant with vitality, but more innocent of human amenity, more barbarous even in lack of physical utilities, than the backwoods areas of North America.

But no culture conquers through its weaknesses. From the beginning the new mechanical system recognised certain essential human needs that the Old World culture, even the highest forms conceived by axial man, either ignored or suppressed.

To begin with, the New World ideology broke through the frozen hierarchies of Old World culture. With its sense of the future, as subject to human plan and control, the New World ideology detached contemporary man from undue subjection to his immediate historic environment. What began in the Renaissance as a return to the more rational classic past now was directed into anticipation of a more rational future. In concentrating on the study of nature and the control of natural forces, the New World ideology promised to remove limitations on human power that had always been irksome: now instead of wishfully dreaming of giants and djinns that could build a palace overnight, the new inventors devised machines that magnified and multiplied all man's powers. Physical energies that once only great monarchs commanded were now at the disposal of the entire collectivity—and in far vaster quantities. Limitations on human action that had once frustrated man's most innocent plans were now removed.

Apart from its practical triumphs, the New World economy offered another attraction: the knowledge it placed within man's reach was not at the mercy of his unconscious. Instead of presenting man with fitful glimpses of the whole, as in moments of mystical insight, the new science systematically put together minute fragments which, when formulated by minds with a high capacity for abstraction, could be worked into intelligible fields of verified knowledge. Where arbitrary revelations had once produced false explanations of natural processes, sanctified by equally arbitrary authority, science provided a self-corrective method for establishing truths, in a new spirit of humility and self-effacement. The criterion of truth ceased to be the authority of the person: 'I say thus.' It rather became the demonstration or the trial: 'It works thus.'

Though the new method did not do justice to human experience in its wholeness, including what was subjective, self-begotten, or unique, it did at least give security and the power of limited prediction over that part which could be externally observed and measured. In a time of extreme subjective disorder and division, which undermined religion, the scientific method offered common ground for all who cared to stand on it. On its own terms, that ground could be expanded in every direction, without limits. So the surface workings of physics finally led to the underground seams of depth psychology.

This new world vision was incarnated in a series of personalities, from Jacob Fugger to Benjamin Franklin, from Bacon and Galileo and Newton to Watt and Arkwright: but its most exemplary incarnation was in the machine itself and in the new kind of organisation the machine made possible. The machine appeared, indeed, as an instrument of salvation, at a moment when doubt and heresy and inner betrayal had weakened faith in the axial means of salvation. Not merely did the New World ideology introduce, in science, a common method of thought: it created a common discipline of life, or rather, it extended the discipline of the axial religions into the common tasks of daily life, hitherto governed by more human standards of interest or boredom, zeal or laziness.

The very element of repetition, long used in religious ritual, proved a means of allaying anxiety. By concentration on the immediate and the practical, the insoluble enigmas that troubled Old World man—the nature of the universe, the origin and destiny of man—were sealed off: the energy that was thus contained could be diverted into business. The New World personality turned to problems that were small enough to be grasped and solved: he addressed himself to activities where his operational skill and method promised an immediate, if not an ultimate, reward. The uniform, the regular, the predictable, just because they narrowed the range of human choice, produced a happy sense of inner security: up to a point everything seemed under control. The end could now be taken for granted: process had supplanted purpose, and 'the going was the goal.' Within a few centuries these ideas took form and passed into action.

In the New World culture the Old World attributes of personality naturally dropped into the background: family inheritance, noble breeding, aesthetic sensitiveness, badges of status, played little part in the success of the merchant or the inventor. The question was: Could he deliver the goods? These new figures prided themselves, often, on being 'self-made men,' and until far along in this transformation many of them were, in fact, self-taught, from Palissy and Franklin to Faraday and Bell. Reading, writing, and arithmetic, ever more widely practised after the fourteenth century, helped to level off old privileges and break through class barriers. Even more, perhaps, than the clock, the printing press was the most revolutionary development of the New World culture. Not merely was the printing press the pattern of all later machines based in standardised replaceable parts: it was likewise the first wholly mechanical achievement in large-scale production. In so far as culture depends on written symbols, the printed book broke the class monopoly of culture. The secrets of the ruling classes, at least the book knowledge that had helped maintain their position and authority since the bronze age were now open to the public.

In the seventeenth century, the extension of the system of education to the whole population by means of the common school had been worked out in principle by John Amos Comenius. His system was based on the feasibility of developing uniform methods that removed the need for personal pedagogical talent and applying these methods in a series of graded steps, which led from the primary school to the university. Uniformity, impersonality, and mass production had never before been applied to education. Surely it is no accident that the first large-scale development of these methods took place in the eighteenth century, not in democratic countries, but under an absolutist militarism in Prussia: a pattern for other public school systems, Napoleonic and later, seeking the fruits of regimentation. We have lived to see both the triumphs of this conception—and its embarrassing limitations—when it is not counterbalanced by the aristocratic impulse toward lonely excellence.

In the reduction of all the phenomena of nature to measurable units the process could not stop abruptly at man. René Descartes pointed out that animals could be treated as if they were only more complicated machines; and though he exempted man from this category, he made it plain that, were it not for the theological conception of the soul, man could be handled in the same fashion. Having reduced himself by the process of mechanical analysis to a mere moving part, New World man treated this definite segment of himself, knowable and controllable, as if it were the whole.

This principle had many practical applications in the army and factory and could be extended, almost indefinitely, outside these realms. In mass voting by ballot, for example, the same mechanical methods were applied to politics, little though the implications were understood. Each individual would be treated as a numerical unit, without respect to qualitative differences of experience, education, corporate affiliation, or personal force. As a democratic check on arbitrary power, the ballot served well; but the political process would have come to a standstill had not effective power and responsibility been exercised by non-statistical methods behind the scenes. Democracy has not yet mastered this weakness.

Yet one has only to put the various elements of the New World culture together to understand why, in spite of its contemptuous denial of Old World principles, it gradually gained a foothold in Europe and during the last century has not merely thinly spread its methods over the earth, but in ancient centres like India, China, Iran now threatens to displace the old tissue of values. By the very simplification that mechanical order produced, it gave a place and a status to the mass of men they had never enjoyed; for in a purely mechanical system, mass and number now counted. Though at first the gains in energy and productivity were slow to reach the common man, mass production, by its very nature, tended to equalise consumption. Was not machine-made jewellery (brummagem), cheap enough for the poor to buy, one of the early products of Birmingham? That fact was symbolic. Whatever the politics of a country, the machine was a communist. As a result capitalism, which had rested on the Old World principle of class differentiation, was finally, as a measure of self-preservation, forced to accept the 'welfare state,' with its far-reaching provisions for equalisation.

The turning from a subjectively conditioned Old World to an object-centred New World was more than a shift from art to technics : it was also a release from a starved and overinhibited life, in which low vitality was almost a token of holiness, to a life of high vitality, marked by expanding appetites, a more varied and abundant diet, and a rising birth rate aided by early marriages as well as the improved care of the young. Even the iron law of wages, invoked to exact profits from the starvation of the worker, did not for long overcome this general tendency. Observe what happened to the seven deadly sins of Christian theology. All but one of these sins, sloth, was transformed into a positive virtue. Greed, avarice, envy, gluttony, luxury and pride were the driving forces of the new economy : if once they were mainly the vices of the rich, they now under the doctrine of expanding wants embraced every class in society. Thus unbounded power was harnessed to equally unbounded appetites.

Now Old World culture had placed limits on all human activities. Physician, priest, and sage united to counsel moderation in every department: the dangers of insolence and pride were as present in the minds of ancient Greek dramatists as in those of medieval theologians. This notion of organic limits, so natural in biology, was summed up by Aristotle: 'To the size of a state there is a limit, as there is to other things, plants, animals, implements; for none of these retains their natural power when they are too large or too small, but they lose wholly their nature or are spoiled.' New World culture, on the contrary, was based on lifting all limits and letting go: laissez faire. Every curb, every restraint, every inhibition, every non-material interest threatened the forces of expansion.

Thus the New World economy, just because it was based on natural human lusts and drives, went by itself as long as the conditions for indefinite expansion existed naturally: its energies flowed downward, as naturally as a river seeks the sea. This ideology needed no director, no controlling deity, no plan of organisation, no visible goal: by a 'pre-established harmony' the most selfish aims would produce socially beneficial results, as long as 'benefits' were equated with expansion and quantification. Under this scheme of life, goals and ends capable of working an inner transformation were obsolete: mechanical expansion itself had become the supreme goal. The machine was both the necessary means and the ultimate end.

In short, New World man flourished by giving in to the very impulses axial man had sought to control and make subservient to the canons of reason and the service of God. So ingrained did the anti-teleological principle become that proposals to slow down or arrest any part of the machinery of production appeared as outrageous heresies.

3

For a time, the material constrictions on mechanical culture were offset by adventures and opportunities that sprang from the New World: oceans and continents that Old World man had, up to the fifteenth century, never explored except in the most timid, desultory fashion now invited occupation. For Western man not merely systematically explored these lands but conquered them: he not merely conquered them, but he settled them and dedicated them to a life radically different from that he left behind.

As with the mechanical phase of New World culture, the materials for the romantic myth and practice had long been in existence. One of the recurrent themes of Old World culture, in reaction against the constraints of civilisation, if not the inhibitions of axial religion, is a return to nature. That note was sounded in Lao-tse and Theocritus, it was repeated in Saint Jerome, when he contemplated leaving Rome behind him: it came forth again in Francis of Assisi, preaching naked before his congregation, and addressing himself, as a brother, to all wild things. In the romantic movement, Old World man sought to recover parts of himself that civilisation had fettered and axial religion rejected: that which bound him organically to all created life.

Nature, for the romantic philosopher, is a process at work in both the cosmos and man: as Lao-tse put it, it is the Way. All living creatures follow the Way; but man, by his civilised institutions and customs, has departed from it; only the primitive and the untutored, the noble savage or the little child, are close enough to the Way to live in the fullness of their own nature, reaching their utmost height and breadth, like a tree in the open that has never been pruned, or constricted by the overshadowing presence of other trees.

To find the Way one must leave behind cities, institutions, ceremonials, the whole business of getting and spending, which limit growth and curb the spontaneous affections. The forest will become one's temple: the brooks and the stones will utter their sermons: the wild creatures will reward one with companionship. In sexual life, particularly, spontaneity and mutual delight must prevail: indeed the 'return to nature' first began in this province, and the romantic canons of the Provençal troubadours were carried into domestic life in the writings of William Penn, well before Rousseau. Considerations of property and status and tribal classification, which afflicted even primitive communities, must be thrown off. Sexual passion flouts such curbs; and the only family that romanticism acknowledges is one conceived and begotten in love. In the cult of the lover and the cult of the child New World man, in his romantic phase, was to leave perhaps his most permanent impress. Yet whatever is wild, wayward, untamed, spontaneous, innocently primitive, whatever has escaped regimentation and uniformity—whether in the soul or in the landscape—owes a debt to the romantics, from Petrarch onward.

But to live in accordance with nature one must live within nature. Here the opening of the New World offered an opportunity that had long been lacking in the more prosperous, densely settled lands of Europe and Asia. The first promise of the New World was that of renewing the vision of effortless plenty that Old World man had wistfully relegated to the long-past golden age. Here were primeval forests filled with game, rich unploughed soils, teeming with wild berries, with new fruits and grains and tubers, notably maize and the potato; here were coastal waters, dense with clams, oysters, mussels, crabs, and schools of fishes, skies that would darken at noonday with wild pigeons.

Before the population had caught up with the food supply and drunken excess had eaten into this plenty, the settlement of the New World lifted the fear of poverty, dearth, overcrowding, that had continued to haunt Old World man. Here nature's bounty for once temporarily exceeded the human demand : provided one asked only for what nature could give, with but a modicum of human aid, and did not demand the refinements of civilisation. The New World offered a veritable horn of plenty; it gave for the asking what mechanical civilisation promised only in return for a life of exacting toil, chained to the machine. Here, for those who had been without property, were equal opportunities, which would presently reveal the natural inequalities of talent and fortitude.

If the villages and towns of the New World were first conceived in the image of the old, by the end of the eighteenth century they had sufficiently adapted themselves to the new environment to produce a new type of man and a new way of life that corresponded to the dreams and prophecies of Rousseau : a Daniel Boone and a John James Audubon, presently a Thoreau and a Lincoln. In the new life of the frontier, where fire and axe preceded the plough, where the hunter and the trapper provided the main source of livelihood, the essential qualities of pre-civilised life were explored again. These conditions fostered the mutual aid and the neighbourly interdependence of the small community, with its contempt for a money economy or the distinctions of status and rank, with its admiration for character and personal worth. That primeval sense of human equality became a New World trait. If nineteenth-century political democracy had been rooted in that soil, expressed ideally in the

New England town meeting, it would probably have brought forth sounder fruit.

For a moment a primeval wholeness seemed indeed restored in this New World culture; and it was restored on a higher plane, with many of its superstitions and archaicisms sloughed off; and with just a sufficient infiltration of ideas and practices from other historic cultures, including the mechanical New World itself, to promote eager growth and adventurous transcendence. In the great works of the Golden Day, in the essays of Emerson and Horatio Greenough, in Thoreau's *Walden*, in Melville's *Moby-Dick* and *White-Jacket*, in Walt Whitman's *Leaves of Grass* and *Democratic Vistas*, the ideal content of this culture, enriched by the experience of three hundred years in the wilderness, was formulated. In the horticulture and landscape gardening of the eighteen-fifties, as in the shingle domestic architecture of the eighteen-eighties, the forms of this culture were significantly externalised and expressed. These original works of art promised even more for New World culture than had already been achieved. But by the time the romantic phase of New World culture was ready to flower, its mechanical phase had crystallised: the implacable spread of the machine began to undermine one by one the varied regional forms.

Yet in the biological sciences—perhaps there alone—the two aspects of the New World ideology came together in a fruitful union: rational organisation and terrestrial exploration reinforced each other. The geographers and naturalists of the eighteenth and nineteenth century, the Bartrams, the von Humboldts, the Darwins, surveyed and staked out the great dominion of life, on a scale that would have overwhelmed Aristotle, Theophrastus, or Pliny the Elder, pushing its origins backward in time hundreds of millions of years, establishing lines of filiation and ascent that brought into relation species hitherto considered independent creations, turning disconnected episodes into organic continuities, and chance associations into closely knit partnerships. Even in the physical character and distribution of the chemical elements, as L. J. Henderson was to demonstrate, the earth itself revealed a predisposition favourable to the unstable but self-directing processes of life, working against inertia and entropy. Man's self-transformation, on this evidence, was part of a much vaster process of organic and cosmic evolution, which both conditioned him and released him for more adventurous departures.

If this effort to produce a human culture in closer relationship both to nature itself and to man's growing sense of nature had had time to take root, it might have regenerated the Old World no less than the New, sufficiently to direct mechanical improvement, when it came, to large human ends. But that 'if' is a vain one : the very discovery of the New World was itself an achievement of science and technics : impossible without the compass, the sextant, the three-masted ship and the sailing chart. The two aspects sprang into existence together and the mechanical phase quickly dominated by promising, not a generous enrichment of life, but an enlargement of profit and power. The lesson of mutual aid was degraded into the struggle for existence; and ruthless practices of Victorian industrialism were projected back upon nature, in a doctrine that confused extermination with creativity, and survival with development. The very instruments that enabled the Western pioneer to conquer the wilderness also overthrew the romantic interests that had partly lured him there.

Five thousand years of 'civilisation' supported that promise; the forces of life were not yet ready to challenge this ancient regimen, nor were the more sinister automatisms and compulsions of mechanical civilisation yet sufficiently obvious to serve as warning. The romantic exodus was blocked by the age-old social prestige of law and order, property and status. Before he knew it, the New World adventurer traded his freedom for security and comfort.

So this aspect of New World culture was only a temporary one : the virgin lands, once penetrated, brought forth another kind of offspring. Vitality gave way before the uniformities of mechanised power, adventure was driven to more distant frontiers, and close behind the valiant conquistadors marched the capitalist enterprisers, girdling the continents with railroads and steamship lines and telegraphs. Instead of entering into reciprocal relations with the peoples he conquered, seeking to prolong and enhance the values that had been repressed by Old World culture, New World man too often showed himself more savage than the most primitive groups whose cultures he despoiled. Imperialist competition and exploitation brought on a cycle of wars that culminated in the twentieth century, making that period the most bloody and brutal epoch in history. With the lands of the New World largely occupied and settled, with population pressing upon food supply throughout the planet, with an ever larger mass of people all over the world caught in the new industrial machine, the compensatory vitalities of New World man sought another, darker outlet. Not freedom and vitality, but power, regimentation, conformity and absolutism have now become the dominant elements in the New World culture: not least in countries where totalitarian automatism is quaintly called 'free enterprise' and generals and businessmen act in interchangeable roles.

In general, New World man wasted the treasures he opened up and he trampled out the very life he had originally quickened to. But some of the artifacts and customs in primitive or archaic cultures nevertheless became part of New World culture. Tobacco smoking and gum chewing, if not the betel nut, spread over the Western world: the dark, sun-baked body of the 'primitive' children of nature became the desired uniform of pale Western skins: the rubber of the Amazon natives transformed the whole technology of the New World, from transportation to contraception. Within their own narrower ambit, primitive peoples had usually preserved, better than those who had submitted to civilisation, their contact with the central modes of life: respect for sexuality and for the phases of bodily growth, communication with their own unconscious resources, welling up in dream and myth, not least the innate joy of being, in a harmonious relationship to nature. Had New World man shown more understanding of the whole range of primitive gifts, too often despised and cast aside, he would have left mankind as a whole both wiser and richer.

4

Because of their close association in time, abetted by their equal rejection of Old World assumptions, the two phases of New World culture had certain common traits. These traits I now propose to evaluate, in order to account for the continuous expansion and ascendancy of New World man. They are, incidentally, a necessary contribution to the next phase of human development.

The first great departure was in the concept of human equality, not as a promise for the axial afterworld, but as a necessary demand of justice in every earthly society. With this denial goes a tacit rejection of the claim on the part of any class or group to a major share of the joint stock of knowledge, invention, wealth, natural resources. The notion of such equalisation was repeated with increasing insistence and confidence from the fourteenth century on: it is the dream of John Bull as reported with sympathetic eloquence by Froissart: it is the ideal state imagined by Thomas Moore in his *Utopia*; it is the cry of the Levellers in the Puritan revolution, as it was of the Anabaptists and the revolting peasants in Luther's time. This idea sounded forth once more, like a thunderclap in the French Revolution, and was accepted by all the feudal estates in their dramatic renunciation of their rights and privileges. Finally, equalisation was the mighty appeal of socialism in the nineteenth century; so strong that it still gives a deceptively humane glow to the realities of communist dictatorships, despite their grim absolutisms, competitive speed-ups, and caste stratifications.

When de Tocqueville, in *Democracy in America*, described the story of the last seven hundred years as the history of the progressive acceptance of the idea of equality, he did not err: he put his finger on the pulse of history, for the principle of equality was indeed 'a providential fact.' This promise of equality was the attractive moral goal of New World culture, in so far as it could be said to have any visible moral objective. It accounts as nothing else does for the way in which this culture captured the popular imagination. Not merely were the goods of New World culture to be open to all men on equal terms: what could not be offered to all men was no longer deemed a good. Thus in correcting an old injustice the new principle introduced a special aberration of its own: the removal of qualitative distinctions and differences.

While New World economy began with a process of grading upward, it tended by its further expansion to become an evening downward, to a dead level of the mediocre and the commonplace. Finally it sought to wipe out all differences between high and low, good and bad, the developed and the degraded, by denying the very significance of values or at least the possibility of arranging them on an ascending scale. But the positive contribution is more important to remember here than this later perversion. In the New World culture the human race as a whole was reinstated: each individual counted at least as a unit, if not fully as a person. And participation in the highest goods of society was no longer confined to the 'elect.' That was a large human gain. The sense of self-respect so promoted in the common man is even now one of the endearing qualities of American culture.

Along with the demand for equality went a fuller dedication to the future. This was part of the general breaking away from the Old World both in time and space. The main weight of New World ideology and enterprise ceased to be on the past, the traditional, the remembered, the established form : all its energies focused on the break, the departure, the innovation, the invention. Instead of being static and bounded, New World culture was dynamic, limitless, bent on moving and changing for the sake of change and movement themselves. The future now had the ideal attributes once assigned to the past. The popular idea of progress held that mankind has moved automatically from a state of ignorance to one of knowledge, from impotence to power; and that this is, in fact, the path of recorded history, visible in the sequence of tools and machines, if nowhere else. 'Let the great world spin forever down the ringing grooves of change.' 'Let us act that each tomorrow finds us farther than today.' Those invocations by two representative Victorian poets, Tennyson and Longfellow, summed up the New World attitude.

Part of this New World challenge was a healthy one, if taken as a corrective. Despite philosophic intuitions like that of Heraclitus, the Old World culture was essentially static : the Jewish conviction that time and history have meaning did not alter a more widespread belief that if change existed, it was fated and bounded, with the end preformed at the beginning, doomed either to a cyclic recurrence or a final terminal event. The highest expression of Old World consciousness was a state of being. In contemplation, a minute was a sample of eternity; and if one lived a thousand years, no deeper meaning would be revealed.

New World culture, revolting from this closed world, treated being as an illusion and made only becoming real : its sole constant was change itself. This was a one-sided interpretation but it opened up the possibility of progress, novelty, emergence, unexpected creativity. Evolution thus created a new kind of hierarchy, continually shifting in place and power, based not on past stratifications but on future emergents.

Mark the contrast to axial culture. The most characteristic works of axial culture appealed to the highest elements in man's constitution, requiring delicate discriminations of taste and feeling and nicely weighed thought : to achieve them or to assimilate them required devoted effort and a lifetime's self-discipline. Even if there had been no conscious effort to establish a monopoly in these matters, axial values presumed, by their very nature, steep differences in grade and achievement. In the end only a minority would be capable of reaching the loftiest points of intellectual synthesis and spiritual illumination.

But though the scientific basis of the New World culture is equally exclusive, equally beyond the reach of the masses, the products themselves are of a different nature: one does not have to understand the mechanism of the telephone exchange in order to talk over the telephone, as one must master Greek vocabulary and grammar if one is to read Greek. In general, one need not reach above ordinary levels of taste and intellect in order to participate in this mechanical culture. Here, to balance off the prescient de Tocqueville's favourable judgment, one may well invoke his negative conclusion: 'The approach I address to the principle of equality is not that it leads men away in the pursuit of forbidden enjoyments, but that it absorbs them wholly in quest of those which are allowed. By these means a kind of virtuous materialism may ultimately be established in the world, which would not corrupt but enervate the soul, and noiselessly unbend the springs of action.'

Yet despite the crudeness of its formulations, such as the belief in mechanical progress as a substitute for purposive human development, New World culture exhibited a buoyant self-confidence that Old World culture, in its senile disillusionment, lacked. The axial religions were essentially pessimistic about life in this world: they sought not merely to turn men away from the false goods they often sought, but also to disenchant them with the real goods life actually might offer: the axial prophets emphasised the impossibility of deliverance here and now, through the exertions of men as they knew them. New World culture shook off this pessimism: its appeal was to the youthful and adventurous, and its heaven lay in the present, or at least in the near future. If it could not assure immortality, it would prolong life by rejuvenation, as Francis Bacon confidently predicted: if it could not remove the cause of pain, it could and did invent anaesthetics. Wherever a biological difficulty or a human evil existed in other cultures, the New World ideology confidently— yes, too confidently—invented a mechanical improvement or remedy.

These improvements were far from negligible: but what the method needed for its human fulfilment were purposes and values that no mere methodology could provide. Power by itself, though available on a cosmic scale, has no meaning in a meaningless world: no value in a valueless culture. As long as Old World culture remained intact, its very existence provided a point of departure and a negative goal for the new processes. One could measure mechanical advances by the distance that they carried one away from the fixed landmarks of the Old World. The accelerated processes of change, confined to the fields of technology, or at least to the technological aspects of every field, moved in one direction only: the expansion of the machine.

New World man, accordingly, lives in an 'exploding universe' of both scientific knowledge and technical invention. The separate members of this galaxy are both increasing rapidly in size and moving farther and farther away from their central nucleus, the human self, where they originated and where they were once held together. And as size and distance increase, the possibility of uniting and rationally directing the separate fragments vanishes. To-day the quantitative increase of knowledge, even within the most limited department of science or technics, exceeds the capacity for effective communication, rational appraisal, or personal assimilation. Except at points where it may be practically exploited for military, medical, or industrial purposes, an increasingly large proportion of this magnificent fund of knowledge remains uninvested for life.

Viewed quantitatively, the New World methodology, detached from human norms and goals, justified itself by its results: no other period in history can show such an increase of energy, population, industrial, and agricultural production, urban organisation, or scientific and scholarly knowledge. This new culture has already succeeded far beyond expectation in solving a problem left almost untouched by Old World culture, once the first advances of Civilised Man had taken place: the problem of poverty and scarcity. But New World man, by his very success, now confronts a new problem of equally vast dimensions: the problem of unlimited quantity. How is he to order this superabundance of energy and vitality so as to avoid indigestion and promote human development—when his own principles deny the validity of controls, limits, norms, goals?

In all organic changes, we know that unregulated growth or random expansion is as dangerous as poverty and starvation: either 'too much' or 'too little' is fatal to life. Physiologically, unrestricted growth brings on tumours, cancers, giantisms; at higher levels mere quantitative increase produces equally inimical forms of disorganisation and disintegration: relapses into the amorphous, the meaningless, the irrational. The quantity of physical energy, of sensory stimuli, or significant knowledge a human agent handles, must always bear some proportions to his capacities and his purposes: this applies equally to a whole society.

By now the pursuit of science and the exploitation of invention have taken on the deceptive appearance of an automatic movement, deliberately divorced from all human ends except the limited goals associated with the pursuit itself. Though the sciences are the highest products of this rational and mechanical culture, they too have been enmeshed in the irrational drive toward expansion and quantification, toward change and movement for their own sake, toward capturing new territory and pushing back frontiers, rather than achieving an orderly basis for stable settlement and cultivation. And at this point, it is difficult to determine which has done the most damage, the process itself, or the sedulously fostered illusion that whatever its plainly human origins it is now beyond human direction and control.

As long as New World culture was embrangled in the old, that is, as long as traditional pieties served as a counterweight to mechanisation, the basic defects in the New World ideology could be concealed: if it neglected subjective expressions, the Old World still provided them, in museum models if not in current acts of creation. As late as the middle of the nineteenth century, the leading prophets of the new way of life had no doubts as to its complete human adequacy: scientific knowledge provided, as Herbert Spencer serenely asserted, the only basis needed for a sound life. Industrialism would automatically supplant militarism, even as science would oust religion; and engineering would do away with the need for other forms of art. Where the New World ideology lingers, many still regard these dubious dogmas as axiomatic.

The studious detachment of science, the singlemindedness of its search for verifiable evidence and viable truths, the priestly remoteness of its more dedicated members from any kind of sordid calculation or even sensible human concern—in short, its otherworldly quality—allied modern science to the high traditions of religion and philosophy, from whence in fact it had sprung. But this inner inviolacy of the scientist, with its tacit claim to social irresponsibility, rested on an illusion. From the start, science served warfare, engineering, industry, medicine, and in pursuing its own private interests inevitably widened their public province. Thus the ideal goals of science, which were wholly innocuous except in their treatment of the pursuit of truth itself as an absolute, acted as an ideological cover for the grosser realities of a mechanised and depersonalised scheme of life.

They had no premonition, these innocents, of what was actually to happen in our own day: that militarism would fetter even science, and that moral delinquency, not confined to fascists but widely shared by more democratic peoples, would threaten the very continuity of life on this planet. They little suspected that the methods of wholesale extermination, devised by Mark Twain's ingenious Connecticut Yankee at King Arthur's Court to wipe out the ignorant feudal hordes surrounding him, might have an even wider practical application. Almost alone of his contemporaries, Henry Adams saw that when the potentialities of this civilisation were expressed, in bombs of 'cosmic violence,' law would give place to force and 'morality would become police.'

Apart from these sinister results of the New World idea, it harboured inner contradictions that made its efforts to supplant all other forms of culture self-defeating. The most obvious contradiction is the fact that, in a finite world, expansion cannot continue indefinitely: there must come a moment when all the unknown lands have been explored, when all the arable soils have been put under cultivation, when even the largest city must cease to spread because it has coalesced with a dozen other large cities in a formless mass in which the very function of 'city' has been lost. If every inhabitant on the planet owned a motor car, rapid movement, the rational reason for the motor car's use, would be almost as impossible in the open country as it is now in crowded urban areas.

What is significant about an economy is not the quantity of goods consumed, but the ratio of consumption to creativity. An economy that supported twenty times the present world population in comfort might prove poorer in creativity than one that rested on half the present population. Without human criteria of development, as a basis for human designs, expansion in any form is meaningless. Quantification demands qualification.

But an even deeper failure within New World culture has already disclosed itself: a failure to sustain its original interest. In its opening phase, it attracted experimental adventurous minds, who delighted to face difficult mechanical tasks. But the very success of mechanisation has put the products of high technology under the control of routineers, lovers of compulsion and conformity, whose chief concern is to keep the wheels running smoothly. Even when they do not win complete control, the process itself becomes automatised—which means that it becomes, from a human standpoint, boring and finally meaningless. Instead of finding the rewards in the day's work, the majority of workers, high and low, look for their rewards outside it: in sport, excitement, luxury.

Ironically, these compensatory processes become subject to business enterprise (the United States, England) or political direction (Soviet Russia, Communist China) and recreations in turn become as standardised as the work routine they supposedly counteract. The steady pressure to decrease the work week, the week-end exodus from every city, the common effort to achieve a cottage and garden in Suburbia—all prove that the mechanical New World no longer holds men's minds. In America, the boasted home of the machine, the young even begin to shy away from mathematics and the exact sciences, the essential pillars of a machine culture. Those who continue to serve the machine demand extra compensations: economic security, sensual indulgences, shorter hours of work and longer hours of play. The buried romanticism of the one-time pioneer comes back in the streamlined rituals of fashionable sport. If the mechanical New World actually reflected human desires, would the effort to escape it be so massive?

5

Let me attempt to sum up this New World transformation, and strike a balance. As long as New World culture existed in a civilisation that had not yet been denuded of its historic accumulations it served man well—did it not challenge stale customs and activate human capacities that had been neglected? The New World technics brought the human race for the first time into a working unity, based on world-wide transportation, world-wide travel, and world-wide communication: necessary agents of larger purposes that embrace humanity. New World agents brought a common law and order, often a common language, to human societies that had been too long self-enclosed, often poisoned by their own virtues, too exclusively cultivated. This culture thus began a mingling of races and peoples, kindreds and nations, cultural forms and artifacts, that opened up a perspective of continuous development, delivered from cyclical repetitions.

Not least, New World culture awakened a new confidence in human powers, and in the possibilities of further human achievement, supported by verifiable knowledge. By unlocking planetary resources that had hitherto been meagrely used, by multiplying energy, from windpower to nuclear power, the New World culture promised to release man from ancient poverty and dearth. By making the separate peoples of the earth conscious of each other, by penetrating deeper strata of the past, the New World revealed cultural wealth even more essential for further human growth. In the institutions of political democracy, which provided an orderly mechanism for achieving equality, the New World repaired one of the most crippling weaknesses of the older cultures. Who shall say that all these were not immense gains?

Philosophically speaking, however, this New World was only a half-world; for the subjective side of the personality was not represented, or rather, only so much was admitted as entered into the processes of systematic reasoning, experimental observation, mathematical symbolism, and technical invention. This culture had no use for the Old World gods, who symbolise cosmic powers beyond man's own, and creative processes that he discovers in himself: above all, the impulse to self-expression and self-transformation. By that very fact, New World culture excluded much of the veritably human, and carried with it no hint of the divine. Its principle of economy—of doing things in the shortest time with the least effort—is the opposite of that at work in the higher realms of life, where elaboration, prolongation, deepening, tend to demand time and prolong effort. Time is the fundamental need of all organic processes; and for some of the most important human fulfilments, a mere lifetime is pitifully insufficient. It is not for nothing that man has so persistently dreamed of immortality: some day, in a fashion we cannot yet foresee, quite different, we may guess, from any simple resurrection of individual souls, he will achieve it. So the alchemists' dream of transmutation—even the more audacious dream of perpetual motion—is now being realised in the unexpected forms of nuclear physics.

Not the machine but the person is the highest emergent in human culture. This truth, which is as old as the New Testament, had been recaptured, with disarming but dangerous oversimplification, by the philosophers of the romantic movement: but it had never penetrated the more practical New World minds who willingly sacrificed their personal lives to the mechanical organisations they served. The art of fabricating an ever-more-human self, projected toward ideal goals and fulfilments to disclose new ranges of human development, was the idea needed to give the New World culture a destination. In learning to understand physical processes and organise natural forces, on a superhuman scale, mechanical man had only, it turned out, begotten a collective automaton. To achieve perfection here he had renounced no small part of what constitutes a satisfactory human career. He was unlovable and incapable of surrendering to love.

Where the archaic and axial components of human culture have worn thin, so that New World criteria are uppermost—as notably in the United States and Soviet Russia—the powers New World man so confidently evoked now threaten to turn against him, as in the tale of the Sorcerer's Apprentice. Mankind now lives under the threat of self-destruction, on a scale hitherto unthinkable by methods heretofore unimaginable. A single homicidal command, escaping such rational controls as remain, might trigger a world catastrophe. Even if that does not happen, an equally dark future seems already visible : the replacement of historic man by a new form : post-historic man. We must face this final threat before turning to a consideration of happier alternatives.

7

Post-Historic Man

I

At this point, we have reached the present; and as soon as we seek to move forward, we are in the realm of myth and projection. Even those who see no alternatives to the dire prospects that the present seems to offer are possibly loading their 'objective' observations with their unconscious wishes and drives, by treating transient social conventions as if they were ingrained natural necessities. For many alternatives do in fact exist; and the very act of assuming that one particular possibility will prevail also implies that the knowledge such observers command is adequate to interpret the situation. This attitude, for all its ostentatious objectivity, is naïve: it fails to allow for the latent forces of life and for the surprises that characterise all emergent processes—forgetting, too, that one of the functions of intelligence is to take account of the dangers that come from trusting solely to the intelligence. Entropy can be predicted, but not creative processes and emergents.

The possible line of development I shall now attempt speculatively to follow rests on the supposition that our civilisation will continue along New World lines ever more exclusively: that it will give increasing emphasis to the practices originally brought in by capitalism, machine technics, the physical sciences, bureaucratic administration, and totalitarian government. These in turn will unite to form a more complete and watertight system, governed by a deliberately depersonalised intelligence. With this, of course, would go a corresponding neglect or suppression of older human traits and institutions, associated with the earlier transformations of man. Under these conditions all human purposes would be swallowed up in a mechanical process immune to any human desire that diverged from it. With that a new creature, post-historic man, would come into existence.

The epithet, 'post-historic man,' was first coined by Mr. Roderick Seidenberg, in his perspicuous book published under that title.

His thesis, reduced to its barest outline, is that the instinctual life of man, dominant all through man's long animal past, has been losing its grip in the course of history, as his conscious intelligence has gained firmer control over one activity after another. In achieving that control, man has transferred authority from the organism itself to the process that intelligence analyses and serves, that is, the causal process, in which human actors are given the same status as non-human agents. By detachment from the instinctual, the purposeful, and the organic and by attachment to the causal and the mechanical, the intelligence has gained firmer control over one activity after another: it now steadily pushes from the realm of the 'physical' activities to those that are biological and social; and that part of man's nature which does not willingly submit to intelligence will in time be subverted or extirpated.

During the present era, on this assumption, man's nature has begun to undergo a decisive final change. With the invention of the scientific method and the depersonalised procedures of modern technics, cold intelligence, which has succeeded as never before in commanding the energies of nature, already largely dominates every human activity. To survive in this world, man himself must adapt himself completely to the machine. Nonadaptable types, like the artist and the poet, the saint and the peasant, will either be made over or be eliminated, by social selection. All the creativities associated with Old World religion and culture will disappear. To become more human, to explore further into the depth of man's nature, to pursue the divine, are no longer goals for machine-made man.

Let us follow this hypothesis through. With intelligence uppermost, thanks to the methods of science, man would apply to all living organisms, above all to himself, the same canons he has applied to the physical world. In the pursuit of economy and power, he would create a society that would have no other attributes than those which could be incorporated in a machine. The machine in fact is precisely that part of the organism which can be projected and controlled by intelligence alone. In establishing its fixed organisation and predictable behaviour, intelligence will produce a society similar to that of certain insect societies, which have remained stable for sixty million years: for once intelligence has reached a final form, it does not permit any deviation from its perfected solution.

At this point, it is not possible to distinguish between the automatism of instinct and that of intelligence: neither is open to change, and in the end intelligence, too, will become unconscious for lack of opposition and alternatives. If intelligence dictates that there is only one right response to a given situation, only one correct answer to a question, any departure, indeed, any hesitation or uncertainty, must be regarded as a failure of the mechanism or a perversity of the agent. 'The party line' must be obeyed; and once scientific intelligence is supreme, even the party line will not change. In the end life, with its almost infinite potentialities, will be frozen into a single mould cast by intelligence alone.*

Post-historic man has long been familiar to the modern imagination. In a series of scientific romances, picturing possible future worlds, Jules Verne and his successor, H. G. Wells, portrayed the attributes of a society created and operated by such a mechanically overwrought creature. In one of his later works, *The Shape of Things to Come* (1933), Wells expressed something akin to worship for that race of flying technocrats who would produce order out of the chaos left by a final atomic war. One might say, indeed, that in the whole lopsided theory of mechanical progress as conceived by its leading exponents in the nineteenth century, post-historic man was the goal to which their most favoured institutional improvements tended. In their notion that mechanical inventions were both the main agents of progress and the ultimate reward—a notion that dates back to Francis Bacon but hardly earlier—they also suggested that the nonmechanical improvements introduced by the arts and humanities belonged only to the childhood of the race.

Post-historic man's existence, on his own premises, will be focused on the external world and its incessant manipulation: both man's aboriginal propensities and his historic self will be finally eliminated, as 'unthinkable.' In more than one passage, H. G. Wells, himself a sensitive and sensual, 'all-too-human' man, by profession one of the ancient sect of seers and dreamers, speaks impatiently of any kind of introversion or subjectivity, disparag-

---

* Though I have drawn freely on Mr. Seidenberg's classic analysis, he is nowise responsible for either my presentation or my conclusions. (See rather his own *Posthistoric Man*. University of North Carolina Press, Chapel Hill: 1950). Seidenberg places post-historic man within a much more extensive field of time than I do, and regards the change as inevitable, on what are essentially biological grounds. Seidenberg's position is that of a humane physician, objectively diagnosing a disease that seems to him incurable. His views must not be confused with those held by those who either innocently or under severe neurotic compulsions are already eagerly culturing the virus that will destroy historic man.

ing the very gifts of emotion, feeling, and fantasy that turned him to literature. The command of natural energies, and the command of human life through the possession of these energies, is the theme of post-historic man. That cerebral direction is only a specialised expression of man's essential autonomy, and is itself the servant of some larger purpose than its own expansion, does not occur to him. Otherwise Wells and his latter-day disciples would have to put the old Roman question: *Quis custodiet ipsos custodes?* Who is to control the controller? Lacking an answer, post-historic man turns out to have no other conception of life than the extensive display of the powers of 'natural magic': instantaneous communication over great distances, swift movement through space, pushbutton commands that produce automatic responses: finally, as the supreme achievement, the reduction of organic capacities and appetites in their infinitely varied manifestations to their more uniform mechanical equivalents.

What indeed is the climactic dream that haunts all the projectors of post-historic man? There is no doubt of the answer: it is that of reviving the obsolete New World motif of terrestrial exploration by creating projectiles for exploring outer space. From Jules Verne's *Trip to the Moon*, through Wells's picture of the Martian invasion of our planet, and from these early sketches to the voluminous outpourings of science fiction, that dream is the dominating one. Even the fantasies of C. S. Lewis, supposedly humanistic or even religious in their bias, picture life as a state of war between planetary creatures who have expanded their territory astronomically but not changed their minds, except in the direction of making them more implacably intelligent.

Coming from fantasy to actual projects now under way, we find scientific ideation and technical skill of no mean order at the mercy of an infantile scheme of life, seeking extravagant supermechanisms of escape from the problems that mature men and a mature society must face. Early escapist dreams of distant exploration and colonisation had at least the saving grace of enabling the adventurers to open up realms actually favourable to life. The wealth of Cathay that Marco Polo reported was no idle dream, and the undiscovered fountain of youth promised less than the real wonders that the Americas disclosed. But no one can pretend, without falsifying every fact, that existence on a space satellite or on the barren face of the moon would bear any resemblance to human life. Those who suppose that there is no meaning to living, except in continued movement through space, themselves reveal the limits of depersonalised intelligence. They show that a highly complicated technique may be the product of what is, humanly speaking, an all-too-simple mind, capable of dealing only by pointer readings with encapsulated realities, divorced from the organic complexities of life.

In our time, these post-historic fantasies, erupting out of the unconscious, have ceased to be merely prophetic: they have already taken command of mechanisation and have been channelled into the most destructive and the most pitifully obsolete of human institutions, war. Meanwhile, in response to the existential nihilism of post-historic man, war itself has been transformed from a limited order of destruction and violence, directed toward limited ends, into systematic and unrestricted extermination: in other words, genocide. Is it an accident indeed that all the triumphs that point to the emergence of post-historic man are triumphs of death? The will to deny the activities of life, above all, to deny the possibility of its development, dominates this ideology; so that collective genocide or suicide is the goal of this effort: unformulated and implicit, yet not always concealed. The post-historic process began innocently by eliminating fallible human impulses from science: it will end by eliminating human nature itself from the whole world of reality. In post-historic culture life itself is reduced to predictable, mechanically conditioned and controlled motion, with every incalculable—that is, every creative—element removed.

Now the supreme achievement of mathematical and physical science in our time was, without doubt, the succession of discoveries that led to the modern conception of the atom and the equation that identified mass and energy: only mind and method of the highest order could have unlocked these cosmic secrets. But to what end was this consummate feat of the intelligence directed? What in fact prompted the final decision that enabled man to start the process of atomic fission? We all know the answer too well: its object was the production of an instrument of large-scale destruction and extermination.

In the course of a decade's wholesale development of this new source of energy, the governments of Soviet Russia and the United States have now produced enough atomic and thermonuclear weapons to make it possible, even on the most conservative estimate, to wipe out all human life on this planet by slow poisoning if not by instant death. While these lethal powers were being multiplied, with all the resources available, the amount of thought spent on creating the moral and political agents that would be capable of directing such energies to a truly human destination was, by comparison, of pinheaded dimensions.

Thus detached and depersonalised scientific intelligence, which boasted its nonconcern with morals or politics or personal responsibility, embarked on a course that must ultimately undermine even its own limited existence. The scientists, who were trained to regard systematic investigation as an absolute, ignored repeated warnings from vigilant observers like Jacob Burckhardt and Henry Adams, warnings that anticipated or accompanied the earliest experiments with radioactive elements. And today, in spite of the threat of universal annihilation that exists, through the possible use of nuclear explosives in war, the nations of the world are hastily embarking on the widest possible exploitation of nuclear energy for peacetime uses—though no practical means for the disposal of nuclear waste products has yet been found, and though the handful of experimental plants that already exist have produced serious pollution. The reckless industrial and medical utilisation of atomic energy alone threatens within a few generations, the National Academy of Sciences warns, to produce grave biological deterioration. These compulsive acts resolutely ignore the fact that errors committed through miscalculation or ignorance in the over-production of atomic radiation cannot be corrected. We may well say of post-historic man, driving himself and all about him to destruction, what Captain Ahab says to himself, in a sudden moment of illumination, in Melville's prophetic *Moby-Dick*: "All my means are sane: my motives and object mad."

For in the end, there is little doubt, post-historic man's animus against life is self-limiting. As a result of his own deep-seated maladaptation, arising possibly out of his conscious self-devaluation and the unconscious self-hatred it begets; he is likely to cut short his own career amost before it has begun. That matter I shall consider more fully, after examining further the present manifestations of his philosophy and practice.

2

To understand how close post-historic man already is, one must realise that he only carries to their logical extremes tendencies already well enthroned in New World culture. In his attitude toward nature, the sense of oneness and affectionate harmony, which induced primitive man to bestow his own vitality on sticks and stones, disappears: nature becomes so much dead material, to be broken down, resynthesised, and replaced by a machine-made equivalent. So, too, with the human personality: one part of it, the rational intelligence, is inflated to superhuman dimensions: every other part is deflated or displaced.

What remains of life for man is the residue that is necessary to keep intelligence, and therewith the machine, in operation. True: ambitious inventions of synthetic substitutes for life sometimes rest on illusions and encounter defeats, when applied even to the simpler phenomena of life. For all science's ability to analyse the chemical components of sea water, laboratory attempts to reproduce it have not yet created a medium in which marine creatures can survive. Despite such setbacks, post-historic man not merely expects to build up complicated protein molecules but eventually to reproduce the phenomena of life within a test tube. Meanwhile, his success in fabricating artificial fibres has led him to predict similar triumphs in converting nonorganic materials into foods. If he succeeds here, he will doubtless ratify that success by breeding a new race that will enjoy such pabulum, or rather will not even know that eating food was once an enjoyment. In time, the human beings necessary to run post-historic culture will be provided at birth with built-in responses, subject solely to external controls: a more economic alternative to the wasteful methods now applied by the political commissar and the commercial advertiser. Under post-historic incentives, frontal lobotomy may be as widely performed on children, to ensure docility and discourage autonomy, as tonsillectomy now is.

In this shift to a world directed solely by intelligence for the exploitation of power, all of post-historic man's efforts tend toward uniformity. In contrast to the organic diversities, produced originally in nature and multiplied by a large part of man's historic efforts, the environment as a whole becomes as uniform and as undeviating as a concrete super-highway, in order to subserve the uniform functioning of a uniform mass of human units. Even today, the faster one moves, the more uniform is the environment that mechanically accompanies movement and the less difference does one meet when one reaches one's destination: so that change for the sake of change, and swiftness for the sake of swiftness, create the highest degree of monotony.

If the goal is uniformity there is no aspect of nature or man that may not be assaulted. Why should post-historic man seek to preserve any of the richness of environmental individuality that still exists on earth and in turn widens the range of human choice: the grasslands, the fenlands, the woodlands, the parklands, the vinelands, desert and mountain, waterfall and lake? Why should he not, on sound post-historic grounds, grind down the mountains, either to obtain granite and uranium and soil and an extra supply of atomic energy or just for the sheer pleasure of bulldozing and grinding, till the whole round earth becomes planed down to one level platform? Why should he not, on the same terms, create a single climate, uniform from the pole to the equator, without either diurnal changes or changes of seasons: so that man's days should be free from such disturbing stimuli? If post-historic man cannot create a mechanical substitute for trees, let him reduce them to a few standardised, marketable varieties, as we have already reduced to a few dozen species the varieties of pear tree—well over nine hundred according to U. P. Hedrick—that were cultivated in the United States only a century ago.

For his own security, as well as to ensure the proper worship of his god, the machine, post-historic man must remove any memory of things that are wild and untamable, pied and dappled, unique and precious: mountains one might be tempted to climb, deserts where one might seek solitude and inner peace, jungles whose living creatures would remind some surviving, unaltered human explorer of nature's original prodigality in creating a grand diversity of habitats and habits of life out of the primeval rock and protoplasm with which she began.

Already, in the great metropolises and spreading conurbations of the Western world, the foundations of the post-historic environment have been laid down: the life of an automatic-elevator operator in a great office building is almost as blank and empty as life as a whole will become once post-historic culture effectually removes every memory of a richer past. At the present rate of urbanisation, the destruction of all natural living spaces, or rather their transformation into low-grade urban tissue, will scarcely require a century before any alternatives to post-historic life will cease to exist. If the goal of human history is a uniform type of man, reproducing at a uniform rate, in a uniform environment, kept at constant temperature, pressure, and humidity, living a uniformly lifeless existence, with his uniform physical needs satisfied by uniform goods, all inner waywardness brought into conformity by hypnotics and sedatives, or by surgical extirpations, a creature under constant mechanical pressure from incubator to incinerator, most of the problems of human development would disappear. Only one problem would remain : Why should anyone, even a machine, bother to keep this kind of creature alive?

The uniform, which was itself, like drill, the product of the oldest system of severe regimentation, that of the army, is fast becoming the invisible costume of an entire society. In the interest of uniformity, every manner of choice is eliminated, even down to the trivial detail of deciding whether one would like a thin or a thick slice of bread. Once the collective decision is made, no individual departure from it, no modification on the basis of personal preference or personal judgment, becomes possible. With the further development of post-historic man, this principle of uniformity must apply to thoughts as well as to things. It is cheaper and more efficient to repress human individuality than to introduce the incalculable factors of life into a mechanical collective. One of the self-limiting facts, indeed, about the development of post-historic culture is that on its own principles it must create slot-machine minds, which admit only the prescribed coin before they eject the uniform, collectively approved product. In the long run, as certain great corporate enterprises already begin to suspect, such uniform organisations no longer create the kind of mind capable of directing them, since cowed conformists and routineers are unable to make the sort of creative decision that originally built the organisation up.

Post-historic man reduces all specifically human activity into a form of work : a transformation of energy, or an intellectual process that furthers the transformation of energy. But under this dispensation, the reward of work is not in the process but the product : instead of elaborating the process of work for the sake of animating it more fully with the human personality in ways that are immediately rewarding by their very exercise, machine technics, in agreement with the whole post-historic ideology, seeks to eliminate the human element. In the case of all servile and repulsive work this is an important human gain : the transfer of such work to automatons is, as Aristotle long ago observed, the main condition for doing away with slavery and giving all men the leisure citizens need for their civic duties and for the direct cultivation of their personal lives.

But post-historic culture goes further : it tends to make all activities automatic, whether they are sterile and servile or creative and liberal. Even play or sport, indeed, must be regularised, and brought under the principle of least effort. Instead of considering work a valuable means of moulding a more highly individualised personality, post-historic man seeks rather to depersonalise the worker, conditioning and adjusting him so as to fit into the impersonal processes of production and administration. Totalitarian conformity springs from the machine, in fact, in every department it touches: the standardised agent exacts a standardised response. The fact is not confined to officially totalitarian states.

In the post-historic scheme, then, man becomes a machine, reduced as far as possible to a bundle of reflexes: rebuilt at the educational factory to conform to the needs of other machines. For this purpose, his original animal nature, to say nothing of the propensities that made him more definitely human, must be made over. All his past achievements and memories, all his urges and hopes, all his anxieties and ideals, stand in the way of this transformation. Only those, therefore, who have been successful in eliminating their more human attributes are candidates for the highest offices in post-historic society: those of the Conditioners and Controllers.

Sympathy and empathy, the ability to participate with imagination and love in the lives of other men, have no place in the post-historic methodology; for post-historic culture demands that all men should be treated as things. Humanly speaking, post-historic man is a defective, if not an active delinquent, in the end a potential monster. The pathological nature of his defect has been concealed by his high intelligence quotient. Disguised in commonplace ready-made clothes, seeming to express equally commonplace, matter-of-fact opinions, these monsters are already at work in present-day society. Their characteristic activities—such as their preparations for 'ABC' warfare—are as irrational as their actions are compulsive and automatic. The fact that the moral insanity if not the practical futility of these preparations has not produced a general human recoil is a sign of how far the development of post-historic society has already gone.

None of the characteristic activities of post-historic man, except perhaps the exercise of pure intelligence, has anything to do with the service of life or the culture of what is veritably human. Post-historic man has already, theoretically, left the human behind him. What survives of that birthright is an embarrassment, which his growing control over the processes of reproduction will in time eliminate, as he now eliminates undesirable qualities from pigs or cattle. One way or another, by psychological conditioning and biological breeding, or by resorting to unrestrained collective exterminations, he will efface what is left of humanity.

Already, these paranoid dreams command the lives of millions of human beings and actively threaten their future. In the current plans for mass genocide, in a 'war' that would inaugurate and close the post-historic period, man's very humanity is the object of attack. By proposing to treat the 'enemy' as if they were vermin, so many million rats or bedbugs, post-historic man would debase both the violator and the victim before bringing about their common annihilation.

3

Is there any better destination for post-historic man than the one I have pictured? Is the ultimate society that he seeks more desirable than the fragmentary parts already in existence? To answer this question one may helpfully bring into rapid review the utopias in which the present mechanisms were first set forth.

Though scoffed at by contemporaries as impossible, the classic utopias since the sixteenth century turn out, like so many ideal constructions, to be almost clairvoyant forecasts of actual processes now at work. From Thomas More on, the classic utopias consist mainly of two elements, one ancient, one modern. The ancient element went back to Plato's *Republic*, and beyond that to the Spartan Laws of Lycurgus: it was an attempt to impose upon a whole community a common military discipline—to drive out the Dionysian love for food and drink and sexual delight, to banish the poet and artist, and to reserve only for the guardians of the state the full exercise of thought. Every form of privacy is either diminished or denied under this system; every form of tender feeling is repressed. The end product is a community unified, centrally directed, uniformly responsive to command: freed from anxiety, insecurity, mischance or error; and by that fact equally freed from possibility of growth and improvement. In the Utopia that pushes all these tendencies to their conclusion, *1984*, George Orwell says: "Orthodoxy means . . . not needing to think. Orthodoxy is unconsciousness." There is no freedom except in Karl Marx's Pickwickian sense: "Freedom is the conscious acceptance of necessity."

In compensation for this wholesale surrender of the attributes of the person, one might even say the attributes of a living organism, the utopians introduced a new element: they called upon science and invention to transform both the physical and the social environment. Bacon's unfinished Utopia, the *New Atlantis*, depicted the spirit that went into both science and invention with remarkable insight, and even precision. In fact, he laid out the entire field of technocratic exploit for the next three centuries, imagining a scientific building half a mile high, the deliberate mutation of species, the acceleration of natural processes, the improvement of instruments of destruction, the creation of international scientific foundations, aerial flight, motion pictures, and even air conditioning. Though Bacon underestimated the possibilities of pure science, one of his seemingly wild conjectures, the subdivision of scientific labour, is not by now unknown in certain laboratories.

Post-historic society is little more than the perfection through even more exquisite technical devices than the imagination, dared picture, of the instruments for human regimentation, originally put forth as benefits by their utopian projectors. One and all, these utopias proposed the replacement of man by a mechanical collective. Not merely is every human activity to be tied to the machine: life is so ordered as to make it difficult to escape the machine, just as even now the machine follows one, in the blare of the radio and the flicker of television, to the farthest wilderness. The result was to be physical security and comfort on a scale far beyond any earlier dream; but the price of those felicities was increasingly abject dependence upon the mechanical collective. What cannot be brought under external control is not considered a worthy form of life.

Yet there were two insidious possibilities that even the liveliest utopian imaginations did not picture. One was an inherent weakness of the system itself: the fact that as each part of the process becomes more mechanised and rationalised, the whole tends to escape human control, so that even those who are supposedly in charge of the machine become its passive agents and finally its victims. Thus man, as Samuel Butler sardonically predicted in *Erewhon*, would in the end become simply a machine's device for creating another machine.

Modern man has already depersonalised himself so effectively that he is no longer man enough to stand up to his machines. A primitive man, in alliance with magical powers, has confidence in his ability to control natural forces and bring them to heel. Post-historic man, backed by all the mighty resources of science, has so little confidence that he consents in advance to his own replacement, to his own extinction, if the price of survival is to stop the machinery or even lessen the amount of power fed into it. By treating scientific knowledge and technical inventions as absolutes, he has turned physical power into human impotence: he had rather commit universal suicide by accelerating the processes of scientific discovery than preserve the human race by even temporarily slowing them down.

Never before was man so free from nature's restrictions; but never before was he more the victim of his own failure to develop, in any fullness, his own specifically human traits: in some degree, as I have already suggested, he has lost the secret of how to make himself human. The extreme state of post-historic rationalism will, we may confidently expect, carry to a further degree the paradox already visible: not merely that the more automatic the means of living become the less life itself will be under human control, but the more rationalised become the processes of production, the more irrational will finally become the end product, man himself.

In short, power and order, pushed to their final limit, lead to their self-destructive inversion: disorganisation, violence, mental aberration, subjective chaos. This tendency is already expressed in America through the motion picture, the television screen, and children's comic books. These forms of amusement are all increasingly committed to enactments of cold-blooded brutality and physical violence: pedagogical preparations for the practical use of homicide and genocide, just as Robinson Crusoe was a preparation for surviving, barehanded, in a strange uninhabited land. Such evil fantasies forecast grim realities that are already all too close at hand.

Yet this is where another factor, unforeseen by the utopians, comes in: the compensating function of mischievous destruction. Just because man is born with the potentialities of being fully human, he must sooner or later revolt against the post-historic plan of life. If man must take his orders from the machine, he still has one form of resistance left. Since he cannot reinsert himself, as a fully autonomous being, into the mechanical process, he may become the sand in the works: if necessary, he will use the machine to destroy the society that has produced it. That prophecy in Dostoevsky's *Letters from the Underworld*—repeated independently by Jakob Burckhardt—is already on the brink of fulfilment. The snivelling hero of those underworld letters, rejecting the order and comfort that the nineteenth century boasted, remembers that one form of freedom is left : that of the criminal, if not the citizen. Dostoevsky predicted the coming of a new character (oddly like Hitler) who will survey all this putative progress, and decide to kick it to smithereens.

If no creative outlet is possible, man is so constituted that he will take pleasure in negative creation : that is, destruction. He will resume the human initiative by utilising violence, committing acts of sadism, exulting in his power to maim and mutilate, finally to exterminate. Was it not in the country most disciplined by militarism, absolutism, and physical science that systematic torture in the form of "scientific experiments" was undertaken? Did not Germany produce the nauseating horrors of the extermination camps? In the combination of cold scientific rationalism with criminal irrationalism the fatal poison produced its equally fatal antidote.

The further we push along the post-historic path, the more ironic confirmations we have of the stupidity and falsity of its human proposals. Already the effect of two centuries of invention and mechanical organisation is to create organisations that work automatically with a minimum amount of active human intervention. Instead of the indispensable leader as a driving force, as in the original ordering of civilisation, this automatic system works best with anonymous people, without singular merit, who are in fact interchangeable and removable parts : technicians and bureaucrats, experts in their own narrow departments, but incompetent muddlers in the arts of life, which demand the very aptitudes they have skilfully suppressed. With the further development of cybernetic controllers, to make decisions on matters beyond the range of human patience or conscious human calculation, because of their complication or the astronomical range of numbers involved, post-historic man is on the verge of displacing the only organ of the human anatomy he fully values : the frontal lobe of the brain.

In creating the thinking machine, man has made the last step in submission to mechanisation; and his final abdication before this product of his own ingenuity will give him a new object of worship : a cybernetic god. This new religion, it is true, would demand an act of faith even greater than in axial man's God :

the faith that this mechanical demiurge, whose calculations cannot be humanly checked, will give only the correct answers. . . .

Let us generalise this result and see it clearly for what it is. By the perfection of the automaton man will become completely alienated from his world and reduced to nullity—the kingdom and the power and the glory now belong to the machine. Instead of participating in a meaningful intercourse with nature to get his daily bread, he has condemned himself to a life of effortless ease, provided he will content himself solely with the products and the substitutes offered by the machine. Or rather, the ease would be effortless if it did not impose the duty of consuming only the goods that the machine now insistently offers him, no matter how surfeited he may be. The incentive to think, the incentive to feel and act, in fact the incentive to live, will soon disappear.

Already, in America, man has begun to lose the use of his legs, as a result of over-dependence upon the motor car. Presently, only a viseral existence, centred around the stomach and the genitals will be left, though there is reason to think that the principle of least effort will also be applied to this department. Are not American mothers actually encouraged by many physicians to make no attempt to nurse their new-born infants? From a post-historic point of view, a 'formula' is far more satisfactory than the pyschosomatic experience of maternal tenderness provided by breast feeding. Will not science also provide an effortless mechanical orgasm, thus doing away with the uncertainties of human affection and the need for bodily contact: a necessary aid to artificial insemination? The contempt for organic processes, the wilful effort to replace them, at a price, with mechanical equivalents, have only begun to show their hand.

To understand the final goal of the post-historic system, let us examine the best existing specimen of the new incarnation: not a nightmare, like a creature from 1984, but a visible reality. Consider an aviator whose vocation is to pilot a plane at supersonic speeds. Here is the new mechanical man, fully accoutred, completely insulated, with his electrically heated suit, his oxygen helmet, his parachute seat that can be catapulted into the stratosphere. Equipped for duty, he is a monstrous scaly animal, more like a magnified ant than a primate: certainly not a naked god. While hurtling through the lonely reaches of the sky, the life of this pilot is purely a function of mass and motion: for all his steely courage, his existence is narrowed down to a pinpoint of sentience by the necessity of co-ordinating his reactions with the whole physical mechanism upon which his survival depends. Loss of consciousness, asphyxiation, freezing, blast, all threaten him more perilously than sabre-toothed tigers and hairy mammoths threatened his palaeolithic ancestors. Apart from this shuttered moment-to-moment existence, dependent on retaining by artificial means a sufficient modicum of his faculties to control the machine, his working life has no other dimension.

Can one call this life? No: it is a mechanically engineered coma. This is but a specimen, small but precise, of the total change in human behaviour that the successful transformation into post-historic man would bring about. The next step in forming post-historic man is to mould all his other activities to the same pattern. We already provide mechanical daydreams and mechanical thoughts, via radio and television, so ubiquitous as to be almost unevadable. We have only to put the still unfettered portions of life under similar control.

Post-historic man's starvation of life would reach its culminating point in interplanetary travel by rocket ship, or in the erection and human occupation of a satellite space station. Characteristically, the purpose of such an expedition would be to collect further data about the physical universe or—and this is what now sanctions the costly research devoted to the subject—it would establish a vantage point from which to work violençe upon a possible human enemy : superhuman powers for subhuman purposes. (What man truly needs is enough insight into his nature to explain why he thinks such data important, at a moment when his own immaturity and pathological unbalance call for his concentrated attention.) Under such conditions, life would again narrow down to the physiological functions of breathing, eating, and excretion : even these functions would be performed on a space ship under conditions that would minimise their efficacy. Yet this is the final goal of post-historic man : the farthest reach of anything that could be called desire, the justification of his every sacrifice. His end is to turn himself into an artificial homunculus in a self-propelling capsule, travelling at maximum speed, and depressing to the point of extinction his natural gifts, above all, eliminating any spontaneous trace of spirit.

The triumph of post-historic man would, one may confidently say, do away with any serious reason for remaining alive. Only those who had lost their minds already could contemplate, without horror, such mindless experience : only those who had forfeited the attributes of life could contemplate, without despair, such a lifeless existence. By comparison, the Egyptian cult of the dead was overflowing with vitality: from a mummy in his tomb one can still gather more of the attributes of a full human being than from a spaceman.

Already, in his ideal projects for flight, as in his subhuman plans for war, post-historic man has lost hold on every living reality: he is the self-appointed victim of inner compulsions leading to death. Even if he should momentarily succeed in his self-transformation, his success would bring on the last act in the human tragedy. For that which is post-historic is also post-human.

World Culture

I

Post-historic man, the wholly subservient creature of the machine, dismally adapted to the pseudo-life of its mechanical collectives, is a theoretic possibility, not a historic probability. For the conflicts between the overrational and the irrational, between the mechanised institutions and atavistic men, are too great to promise more than an increasingly erratic oscillation, ending in a final breakdown. Whatever his powers and numbers post-historic man has a short expectation of life.

One cannot, of course, deny that large tracts of our life have become increasingly bovine, vulpine, and simian. The age of the 'men who are ten years old,' long ago predicted in the Pali texts of Buddhism, is already visible. 'There will be a time when children will be born to men who only reach an age of ten years; and with these men, girls of five will be fertile. . . . With these men of an age of ten, violent hatred against each other will predominate, violent enmity, violent malevolence, violent lust for wholesale killing.' The terrible triviality of this ten-year-old culture, already visible in more than one place, might be symbolised by an atomically powered juke box; for its most exquisite scientific and technical devices are at the service of infantile fragments of the human personality. Once these impulses get the upper hand in government—as they did in Central Europe under Hitler and Himmler—the end will come swiftly. In short, the purely instinctual attempt to compensate by irrational and primitive means for the repression of human vitality under post-historic culture cannot hope for the kind of success achieved in early civilisations. Rather such an attempt must now bring the whole process to an end : for the mixture of the automaton and the id is an explosive one.

An apocalyptic termination of all human development has become possible in our day; far more so than in the comparatively innocent times of John of Patmos. With our present lethal weapons the swift suicide of post-historic man is even more likely than his gradual triumph, through his conditioning the human organism into becoming a nonentity. Plainly the 'realists' who see no happier future for mankind than the indefinite prolongation of this self-punishing and self-defeating regime, whose destiny is to have no destiny, underestimate both the inner resistances and counter-measures and the external dangers.

But though the future is of necessity partly conditioned by the past and to that extent is already present, what portions of man's heritage shall be actively called into play is not predictable, for this is increasingly dependent upon the ideals and goals that man projects into the future. If man's own designs for himself exclude the post-historic transformation, all the forces that now seem so implacable and so inevitable will weaken, as the forces of Roman imperialism suddenly weakened from within when confronted by the new image of the Christian self. As we see in that revealing third-century dialogue, the *Octavius* of Minucius Felix, common sense and inertia were on the side of the 'Roman way of life' : but deeper sources of life had already projected a new kind of self, in the person of the Christian, and this new ideal had the vitality needed to dominate the pagan world for the next thousand years.

Man's present consciousness of his own long development and his deepened understanding of his own potentialities—both new facts in human history—may become the impetus that will prompt him to take protective action, before the 'men of ten years,' who have learned their new ABC's of Atomic, Bacterial, and Chemical extermination, wantonly attack all life on this planet. But to overcome the blind drift to automatism mankind as a whole must deliberately resume the long effort that originally turned hominids into men.

Man's principal task today is to create a new self, adequate to command the forces that now operate so aimlessly and yet so compulsively. This self will necessarily take as its province the entire world, known and knowable, and will seek, not to impose a mechanical uniformity, but to bring about an organic unity, based upon the fullest utilisation of all the varied resources that both nature and history have revealed to modern man. Such a culture must be nourished, not only by a new vision of the whole, but a new vision of a self capable of understanding and co-operating with the whole. In short, the moment for another great historic transformation has come. If we shrink from that effort we tacitly elect the post-historic substitute.

The political unification of mankind cannot be realistically conceived except as part of this effort at self-transformation: without that aim we might produce uneasy balances of power with a temporary easing of tensions, but no fullness of development. Fortunately, this unification is not a sudden desperate move, prompted only by the threat of universal extermination. So deeply is it bound up with the whole broad movement of culture that it has long been taken as the goal of history by many prophetic minds: by Isaiah, Mo Ti, Joachim of Floris, to mention only a few, widely separated. Not merely the general idea, but many of the institutions favouring this transformation, are already in existence: indeed many social agents that now work to the undoing of man, like science itself, will actually contribute powerfully to this transformation, once the seminal ideas, with their unifying images and designs, have become clarified.

Admittedly, the very situation that has made this self-transformation imperative discourages any quick, fulsome hopes. Though man has now for the first time the technical means of achieving and perpetuating a world culture, he has already become seriously frustrated, indeed deeply discouraged, by the current miscarriage of these means. That miscarriage is recorded in two world wars, which brought premature death by military combat or genocide—leaving out those who succumbed to epidemic diseases—to between thirty and forty million human beings within thirty years. This decimation cancelled out a century's gains in lowering the death rate from preventable disease.

In consequence of this disintegration, all the forces that made for insulation, non-co-operation, aggressive hostility, and totalitarian absolutism have reformed their ranks. Even the axial religions, still largely unchastened by this spectacle, remain as divided as national states that do not make any of their claims to universality. In assaying the world's weaknesses they have not yet come to terms with their own. Not least, the unity of the sciences has broken down: even within the domain where they had once established a consensus, they have violated their most sacred canons, the free exchange of knowledge and the submission of truth to open judgment. The very knowledge needed to protect mankind against the misuse of nuclear power, in peaceful industry no less than in war, has been suppressed by highhanded government agencies, concealing their own fallible decisions from public inspection—as yet without effective challenge by corporate bodies of scientists or citizens.

Considering these conditions, one may doubt if any factors now known will be capable of bringing about the needed transformation of man in time to avoid the self-destruction of the human race—either by swift thermonuclear annihilation, by slow atomic pollution of air, soil and water, or by the insidious conditioning of man to post-historic compulsions. If viewed on purely rational terms, one might be tempted to accept the dying judgment of H. G. Wells as something more than senile hallucination: 'Mind is at the end of its tether.' A more benign alternative would call for something like a miracle.

Therefore let us consider miracles. At rare intervals, the most significant factors in determining the future occur in infinitesimal quantities on unique occasions. Such behaviour is too erratic and infrequent to lend itself to repeated observations and statistical order. But the reality of these individual events cannot be dismissed because they are incalculable in both their origins and their consequences. Under this canon, we must allow for the possibility of miracles, on the scientific grounds developed by Clerk Maxwell in his famous essay on Singular Points. By a miracle we mean, not something outside the order of nature, but something occurring so infrequently, operating through such insignificant forces, and bringing about such a radical change, that one cannot include it in any scientific prediction.

Maxwell's doctrine gives exactly the insight needed into the present situation. He pointed out that even in the simplest physical systems at rare intervals there are moments which he called singular points. At these points an infinitesimally small force, through its character and position in the whole constellation of events, is able to bring about a change of almost unbelievable magnitude, as with a pebble starting a landslide. This doctrine allows for the direct impact of the human personality in history, not only by mass movements, but by individuals and small groups who are sufficiently alert to intervene at the right time and the right place for the right purpose. At such moments —do they not obviously account for Gautama, Jesus, Mohammed?—a single human personality may overcome the apparently irresistible inertia of institutions. Happily, as Maxwell pointed out, the higher and more complex the system, the more often do singular points occur in it: there are more singular points in biological systems than in physical systems, more in man's life than in an ant's. So our sense of what is now possible is not in fact sound unless it makes due allowance for what, on the basis of the known, the typical, the predictable, would be an extravagant impossibility.

Naturally, the odds against a beneficent, world-transforming miracle are probably many million to one: so I can sympathise with those who would impatiently dismiss this whole argument as nonsense. Even if a singular point should come and find leaders capable of actively riding this 'tide in the affairs of men,' to repeat Maxwell's quotation, the significant moment itself is so difficult to identify in the mass of events that it may long escape even retrospective identification. (How many Romans as late as A.D. 150 could identify Jesus or anticipate the coming triumph of Christianity?) Those who like to lay their wagers on sure things may perhaps play safe by betting on an early catastrophe of planetary dimensions; for that, it seems to me, is somewhat more likely than a continuance of the *status quo*, with its own dreadful natural terminus, the ascendancy of post-historic man.

Yet if mankind abstains from self-extermination and actually begins to move toward the fabrication of a world culture, the separate contributions to this process, many already in existence, will carry with them an air of quiet inevitability. It is the formal sequence of events, and the ideas and agents that will transform the human self, and above all, the new design that will emerge, that are so difficult to imagine in advance. At a moment of ripeness, the unseen will become visible, the unthinkable thought, the unactable enacted; and by the same token, obstacles that seem insurmountable will crumble away.

This experience has many parallels in human history. Suddenly, at what seems the peak of their efficiency and power, dominant institutions lose their hold on their most devout supporters or their most favoured beneficiaries; while at the same time, millions of people who seemingly conformed with docility to these institutions throw them off, like a dirty garment. In such a situation ideas that were hardly more than shadows a moment before become solid landmarks on a well-paved road.

Now, if belief in the next transformation of man required a detailed account of the immediate agents and means that will promote this growth, one might prudently forgo the task. That kind of prognosis lies beyond both imagination and predictive intelligence. But the goals of this world culture have long been plainly in view; and one may redefine those goals and even enlarge them with at least as much confidence as the Franciscan friar, Roger Bacon, when he depicted technical advances whose simplest mechanisms lay far beyond his own skill as inventor. Bacon could not foresee the Black Death of the fourteenth century, or the fact that it would create a shortage of labour, which would undermine serfdom and place a premium upon labour-saving devices—or yet the steady succession of mechanical inventions that would finally make possible the horseless carriage and the flying machine. Yet Bacon's technical anticipations were sound: they pointed in the direction toward which the forces of civilisation, largely invisible when he wrote, were to move. This must be my justification for following through the most pregnant set of ideal possibilities that the present situation opens up to us.

Let us make one basic assumption: the destiny of mankind, after its long preparatory period of separation and differentiation, is at last to become one. Our survey of man's successive transformations has disclosed the fact that the widening of the base of human community, though fitful and erratic, has nevertheless been one of the cumulative results of human history. This unity is on the point of being politically expressed in a world government that will unite nations and regions in transactions beyond their individual capacity: it will be spurred to these difficult tasks of political and economic unification by common ideals of human development. The words that G. A. Borgese applied to one aspect of this movement may now be applied to the whole task of building a world culture: 'It is necessary; therefore it is possible.' And one may add: If it were easy, it would hardly be necessary.

At the outset, this conception rejects the continued extension of a purely extraneous and technical kind of universalism, such as would be conceived by post-historic man. The new unity we conceive lies at the other end from totalitarian uniformity: it is one that seeks to enrich and enhance, in the very transactions of world society, the human values that differentiation has brought into existence. That is why, in opposition to certain thinkers whom I otherwise respect, I do not conceive that the means for bringing about unity lie, willy-nilly, in the further development of mechanical collectives on a planetary scale. One of the positive incentives toward bringing about world unity, indeed, is the necessity for finding alternatives to an integration based on mechanical uniformity.

As we have seen, the need to enlarge the area of intercourse and human co-operation had its rise in the earliest civilisations. Even the crude attempts to produce unity by economic expropriation and military conquest achieved a post-factum justification by actually subserving man's higher development: in that sense Augustine could even justify the military exploits and material organisation of Rome, as providing a means for disseminating the Christian gospel. As for the axial religions, they were even more consciously dedicated to unity than the great empires: part of their dynamism was due to their belief that, as Pascal put it, the whole history of mankind, for all its diversity, may be treated as the biography of a single creature, man.

In coming to One World culture, we naturally build on these earlier efforts at universalism. But we go even further, because we must assume, as a result of our historic analysis, that none of man's past can in fact be left behind. With this assumption, we rectify the serious error that the New World ideology made, alike in its utopian, its utilitarian, and its romantic philosophies. Even if we deliberately chose to make no use of the funded values of history, the living past would still be present under the surface, deflecting seemingly autonomous decisions, holding back fresh advances, working all the more effectively because of our failure to be conscious of these pressures. We may with good reason, for example, plan to wipe out the institution of war, as earlier societies wiped out the practices of cannibalism and incest: but if we chose to forget the fact of war, desiring to dwell only on the pleasanter aspects of man's record, we might usher in the day when our very innocence might encourage a reappearance of this evil in a new guise. And if we failed in our education for peace to include the dedication and discipline of the soldier, his readiness to undergo hardship and face death, we would forfeit one of the most important attributes of a noble character, essential for world culture.

But note: no part of the past can enter world culture in the form that it took independently in an earlier situation. As with every other fresh integration, each part must die to its old form, in order to be born anew within a larger whole, and become viable in terms of the new self and the new culture we are putting forward. The failure to undergo this regeneration is what made the earlier clinging to venerable historic examples so burdensome to the Egyptians, the Jews, the Chinese, to say nothing of other peoples who idolised their dead selves. While the ability to select, to revaluate, and to rethink the past in terms of its further development in the future is what has given vitality to every true cultural renaissance.

Now this change toward world culture parallels a change that seems also on the point of taking place within the human personality: a change in the direction of wholeness and balance. In the new constellation of the person, as we shall presently see, parts of the human organism long buried or removed from conscious control will be brought to light, recognised, accepted, revaluated, and redirected. The ability to face one's whole self, and to direct every part of it toward a more unified development, is one of the promises held forth by the advance both of objective science and subjective understanding. Wholeness is impossible to achieve, in fact, without giving primacy to the integrative elements within the personality: love, reason, the impulse to perfection and transcendence.

Without a concept of development, without a hierarchy of values, the mere lifting of unconscious repressions might simply produce, as it has often done in our day, a wholesale eruption of the libido, which would turn the mind itself into an instrument for slaying the higher impulses. Perhaps the greatest difficulty today, as a result of the general hostility to values brought in by seventeenth-century science, is the failure to recognise that wholeness demands imperatively that the highest elements in the human personality should be singled out, accepted and trusted, fortified and rewarded. The integration of the person begins at the top, with an idea, and works downward till it reaches the sympathetic nervous system, where organic integration in turn probably begins and works upward, till it emerges as an impulse of love or a vital image. In this replenishment of the whole self under a formative idea lies the promise of reducing the distortions, conflicts, isolationisms, infantilisms, and obsessions that have limited human growth.

The relations between world culture and the unified self are reciprocal. The very possibility of achieving a world order by other means than totalitarian enslavement and automatism rests on the plentiful creation of unified personalities, at home with every part of themselves, and so equally at home with the whole family of man, in all its magnificent diversity. Unified man must accept the id without giving it primacy: he must foster the superego, without making it depress the energies it needs for its own fuller expression. Without fostering such self-knowledge, balance, and creativity, a world culture might easily become a compulsive nightmare.

To be on friendly terms with every part of mankind, one must

be on equally friendly terms with every part of oneself; and to
do justice to the formative elements in world culture, which give
it greater significance and promise than any earlier stage in man's
history, one must nourish the formative elements in the human
self, with even fuller energies than axial man applied to this task.
In brief, one cannot create a unified world with partial, fragmentary, arrested selves which by their very nature must either
produce aggressive conflict or regressive isolation. Nothing less
than a concept of the whole man—and of man achieving a consciousness of the whole—is capable of doing justice to every type
of personality, every mode of culture, every human potential. At
this point a further human transformation, so far not approached
by any historic culture, may well take place.

2

What is the integrating idea behind world culture? Its purpose
is to provide a means of bringing into relations of reciprocity and
willing amity the entire family of man, so that they may share,
as never before, not only what they have gained through their
historic experience, but what they have still to create through
their deliberate intermingling and cultural interchange. Peace
would be the by-product of such an effort, rather than its principal justification. Beyond that lies the interchange and utilisation
of the entire experience of the race, past, present, and potential, so
that the whole horizon of life will widen, as it does to a flier
soaring in the stratosphere, and so that the obscure depths of life
will be penetrated, as they are penetrated by the diver exploring
dark underseas lairs into which creatures that inhabit the surface
have never yet peered. Up to now man has not been sufficiently
united to approach himself as a whole. ·
Compared to the world that now opens up for man's exploration and cultivation, all man's past knowledge seems petty, and
the best achievements based on it seem circumscribed. So, too, the
circular, self-limiting courses pursued by earlier universal states
and universal churches seem pitifully stultifying. Thus far, even
the mightiest of civilisations have lived only an impoverished,
half-awakened life: only a fraction of their populations had a
chance to develop beyond their narrow animal role; and even
their favoured elite stumbled and halted long before they had
reached their conceivable natural limits. As a further handicap,

the great civilisations were but islands, cut off in space from their immediate neighbours, and even more seriously cut off in time both from the riches of their own past and that of the rest of mankind.

So far we have only skimmed the surface. Nourishment for the fullest human growth, a growth that was hardly imaginable in any earlier culture, even for its chosen few, is now at hand in almost every part of the world. And this spiritual sustenance is open to a far larger portion of the population, once we are ready to tear down man-made barriers of law and custom that once kept the masses of mankind in a deliberately stunted state. Above all, when we recognise that personal creativity is more significant than mere industrial productivity. What is properly human can no longer be confined, as the old prophets well knew, to a single culture, no longer adequately cultivated in a single place, no longer confined to a single happy moment or two in history.

All human history, up to the present time, has been a zigzag advance, frequently halted, hardly even yet deliberate, toward this goal. The lack of consciousness of what was happening and what might happen itself was one of the main obstacles to development. Every constructive effort, whether practical or spiritual, has involved a widening of the means of communication and communion and co-operation, a building up of common institutions, now an empire, now a church, now a great city, in which ever greater numbers of men could come together in meaningful and purposeful association.

The wider such a community, the greater the need for active intercourse and for a diversity of agents to promote that intercourse: likewise the greater richness of the total contribution to the common heritage. Up to the point where excessive numbers bring about disorganisation and an intensified struggle for existence—possibly the world has already reached that point—an increase of quantity brings with it the possibility of higher quality, as much in social life as in the biological crossing of diversified genes. And as is true in biological hybridisation, even 'poor' stocks, or primitive species, may greatly enrich the possibilities of inheritance.

While primitive man, insecure even in the achievement of his humanness, was forced to repeat and re-enact his past, One World man may give equal attention to the future: indeed, he may attempt enterprises that no civilisation seeking mainly to exploit immediate economic advantages would entertain : launching projects and experiments whose outcome may await centuries. Beside such efforts, the static eternity of the Egyptian pyramid would seem trivial, and the records of such admirable time-extended experiments as those of the Rothamsted Experimental Station in England would seem meagre. The margin of free time, free energy, and free vitality that modern man may command is so great that, instead of devoting most of his days to mere biological survival, he now has capacities for self-development that were once confined to a minuscule ruling class.

So far, this margin has been largely dissipated in a thousand extravagant devices, far less impressive than pyramid building : devices profitable to the purveyor but noxious to the user, in that their exclusive use arrests human development, even if it does not degrade it. But these perversions need not become permanent. If the present way of life of so-called civilised man does not reflect the immense possibilities that have already opened up, it is because his 'expanding economy' based on waste and war has only two ultimate outlets : rubbish heaps and ruined cities. We shall not enter into our full human inheritance until we find in ourselves the purposes and plans we so far have sought to derive from the machine.

3

In considering the new pattern of One World civilisation we must take into account two matters that hold at every stage of man's self-transformation. One is the nature of emergence; and the other, which qualifies it, is the 'fibrous structure' of human history, and perhaps of all forms of organic inheritance.

The advance from the present constitution of society, with its confused mixture of the tribal, the civilised, the axial, the mechanistic, the national, will not be the outcome of any series of slight modifications or readjustments. Rather, the next transformation, it seems clear, will involve a leap from one plane to another. This will be similar to the decisive historic leap from the neolithic tribal community to a centralised state organisation, focused in cities, capable of dominating and ordering a whole river valley. This emergence of a new system brings a change, not only in individual details, but in the over-all design.

Because One World civilisation will be a true emergent, its

most characteristic features will probably escape forecast. Mendelejev's periodic table enabled all the chemical properties of radium, including its atomic weight, to be forecast, except its one emergent element, unknown up to that point: namely, its radio-activity. So who could have predicted in 1492 that the European discovery of the Americas would bring about, not the enslavement of native Indians, but the transportation of thousands of black slaves from a distant continent, then almost unexplored? And who can guess now whether the breaking down of national and racial barriers will lead to a wider blending of races and cultures, as in Hawaii, or to a concentration upon intimate cultural values that had once, under the impact of imperialism, been lost, a reaction that took place in Provence under the *Félibrigistes*?

The one thing that can be predicted of any true emergence is that its results cannot be predicted. In any emergent stage, the change in the basic pattern radically alters the nature of the constituent elements through their very shift in position in the design, as well as by the fact that scattered mutations then become dominants, and forces that were once dominant become recessive or subordinate.

But if it is all too easy in thought to falsify this change, by conceiving One World culture as a mere enlargement of familiar processes and institutions, one would equally misinterpret the nature of the transformation if one overlooked the elements of continuity and renewal that will in fact be present. Was it not indeed the failure to take account of these persistent factors, assuming that stage three left stages one and two completely behind, that made all the simple schemes of progress, such as those of Auguste Comte and Herbert Spencer, so inadequate? And though Marxian dialectic has sought to overcome this error, by including the original thesis as well as its antithesis in the new synthesis, it has no place for forces or institutions that do not take part in the dialectic struggle.

To correct the partial interpretations offered by the doctrines of both progress and emergence, we must accordingly take note of the fibrous structure of society: the fact that parts of man's life send forth threads and strands that penetrate through all the strata of time, modifying each new stage with the fibres of both organic and social memory. The doctrine of evolution, as distinct from the more mechanical one of progress, sought to reckon with this fibrous structure: both comparative embryology and comparative anatomy show us that certain decisions about the organs of the body, made as early as the amphibians, have governed every succeeding event. This includes, for example, the topographical association of the organs of reproduction and excretion, unimportant in the sexual life of frogs, but somewhat embarrassing in the more elaborate love play of men and women. While the doctrine of emergence takes account of a radical change of form like that which marked the ascent from the reptile to the bird, the corrective doctrine of fibrous continuity is equally needed.

In the transformation of man, we do not begin with the static, self-enclosed village and clan and move through a series of stages, each new one leaving the old behind, till we end with a single dynamic structure, without walls or frontiers, that embraces mankind. The communal polity of neolithic times, the urban civilisation of antiquity and later, the axial and national cultures that succeeded them, and the mechanical models of the New World are still with us in one form or another; and will long remain with us. Even when we seek to weed out their residual fixations and atavisms, we must still make use of their helpful contributions and renew them. For these stable social structures produced the materials that have gone into the making of the human personality. Even those human ventures that left behind only fragmentary symbols and monuments may be as important to psychological development as chemical trace elements are to physiological growth. Without these agents of continuity, we should be forced to live on the cold asteroid of post-historic culture: indisputably new, mechanically efficient, slickly uniform, but incapable of sustaining human life.

4

In order to bring out more clearly the emergent character of world civilisation, let us first look at the older threads that will give strength to the new fabric, and age-tested colours to the new pattern. In each case, we must assume that there is enough life in these old institutions to enable them to undergo renewal, if not spontaneously, then with conscious effort, prompted by our present sense of need.

And to begin with: the old communal unit, the primary association that began with the family and kin group, and established itself with the invention of agriculture in the village. This primary community on the undifferentiated human level rests on simple cohabitation in a common environment and a sharing of the means and the unspoken meanings of life. Language itself was one of the most precious attributes of this early group; so it is only natural to find that each attempt to reassert its integrity against the centralised domination of the state, as in the various regionalist and nationalist movements of the nineteenth century, begins with a recovery of the folk language. But it is above all through meeting face to face, eye to eye, day after day, through a sense of being 'all in the same boat,' that an understanding is achieved that goes far deeper than words. That animal faith, as we found in the Second World War, often enabled the small military unit to survive, through exemplary acts of love and sacrifice and devotion, when all other appeals had become meaningless.

Family, household, neighbourhood, work group may all in future take new forms, due in part to our growing sense of their meaning and value; but the intimacies that they share, the co-operations that they pledge, are essential to the development of man's basic humanity. To create organs for neighbourly help and initiative, to meet face to face for personal assessment and vivid discussion, to take part in communal celebrations, not in vast anonymous masses, but in a circle of identifiable faces and persons, all these survivals of aboriginal village life are still necessary. They keep intact the close chain of sympathetic responses in which man first securely established himself as irrevocably human : these friendly eyes are the indispensable mirror in which the self beholds its own image, and establishes its own identity.

The more readily we conceive the planet as a single unit and move about it freely on missions of study or work, the more necessary it is to establish such a home base, such an intimate psychological core, with visible landmarks and cherished personalities. The world will not become a neighbourhood, even if every part of it is bound by instant communication and rapid transportation, if the neighbourhood itself as an idea and a social form is allowed to disappear.

Such primary communal groups persisted in at least a dormant traditional form through the submerged existence of archaic culture, right down to our own time : so spontaneous, so unartful, that they seemed the products of nature rather than deliberate associations evoked by human need. But these elementary groups were fated to be swallowed up by the spawning of mass civilisations before their absence was missed or their positive functions—above all, their educative and man-moulding functions —were evaluated. If we now re-establish the intimate communal groups and widen their activities, it will be because we have become aware of their indispensable role, and realise the constant part it plays in the development of human character. Precisely because of their varied nature, due to the mixture of ages, of sexes, of life experiences, the communal group represents man as no specialised association, formed for a more definite purpose, or based on a single vocation or age group, can do.

The pattern of the village and the family group, brought in by neolithic culture, is still a fundamental one: more needed today perhaps than ever. It is only in the close, mixed society of families and neighbours, or workfellows and playfellows, that the intimacies, the solidarities, the basic understandings and unanimities needed for human growth, can take place. The perception of this fact was the great contribution of the American sociologist, Charles Horton Cooley; and it has been independently translated into practical proposals by many isolated minds, from Peter Kropotkin and Ebenezer Howard to Clarence Perry and Adriano Olivetti. In the course of the coming century, if One World culture is to grow, this principle must assume greater importance.

The fact that an increasing fraction of the population is more nomadic today than perhaps ever before has not altered the picture: rather, it is precisely because of the fact that distances have expanded, and that the role of the secondary association, based on specialised functions or purposes, has increased. Because we must have constant transactions with people we shall never see and because so much of our daily life must be lived at second hand, or even more remotely, we need a quickening of the direct I-and-thou relationship. Without this intimate relationship, men presently become things, that is, human nonentities. Above all we need, particularly as children, the reassuring presence of a visible community, an intimate group that enfolds us with understanding and love, and that becomes an object of our spontaneous loyalty, as a criterion and point of reference for the rest of the human race.

As for the unstable nature of the modern urban environment today, seemingly hostile to such solidarity and continuity, two things may be said. Part of its discontinuity and transitoriness, with its perpetual shifts of jobs and homes, its broken marriages and its atomised family relations, is due to the failure of our dominant institutions to give durable satisfactions or respond to persistent human needs. But granting that some of this mobility is not merely inevitable but desirable, not only desirable but often imperative, this fact does not by itself wipe out the possibility of intimate associations and warm loyalties. There are no modern cities that change as completely in population as a college, where a quarter of the community, roughly, moves away at the end of four years. Yet because of the close inner unity of the college, particularly the small college, with its living traditions, its venerable buildings and boundaries, probably no other institution in our civilisation promotes more lifelong loyalties or gives a deeper sense of 'belonging' to most of its members.

The community that has achieved the highest degree of solidarity and continuity in human record, enduring changes that wiped out empires and turned cities to rubble, is that of the Jews. Perhaps the secret of that ability to stand the shock of repeated displacements and persecutions, from the Babylonian captivity onward, was the synagogue: the congregation of those who met once a week, at least, face to face, the young and the old, the learned and the ignorant, the poor and the rich. With this small primary community as a basis, the Jews never became the human dust that drifted aimlessly about the great metropolises in the disintegrating phases of every civilisation.

When Roman civilisation went under, it was again in such a community of Christian believers, modelled after the synagogue, that the human spirit was fortified to face its ordeals. This local structure was never discarded by the Universal Church: in fact, the highly centralised organisation of Christendom up to the sixteenth century was made possible by the complementary neighbourhood unit, the parish, which was no mere organ of administration but an independent expression of community life.

In short, the primary attachment within a local group is the natural breeding place for every higher and wider loyalty, including that to the world community. Only when these elemental ties are firmly re-formed will the kind of detachment and free choice made possible by world organisation become feasible. The invention of new facilities and new procedures for the intimate local group, considered as a basic political and social unit, remains one of the prime tasks of the coming generation. In factory councils, co-operatives, *kibbutzim*, community associations, neighbourhood units, we have only begun the larger exploration—and, even more, experimentation—that is demanded.

Present-day society still bears the scars of the military and industrial absolutisms that accompanied the New World regime. These absolutisms broke down primary ties and loyalties, lest they should demand a share of centralised political or financial power. Under the principle of democracy that share belongs to them by right; and it will be fostered by the growth of local communities, with definitely established responsibilities: not separate from the larger whole, but self-affirming and self-actualising.

Plainly, no isolated, archaic form of communal life will meet the new demands of an emerging world society: the flag of the United Nations should fly in every neighbourhood, as a reminder of the greater community in which it functions. The forms that simpler communities evolved for themselves over many centuries, once rediscovered, must be deliberately renewed and remodelled, through the application of political intelligence, social tact, and psychological skill. But by now it is fairly plain that without such definite cellular structure only a cancerous kind of social growth can take place.

Beyond this renewal of the primary community, something more remains to be done with the most ancient sources of human culture. When the planet was first opened up by Western navigators and explorers, they had no notion of the importance, either for biological knowledge or for practical use, of the wild species they trampled on and often exterminated. Before modern man understood the value of this primeval environment—even its sheer economic value for breeding new plant species and anti-biotics—he had wrecked it. So with the primitive peoples he conquered and contemptuously de-cultured: peoples who still carried in their folk-ways the relics of ancient habits of mind that civilised man had partly discarded.

Only belatedly have anthropologists begun to appreciate the values of the cultures that primitive man, by his very resistance to more universal patterns, retained and developed. The philological examination of the structure of primitive languages, for example, has revealed a diversity of grammars and of logics, indeed, of metaphysics, radically different from those of the main civilised stocks. From this vantage point, we have only now become acutely self-conscious of our own ideological peculiarities and prepossessions, which had hitherto been regarded as ingrained in our common nature. This discovery is as illuminating and liberating as the discovery of the possibilities of multi-dimensional space, in contrast to the geometry of Euclid. So the examination of primitive folk-ways, rites, fantasies, and aesthetic forms discloses modes of creativity that promise, when assimilated, to enrich the common store of our culture. Though vast tracts of life have been irreparably damaged, enough remains, both in record and in life, to provide fresh stimulus for a human growth that shall be strengthened through the use of primitive elements man had long ago too flatly rejected.

This selective assimilation of primitive cultures, now only beginning, is one of the many elements that may help bring One World man into existence. Modern man's embracing of the primitive is not merely an act of moral reparation : it is a step in the reciprocal development of both his higher universal culture and that of the surviving primitives and archaic types. On one hand, as C. G. Jung has suggested, it provides a needful counteraction to his over-rationalised picture of the world, too exclusively the product of a detached intelligence, hostile to other manifestations of life; on the other, it not merely will restore the primitive's own self-respect, but will enable him to absorb, without fear and hatred, the rational world culture that otherwise seems to him—and too often actually is—inimical to his basic sense of life.

Not that the untutored 'noble savage' is to be preserved in amber : quite the contrary, the primitive has many retarding superstitions to slough off, and much to gain from his own selective absorption of world culture. The Western importation of flowering plants into Hawaii alone made possible the conversion of the shell lei, a traditional badge of aristocracy, into the charming folk custom of the flower lei. So, too, it was the introduction of the Western musical scale that provided a rich melodic basis for new strains of music, characteristically Hawaiian, but impossible in their primitive music. Both cultures profited by this cross-fertilisation : pioneer achievements prophetic of much wider interminglings.

In short, to help restore the primitive's self-respect and give him confidence in his own further development, one must be willing to learn from him, to receive as well as give. This applies to the primitive elements in the human psyche and to the primitive peoples who, so often in Western fantasy, represent the dark side of man's nature. One World man, far from rejecting the primitive or seeking completely to make him over, will join with him in building their higher common culture. This involves no mere muddy mixing of regional cultures and racial stocks, though an unpredictable degree of blending will doubtless take place, as already in Hawaii or Brazil. Through an intensified interest in the indigenous inheritance, the frayed and soiled threads of local cultures may partly recover their old colour and strength, and in their re-weaving on the loom of a world culture achieve a hitherto unattainable richness of pattern.

5

As for the contributions of 'civilisation,' in the special sense that we have defined this stage, we must assume that these original disciplines will be widened, rather than narrowed, in a world culture. But they will carry less weight. As an agent of mechanical uniformity, civilisation has extended the realm of law and order far beyond its original boundaries: it has now produced a system of uniform measurement in the all-but-world wide metric system; and even a rational world calendar and a supplementary universal language are at length plainly in prospect. This kind of uniformity may be profitably extended to other departments. As man brings the machine to perfection, in conformity with his own values, in response to his own purposes, it will assume platonic forms, immune to stylistic perversions, which will remain stable perhaps for centuries.

Such devices widen the area of effective co-operation without lowering other human values. The aviator, seeking a landing lane in a strange airport, is grateful for the familiar layout and the international signals that add to his safety. The maintenance of meaningless differentiation is almost as repressive of life as the wiping out of meaningful differentiation. So we may look forward, without anxiety, to the continued extension of such uniformities; for they but carry further the widening of the area of predictable conduct and common understanding that civilisation, in its first phase, introduced—albeit at such a heavy price. Through such standardisation, the higher functions of society are released, as the higher functions in an organism are freed by the reflexes, which helpfully increase the amount of behaviour that no longer requires conscious thought.

Above all, in law, the establishment of certain rights and duties as members of a universal society is but a final extension of the age-old juridical process. The basic human freedoms, freedom of thought and belief, freedom of expression, freedom of association, freedom of movement—which may be summed up as freedom for self-actualisation and autonomous action—are the very anchors of world government. So, too, with the basic securities: security of life and property, security from arbitrary arrest and coercion, security from random violence. These have become the minimal foundations for all modes of association; and until they are recognised and secured no world community can hope for stability.

By the same token, the axial fibres will not be lacking in a One World pattern. Axial culture, as we have seen, is marked particularly by ideal allegiances that seek to promote universal fellowship, by the direction of life toward superpersonal ends. It attempts to pass beyond the boundaries of both the natural community and the organised state by centering growth within the human personality, in accord with its ultimate hopes and expectations. Wherever this kind of choice is deliberately exercised, so that the ties of fellowship are widened, without respect to birth or caste, to property or power, the axial ferment in effect is still at work. But to make world culture possible, the axial religions in turn will need to disavow their naïve claims to special revelation or exclusive spiritual leadership: still more their demand for temporal authority based on such assumptions. They will rather soften those features that identify them with a particular culture or political society, in the way that the Jesuits did in China in their original missionary enterprise.

The day of the axial religion as a transcendental union of souls seeking salvation, taking over in the name of their divinity a disintegrated material society of inert corporate bodies and degraded or unawakened men, has now passed. Neither 'matter' nor divinity, neither corruption nor salvation, can now be soundly interpreted in such terms, nor can such salvation seem more than an anodyne that has been administered once too often. Today we not merely seek to lessen the pain: we seek to diagnose the disease and cure the ailment. The recurrent illuminations and debasements of the universal churches, which in time traduce the universality that they originally proclaim, even if they do not sink into selling spiritual salvation in the market place, carry no greater promise than the cyclical repetition of secular states. If, as Tonybee urges, the second is always 'a vain repetition,' must not a sufficiently chastened judgment say the same of the first? On the premises that each of the world religions has hitherto held, none of them can hope to embrace within its fold the entire body of humanity.

This means, then, that for the axial religions the moment of general detachment and dematerialisation has possibly come: a carrying further with even bolder faith the movement begun three centuries ago by the Society of Friends. Yet because the axial religions endowed all life with meaning and purpose, and gave man the ability to conceive of a higher self than his social efforts and secular institutions had yet achieved, the axial impulse will remain at work in all self-transcending endeavour. Though we can no longer minimise the difficulties of achieving a higher self, though we must bring to that task help from other quarters, both the original impulse and the intuition are precious. Axial religion remains the starting point for an even higher form of community than any universal church achieved, except in dream: a starting point but not a terminus. What the axial religions sought originally to effect through verbal exhortation, miraculous myth, and conversion will in future be attempted by ampler means, in which science and technics, at last oriented to life, will also play a part.

But this qualification of the orginal role of the axial religions carries with it a compensating promise.

Only in fact through world society and in the person of unified man will the axial religions themselves overcome their own disabling compromises with tribal gods and civilised iniquities. Once redeemed from a sordid concern with their own survival, the vital spark they brought to man may blaze up again. Without the sense of infinite significance and infinite possibility that the axial religions have kept alive, the passage to world culture would hardly be worth the effort it demands; for the limited goals of peace, order, power, security, wealth, knowledge, would be only disheartening mirages that left the thirsty soul dry, if they were regarded as life's ultimate consummations.

6

The persistence of the original New World impulses and institutions must likewise be counted on: it is only when they crowd out other needs that they threaten human growth.

World culture, even more perhaps than today, will rest on the constant activity of the sciences in every department of life. No longer are the exact methods of observation and operation, the refined conceptual analyses of the scientist, confined to the 'physical world.' These salutary habits of thought must in time effect the practice of every art, and so exert a constant moral discipline upon the human personality. In turn the scientist will consciously utilise impulses and intuitions hitherto formally excluded—though never absent in the best minds—from the rationale of science. The release of the imagination through science not only widens the potential field of human action, but creates an aesthetic realm that, by reason of both form and meaning, is enchanting to the human spirit. In the world that the mathematicians, the physicists, and the astronomers have lately disclosed, the mystery that religion first acknowledged has only deepened. These insights will become more valuable, not less, when man himself firmly resumes his central position as interpreter and active director of the multitudinous forces that play over his existence: no longer a mere seeing eye, a manipulating hand, or a detached intelligence.

Hitherto science has prided itself on its depersonalised 'objectivity'; that is, its capacity to treat subjects as objects, organisms as mechanisms, and persons as things. But it will complete its own maturation and achieve a truly objective grasp of phenomena that were excluded originally from its province, when it recognises the full implications of the natural order of organic development and emergence. In this order the physical, biological, social, and personal appear in an ascending hierarchy. Causal interpretation holds most completely at the physical end, while telic interpretation in terms of values, purposes, and goals, becomes increasingly more important at the personal end. Yet at the lowest level life and mind exist as potentials, and being of any rank constitutes a value; while even at the highest, causal determination and organic inertia must be taken into account. In a fully unified science, the methods of reductive analysis and constructive synthesis will no longer be mutually exclusive, nor will they be regarded as the separate provinces of science and humanism.

In turn the scientist himself, restored as whole man, will move as easily from one phase of existence to another as Christopher Wren or Goethe did. He will cease to idolise, as his model of 'objectivity' the specialised, depersonalised self he took over all-too-uncritically from Civilised Man. And what was originally an over-strict division of labour, maintained for productive efficiency, will give way increasingly to a generous sharing of experience, freed from the bristling jealousies of departmentalism and the authoritarian arrogance of the specialist and the expert. Works like D'Arcy Thompson's *Growth and Form*, or Hermann Weyl's *Symmetry* will no longer stand out as exceptions, admirable but inimitable.

In both science and technics, then, One World culture will not forfeit a single sound advance that has been made during the last five centuries, from the printing press to the cyclotron, from the glass hothouse to scientific soil analysis and plant breeding. Rather, it will turn every new invention or new truth to the fullest rational use; and it will push fresh investigations in departments that have been often neglected because they promised no profit to established groups or vested interests. In liberating both science and technics from their original unconscious drives, One World man will in fact re-establish both activities on a firmer basis, as essential contributions to human education and development.

So, too, we cannot easily spare the sense of adventure, the love of freedom, the self-reliance and self-respect, the readiness for audacious experiments, that have come in with New World democracy. Many of the New World values one finds in Emerson and Whitman and Thoreau must be recovered and replenished as contributions to an even larger development. Passage to India!— and passage to more than India.

But the field of adventure is no longer that of the old explorers and pioneers, swiftly staking out the surface of the earth: we must now tunnel downward in chosen areas and deal intensively with many matters that the New World mind, in its first moment of expansion, could touch only superficially, if indeed it did not completely neglect. In this concentration and intensification of interest, the New World ideology must itself undergo a change that will rescue it from the shallowness of its original vision and technique. Not expansion and conquest but intensive cultivation, not 'freedom from' but 'freedom for,' not wholesale mechanisation for the sake of power, profit, productivity, or prestige, but a mechanisation measured by human need and limited by vital norms—this will dictate the nature of economic and social enterprises. This means a general change from a money economy to a life economy.

The old exploration is now at an end. Under One World guidance 'the new exploration,' as Benton MacKaye has called it, will begin : the assemblage of all existing knowledge and values toward the creation of an integrated plan of life. This new exploration has a wider province than the geographic one; but its application to the earth is important. For a survey of the possibilities of human existence, in a new ecological pattern, region by region, is the necessary basis for the resettlement and recultivation of the planet. That will be more than a reversal of New World habits: it will be a moral atonement for four centuries of ruthless exploitation and desecration.

This new adventure demands psychological maturity, as the boyish heroism of the old adventurers did not; for it is an exploration in depth, to fathom all the potential resources of a region, geologic, climatic, vegetative, zoological, historic, cultural, psychological, aesthetic, and to assess its possibilities for continued human enjoyment and for further improvement. The kind of intensive study of the local environment that Henry Thoreau began now needs to be done systematically throughout the planet; and, though it necessarily enlists all the resources of science, it need not, as Patrick Geddes showed through the regional survey, be the work of specialists alone: it is above all an instrument of education in which every member of the community may be enlisted, not least school children.

Man has lived on this planet for perhaps half a million years; yet many of the earth's potentialities are still unrealised. Much that has been overlooked so far has yet, for the first time, to be brought to light and properly valued. Much that was once coarsely violated, through ignorance or greed, will be restored. Much that is still uncouth must be reshaped by art, as the great English landed proprietors of the eighteenth century transformed their domains, so that every vista disclosed an enchanting picture. And much that exists only to be contemplated and admired without any effort at alteration will at last perform this office, freed from the menace of technological 'improvement.' Mountain tops once invaded by funiculars or motor roads will be cleared of these encumbrances, to give the aristocratic rewards of solitude and far horizons to those capable of earning them by their personal efforts.

Perhaps not the least contribution of New World civilisation, once it transfers its old impulses into more humane common channels, will be in the reversal of its original mistakes: the resettlement of people, the replenishment of resources, the recultivation of landscapes: in short, a general undoing of its blind assault upon both the biological environment and the cultures of primitive peoples, and its present wiping out, by heedless urban expansion, of the very rural background necessary to the enjoyment of life in cities. At last sufficient knolwedge is available to rectify the results of importunate greed and to remodel an environment that had been degraded by the engineer's over-confidence in machine-made plans.

Since George Perkins Marsh's classic work on *Man and Nature* appeared in 1864, the need for regenerating and replenishing the earth has been more widely recognised. As a result many wilderness areas, which are essential preserves for the human spirit as well as for wild-life, have belatedly been protected or restored. But this whole process requires a much wider base than the most dogged of conservationists has dared to outline. When, in seeking human balance, we go on to provide a balanced environment, we shall have, in most of the busiest centres of population, to undertake widespread acts of demolition, in order to restore, in a century or so, some of the basic natural ingredients for a full and rich human life. The notion that mechanisation and urbanisation, as they have existed during the last century, are subject to indefinite acceleration is a superstition foisted by those who have made the machine their god. A world culture, in establishing a common human norm, will not merely slow down these processes —it will often reverse them.

In America, we have recently witnessed a blind surge of population into the favourable environment of coastal California. Because this has happened without social foresight or wise political direction it has already, in large areas, wiped out the natural advantages that drew the newcomers to this area. In a world civilisation, the need for controlling such flows of population into regions of advantage will doubtless present some of the most vexatious problems for statesmanship to settle: as difficult to arrive at, by applying rational criteria, as the achievement of an optimum level for any particular region.

In both cases, what cannot be settled wholly by conscious intelligence must be settled by developing a collective conscience about the environment, as a work of art whose own formal outlines must be respected. Here the confidence of New World man in the ultimate reasonableness of his fellows may prove valuable in setting the tone for decisions—as it actually does, for example, in matters like public health, where the dictates of science, though fallible and often burdensome, are generally accepted. Changes in the internal texture of national life, creating mixed populations rather than stridently nativistic ones, may slacken local tensions that would otherwise test to the utmost the political sagacity of a world parliament. Otherwise, the freedoms of an open world would raise, on an even more staggering scale, the very real problems that the Puerto Rican migration has unloaded on the unprepared municipality of New York.

7

So much for the persistent elements in the historic fabric: the threads that may be respun and rewoven, yet cannot, except to our impoverishment, be entirely discarded.

But it would be naïve, in dwelling alone on the more familiar parts of One World culture, to give a purely optimistic picture of the series of adaptations and renewals that are called for. Though each of these original components is needed to create One World Man, that need will often meet heavy opposition from man's earlier selves. Many of the burdens and evils of the past will persist, along with the goods: after the universal framework of human culture is established, unregenerate impulses derived from earlier stages will continue to attack and undermine the new society. Though in future nationalism may be as speedily deflated as it was resurrected after 1914, the needful detachment of national and regional cultures from the power complex may require generations. Plainly, those peoples who have awakened to national consciousness late seem to take it—almost like a fresh disease to which they have built up no immunity—in its most virulent form, regressing to the tribal instead of moving forward to the human.

So, too, the axial religions may stubbornly refuse to lessen their theological particularity, even to gain wider influence. Has not the largest single body of Christian believers officially, during the last century, proclaimed a new series of self-isolating dogmas and miraculous translations, and condemned as heresy every effort to give a poetic, universal meaning to beliefs that, more literally interpreted, insult the mind? And again the dogmas of totalitarian 'communism' may for long resist any change that seeks an inclusiveness, a variety, a freedom, based on man's historic nature, that would modify their self-sealing system of doctrines, masquerading as ultimate truths.

Yes: as world civilisation emerges, the reaction against it may grow more sharply vicious: we have seen this happen during the last decade in the United States. In addition, temptations to one-sided seizure by a nation or class, to sunder again what has been only imperfectly united, will long require vigilance: that problem has not been satisfactorily solved, even after almost two centuries of experience, punctuated by a bitter war, in the American system of federated union. Obsolete modes of government, still flatulent with undigested power, may promote more than one uprising against the common decisions of the United Nations; and they may have to be summarily put down, by show of force if they are deaf to persuasion.

In the end, it will become plain that the very survival of older institutions is bound up with the development of a comprehensive world civilisation, capable of protecting whatever local value has moral vitality or the potentiality of renewal. But what A.E. said long ago about national unity holds with even greater force for world unity: one cannot expect, merely by achieving this marriage, to live happily ever afterward. Those who cherish that utopian dream are not yet fit for world government.

But the very fact that the world order will be an inclusive one makes further expansion, in a physical sense, impossible. All the resources of the planet are finite and limited. At some point, as yet indeterminate, world population must be stabilised: possibly, if the higher development of man is fully considered, at a lower number than the present one. So, too, fundamental biological wants, particularly that for food, will be normalised; and the economy that satisfies these wants will be put on a replacement basis. When that point is reached, the vast gains in energy and productivity, already achieved, but diverted mainly to military preparation, aimless material expansion, and consumptive waste, will flow directly back into life: into the remaking of cities; the wider cultivation of landscapes for beauty and enjoyment, as well as food; the fruitful use of leisure in the arts and sciences and humanities; and not least in the still only half-explored offices of love and friendship and family activity.

'One World' will by definition be an open society. Coherence will be achieved, not as in the past, by walled isolation and hostile exclusion, but by concentration upon common purposes, polarisation toward common centres, mobilisation toward common actions, with a relaxation of tension and a dispersal of forces again once the objective is won. Those who are used to more definite boundaries, more constant compulsions, may feel ill at ease when confronted by the hospitalities and freedoms of this open society. In the present trough of political reaction and apathy, the implications of an open world may seem the emptiest of dreams: for by now even historians, with the exception of an occasional Ferrero, have almost forgotten the open world that actually existed before 1914. Too easily they treat as a permanent and natural condition the limited freedoms of the present world. Yet those of us who are over fifty can remember many features of that older world that now seem ideal, including travel without passports and a sense of virtually absolute immunity to violence and arbitrary power on the part of civilised governments.

There is a practical reason for recovering these freedoms as the very condition for maintaining a world order. Only one ultimate security exists against secret preparations by ruffianly minorities to seize power. This threat now holds possibilities of appalling blackmail, even if without governmental backing, once atomic energy becomes commercially producable and purchasable. The only safeguard against such a threat lies in the fullest freedom of travel and intercourse. No police agency can be sufficiently numerous and widespread to ferret out such criminal activities without counting upon the effective surveillance of each citizen in his comings and goings about the planet. It was a wandering geologist, Professor Bailey Willis, who discovered in the late nineteen-thirties that the Japanese had built a secret military road for the invasion of the Philippines. And it was a code clerk in the Russian embassy in Canada, not official spies or the ubiquitous U.S. Federal Bureau of Investigation, that revealed the presence of Communist atomic scientists who transmitted information to Russian agents.

Only in an open world, where every nook and corner is exposed to the curiosity of the chance visitor, where every citizen may be freely heard if he raises his voice, can mankind sleep safely, even supposing that it had achieved a firm basis for coexistence between governments now hostile to each other. To put faith in any purely official system of inspecting armaments is to nourish bureaucratic illusions. Not till every citizen is, as citizen, a policeman, and the wide world is his precinct, shall we have the minimum security needful against possible outbreaks of private or collective criminality. No local system of law and order has yet done away with the common law-breaker; and it would be childish to assume that world law and order will be less open to such disruptive threats.

8

Within the One World economy, accordingly, there will be a polar relationship between the universal and the regional : one will not exist through the neglect and sacrifice of the other. But one must recognise that nature has unevenly distributed the advantages of soil, climate, natural resources; and that the uneven historic development of communities has often pushed further this inequality. To bring an end to the miseries of impoverished regions and the resentments of the poor and the dispossessed, a life economy will aim to even out gross inequalities. The present programme of technical aid to backward countries is a makeshift attempt to achieve quickly, often for low ulterior purposes, what only a more fundamental and continuous process of equalisation will bring about. World civilisation, as a measure for fully utilising the resources of the planet, may well introduce a graduated world income tax, payable by each state, to rectify the blind favouritisms of nature and provide a basic minimum of the necessaries of life to every people.

World economy, in other words, means both a progressive equalisation and a dynamic equilibrium, not as a matter of prudent philanthropy, mere doles resorted to in moments of crisis in order to forestall an uprising, but as a matter of justice. Precisely as the higher income groups, in commonwealths like the United Kingdom and the United States, are now heavily taxed in order to provide domestic social services that redress in no small degree the inequalities of earned income, so will the more prosperous nations be heavily taxed, in order to make possible the capital investments and the subsidies that may be necessary to give a just share of the planet's ill-distributed wealth to every community.

No monopoly advantages based on the 'law of rent' can be justified in a world economy. Justice demands continued adjustment. What makes adjustment a matter of principle, not mere expediency, is the idea of balance itself as the precondition of life and growth, and chronic unbalance, however orderly in form, as a forerunner of disintegration. In a world economy the factors to be balanced are natural energies and human vitalities, populations and resources, areas of living and specialised facilities for production. Their constant reapportionment is both the condition

of having a sound life and the price of peace : for the older kind
of stability, which rested on ignorance and isolation, is gone.
With little more than a transfer of funds from the present
national war budgets to a world peace budget this change could
be begun.

But before a new framework for political and economic activity
is created, in harmony with One World principles, many of the
residual superstitions of classic capitalism and monolithic communism must be scrapped. New criteria of practicality and profit-
ability, conceived in terms of human development, must be
introduced : the good life must replace the 'goods' life as the
motive force in industry.

Happily, almost every government has been forced—covertly
or openly—to accept the standard of human welfare as superior
to the rights of property, when they are in conflict, not merely
in emergencies but in everyday concerns. But because of a failure
to formulate a life economy, too often these non-capitalist
methods of ensuring production or consumption take a distorted,
even antisocial, form. Witness the fixed agricultural subsidies in
the United States whose grotesque workings penalise the consumer three times over. This kind of market-economy irrationality
vies with the irrationality of war. Hence we have now to found a
new economy on John Ruskin's principle : There is no wealth but
life. And we have to consider the gifts of nature, from uranium
mines and oil wells to the surplus products of farm and factory, as
common possessions, to be distributed according to human need :
not as profits and earnings parcelled in accordance with the laws of
property to a privileged minority. The coming triumph of auto-
mation in mechanical industry only makes this change more
imperative.

These facts form a solid basis for turning formal co-existence
between the communist and capitalist states into active understanding and co-operation. Communist regimes, if they accept the
flexibility and diversity of a mixed system of production as a
means of increasing efficiency, will tend to become responsive to
popular control and more open to the give-and-take procedures
of democracy. Similarly with 'capitalism.' In accepting equality as
a necessity of mass distribution, whether by job insurance, wage
rises, fixed annual wages, or outright gifts, systems of production
once rigidly capitalist have already absorbed many of the ideal
features of communism. Instead of maintaining their ideological

purity, each regime, seeking a dynamic equilibrium, will tend to take on more of the diversified attributes of living systems.

Though this change from a money economy based on power and productivity to a life economy based on participation and creativity will solve many of the vexatious problems that have haunted the industrial world, in crisis after crisis, other problems will press for attention. For to make the world as a whole a theatre of human activity will immensely increase productivity, hitherto curbed by considerations of marketability. What was done automatically in earlier societies, through sheer poverty of means or natural barriers to intercourse, must now be done through conscious control.

A life economy, in order words, demands a life plan, conceived in terms of man's higher needs: a standard of living formulated, not with reference to the capacity for production alone, but to the capacity for rational assimilation and creative utilisation. The Economic Man was, by definition, a voracious consumer, fettered to the dogma of increasing wants. The whole man, to the extent that he is a creator, will change both the direction and tempo of the whole economic process: indeed, in the interest of wholeness, he may carry further the movement that has already started in America: the do-it-yourself movement. As I suggested long ago in *Technics and Civilisation*, the final effect of rationalisation, specialisation, and mechanisation may be to evoke, as an indispensable counter-weight, the amateur.

Already, even within the relatively narrow theatre of the national state, our capacity to absorb all the materials needed for human growth—without being choked by surfeit—taxes our system of education. There is no field of knowledge in which the superabundance of available data does not tend to produce ignorance, impotence, and confusion; just as there is no field of production where an excess of goods does not produce repletion, boredom, and wanton caprice, sedulously fostered as 'fashion.' So in order to make use of the far vaster resources that a world culture will open up, we shall need a new kind of personal centrality and rootedness: a firm inner discipline and a habit of self-directed, purposeful activity. The great field for unified man's activity is not production but education; and the productive process itself will be considered mainly as an auxiliary to human culture.

Without this firm inner core, we should be threatened with a welter of images, symbols, ideas, proposals, stimuli, activities which, in addition to our present materialist surfeits and extravagances, would defeat all creativity. The ability to select, to inhibit, to choose, is essential to a life economy: indeed, the restriction of consumption is one of the essential conditions of creation; and only an economy that remains stable under such conditions is worthy to survive.

In short, world civilisation will have its own tensions, difficulties, even perils, peculiar to itself; and the solution of these problems will call for political imagination of the highest order. Many of its problems will prove insurmountable, indeed, until the same needs that have produced the beginnings of these institutions bring forth, in the fullness of time, a higher order of personality, capable of perfecting them. Both the agent and the goal of this transformation is unified man. His mission will be to create an open synthesis and an open self. Through him the forces of life will be replenished and brought into a dynamic equilibrium, visible in every part of the planet. That equilibrium, once achieved, may serve as the starting point for an extensive—but, still more, an intensive—process of human development.

9

Human Prospects

I

The development of a world culture concerns mankind at large and each individual human being. Every community and society, every association and organisation, has a part to play in this transformation; and no domain of life will be unaffected by it. This effort grows naturally out of the crisis of our time: the need to redress the dangerous over-development of technical organisation and physical energies by social and moral agencies equally far-reaching and even more commanding. In that sense, the rise of world culture comes as a measure to secure human survival. But the process would lose no small part of its meaning were it not also an effort to bring forth a more complete kind of man than history has yet disclosed. That we need leadership and participation by unified personalities is clear; but the human transformation would remain desirable and valid, even if the need were not so imperative.

The kind of person called for by the present situation is one capable of breaking through the boundaries of culture and history, which have so far limited human growth. A person not indelibly marked by the tattooings of his tribe or restricted by the taboos of his totem : not sewed up for life in the stiff clothes of his caste and calling or encased in vocational armour he cannot remove even when it endangers his life. A person not kept by his religious dietary restrictions from sharing spiritual food that other men have found nourishing; and finally, not prevented by his ideological spectacles from ever getting more than a glimpse of the world as it shows itself to men with other ideological spectacles, or as it discloses itself to those who may, with increasing frequency, be able without glasses to achieve normal vision.

The immediate object of world culture is to break through the premature closures, the corrosive conflicts, and the cyclical frustrations of history. This breakthrough would enable modern man to take advantage of the peculiar circumstances today that favour a universalism that earlier periods could only dream about. But the ultimate purpose of One World culture is to widen the human prospect and open up new domains—on earth, not in interstellar space—for human development. If the chief result of a world civilisation were only to provide each individual with a television set, a motor car, a social security card, and a one-way ticket on a spaceship, one might as well turn the planet over at once to post-historic man.

The resources for this human transformation have been available for only little more than a century; and many of the technical instruments and corporate agencies have still to be shaped. But for the first time in history, man now begins to know his planet as a whole and to respond to all the peoples who inhabit it: that is, he begins to see his own multiple image in a common mirror, or rather, in a moving picture that traverses backward and forward the dimension of time. Since the exploration of the earth was undertaken by Western man before he was spiritually prepared for it, the peoples and regions that were drawn together by trade, colonisation, and conquest lost many of the most precious attributes of their cultures and their personalities. The New World expansion debased the conquerors instead of elevating the conquered. By the same token, Western man impoverished his own future development, too, for the heritage he mangled and often extirpated was also his own, as a member of the human race. In his land hunger, in his greed for gold and silver, for coal and iron and oil, Western man overlooked far greater riches.

Though our dawning sense of interdependence and unity comes too belatedly to repair all the damage that has been done, we see that even the residue of past cultures still holds more values than any single nation has yet created or expressed. By his very consciousness of history, modern man may free himself at last from unconscious compulsions, derived from situations he has outlived, which continue to push him off the highway of development into rubbish-filled blind alleys. Yet if he achieves a fresh understanding of the potentialities he has buried through his own failure to know himself, he may repair his shattered confidence in his future and throw open new vistas.

The survey of human existence as a whole that has gone on systematically only for the last four centuries has not alone naturalised man by bringing him within the cycle of cosmic, geological, and biological processes: it has likewise humanised nature and made it more closely than ever before an integral part of human consciousness. Man's own creative works, whether they are a temple, an atomic pile, or a mathematical theorem, are themselves expressions of nature and witnesses of potentialities that were latent in the atom and in the formative process that built up, in rhythmic series, the stable elements.

Whatever the ultimate realities, that which man knows of nature is conditioned by his self, and it changes from moment to moment and age to age as his experience matures and his capacity for symbolic interpretation grows. His feelings are as much a part of this reality as his thoughts, for his very concept of an 'objective,' neutral world without feelings and values was itself the product of a particular moment in his own self-development and is no longer as important as it once seemed. Yet whatever man knows of himself is conditioned by nature: so that the more exact, the more self-detached, becomes his perception of natural processes, the more fully does he free himself from the delusions of arbitrary subjectivity. Brahman and Atman are indeed one, once they are conceived in dynamic interaction: the self-creating world and the world-creating self.

This exploration of nature has naturally opened up man's inner history, too. Within the individual soul man finds in symbolic form a whole universe that seems to contain the scattered debris of past cultures and the germinal nodes of future ones. Here, within himself, he finds primitive urges and civilised constraints, tribal fixations and axial liberations, animal lethargies and angelic flights. Through the agency of culture, if not through any more direct impress upon the psyche, all of man's past selves remain disconcertingly alive. Just as man's interpretation of the so-called physical world has now become multidimensional, spanning the whole distance from inter-stellar to intra-atomic space, and including an exact knowledge of phenomena, like ultraviolet rays, which are outside his sensory experience, so with the inner world of man: it ranges from the depths of the unconscious to the highest levels of conscious ideation, disciplined feeling, and purposeful action.

Our view of the self now includes earlier interpretations that New World science, in its confident externalism, had discarded. Augustine's picture of the mind is closer to Freud's than is John Locke's, and St. Paul's description of human nature seems far more adequate than Jeremy Bentham's. Heaven and hell, as the ultimate destinations of creativity or disintegration, are necessary cardinal points in any description of the human soul. It is not through scientific description, but through sympathy and empathy, through parallel acts of re-creation, that one explores this world, even after it has been opened up to other men in the symbols and forms of art.

Now the persistence of old biological or historic residues, whether active or inert, does not mean, as many still falsely suppose, that they have a preappointed or fated outcome. If certain aspects of man's nature are relatively fixed, since they are structured in his organs, they function like the warp in the loom : not merely is there considerable play in the fixed threads themselves, but the shuttle that weaves the fabric lies in man's hands, and by his conscious efforts, introducing new colours and figures, he modifies even the over-all design. Every culture attaches different estimates to man's nature and history; and in its creative moments, it adds new values that enlarge the human personality and give it new destinations. Though man's release from nature's conditions or his own past selves can never be complete, the effort to achieve it is what gives individuality to every historic form : this indeed is what keeps even the most repetitive movements of history from being entirely meaningless. The making of the future is an essential part of man's self-revelation.

The problem for man today is to use his widened consciousness of natural processes and of his own historic nature to promote his own further growth. Such knowledge must now be turned to fuller uses, in the projection of a fresh plan of life and a new image of the self, which shall be capable of rising above man's present limitations and disabilities. This effort, as we have seen, is an old one; for even before man achieved any degree of self-consciousness, he was actively engaged in self-fabrication. If 'Be yourself' is nature's first injunction to man, 'Transform yourself' was her second—even as 'Transcend yourself' seems, at least up to now, to be her final imperative. What will distinguish the present effort to create world culture, if once it takes form, is the richness and variety of the resources that are now open, and the multitude of people now sufficiently released from the struggle for existence to play a part in this new drama.

2

The readiness to face existence in all its dimensions, cosmic and human, is the first requirement for human development today.

This readiness is itself a new fact, for even scientists, whose curiosity seems boundless, for long recoiled in fear against any exploration of the subjective self that penetrated beyond the threshold of isolated stimuli, abstracted sensations, and measured responses.

Not without a certain irony, the scientific rationalism of Dr. Sigmund Freud, with its fine surgical indifference to the seemingly morbid, brought to light the areas of the personality that positivism and rationalism had dismissed as 'unreal'—the wish and the dream, the sense of guilt and original sin, the elaboration of fantasy into art; and by carrying this inquiry further, into the normal and healthy manifestations of these inner states, Dr. Carl Jung disclosed the integrating functions of the symbol, and thus opened a passage from self-enclosed subjectivity to those common aesthetic expressions and practical constructions that can be shared, in a spirit of love, with other people.

This opening up of every part of the psyche coincides, it would seem, with the new relationship that has begun to develop between cultures. This is symbolised by an appreciative awareness, hardly a generation old, of the aesthetic values of African or Polynesian or Aztec or Andean art, following an equally radical change in Western man's attitude toward the great arts of Egypt, Mesopotamia, Persia, India and China, once considered too far below the absolute standard of Greek art to merit study, still less appreciation. That change might, of course, lead to an abortive cultural relativism, innocent of any principle of development, were it not attached to the emergent purposes of world culture. The partial and fragmentary selves that man historically achieved sacrificed completeness for the sake of temporary order; and in the most partial and fragmentary form of all, that now sought by post-historic man, the order would be almost absolute, because so much that was essentially human would be left out of it.

From this negative universalism the acceptance of man's whole self, disclosed only in the fullness of history, helps to rescue us; for organic wholeness itself is impossible unless the creative and integrating processes remain uppermost. Religion and art, if not science, remind us of the constant reappearance of angelic saviours and redeemers: Promethean heroes who bring fire and light, defying the tortures of the envious gods: mother images of succour and loving devotion. We have learned nothing from historic experience if we have not learned that man lives by more than his applied intelligence alone.

Out of the depths of life itself come the superego, the conscience, the idealised image and the imagined ideal, the voice of reason and the promptings of divinity: all as integral to man's present nature as breathing or digestion. For it is not just the animal past that lives on in man's unconscious: the emergent future that has not yet taken form is likewise present: all that promises to release man from fixations and regressions and to open up untested modes of being and becoming, of transfiguration and transformation. Though no small part of human history has been preoccupied with the exploration of this inner world, even to the detriment of man's control over the external world, it has yet to enlist man's fullest capabilities. And as with the discovery of the New World there is an even more difficult stage that follows the surveying and mapping of the unknown area: that is, its settlement and cultivation.

3

With respect to man's inner development, we have seen it go roughly through four main stages: each of these has left a mark on both his ideas and his institutions.

In the primitive stage, the stage of magic and myth, he was innocent of self-consciousness, because his self, as an entity apart from the group, was still nonexistent; and he therefore lacked the capacity for independent action and invention which became feasible only after a certain separation had taken place. Subjectively, every part of human experience held together, expressible in meaningful images and symbols; but the price of this unity was insulation from any possible contradictory reality. Primitive man, as we piece him together from the myths and relics that remain, was relatively whole; but in transcending his animal state he had left the real world, since he no longer recognised otherness: what he saw and felt and reacted to were his own projections, his own externalised feelings and urges, into which all outward events were somehow converted.

Civilisation placed external curbs on this subjectivity: it exacted external obedience to powers other than his own, to gods and kings if not to actual conditions of nature; and it provided all human activities with a mechanical basis of order. The metes and bounds so provided secured man, in some degree, against subjective dissolution. To the extent that civilisation made man recognise his own limitations, and released him from purely wishful fantasy, it enlarged the human grip on reality. But in recognising as absolute claims outside the self, civilised man ceased to live in a unified world: the fragmentary man, with his split and contradictory selves, came into existence: the innocent paranoia of primitive man gave place to the schizoid state seemingly chronic to civilisation in every phase.

With the development of axial religious consciousness a new self came into existence. In a determined effort to achieve wholeness, the inner man split himself off from the outer world and its imprisoning institutions. So real became the vision of a single unifying God, omniscient and omnipotent, that the outer world seemed, in comparison, trivial and unimportant. Meaning and value were attached to the inner, the disembodied, the subjective; and such aspects of nature as were manifestly part of another system were the expression of God's will and mind, not man's. This innerness was even more audacious in its revelations than that of primitive man; and it restored man's sense of his own self-importance, after civilisation had reduced him to a mere fraction, virtually a nonentity, paralysed by power and authority external to him.

But if axial religion escaped the fragmentation of the civilised order, it did so only by creating a dualism between 'this world' and the 'other world.' This disturbed both inner tranquillity and practical effectiveness. Every external display of human order and power or even intelligence involved a betrayal of the inner man, or at least was a threat to his existence. That inveterate, underlying dualism of the axial self was challenged by another conception, first formulated in Ionia in the sixth century B.C., which shifted meaningful experience from the inner world to the outer world. This philosophy denied, in effect, the importance of the soul as an independent entity, with its conscious values and ideal goals, and gave weight only to the external manifestations of 'earth, air, fire, and water,' devoid of purpose or goal, and detached from any self-consciousness except that exhibited by rational intelligence. The self was thus reduced to the knower, and reality was reduced to that which could be known.

Unfortunately this view, which came to maturity in the seventeenth century, was only a dualism in reverse: it achieved unity by suppressing or ignoring every subjective expression except its own kind of thought. The conscious inner world that was thus brought into existence was ostentatiously antiseptic, like the operating theatre in a hospital: within this special room, with its refined mechanical facilities, the mind learned to operate with a deftness and precision that only the rarest spirits had mastered before. But outside in the corridors there was dirt and disorder and disease: the rejected parts of the psyche were in a worse state under this new dispensation than the rejected parts of the physical world had been under the axial self.

At all these stages in the development of the self, only a small part of man's potentialities were consciously represented in image or idea. Fortunately, the repressed or neglected aspects, even in primitive society, were not effectively excluded from living experience. However well fortified the inner world, some of the outer world is constantly breaking through, making demands that must be met, offering suggestions that, even if unheeded, produce a certain effect. So, too, however heavy the crust formed by external nature, by human institutions and habits, the pressure from the inner world would produce cracks and fissures, and even from time to time explosively erupt. By no attention to magic formulae, by no probing of the unconscious, can one shape a tool. Similarly, by no feat of mechanical organisation can one write a poem. In other words, by the very act of living men have always in some degree escaped the imperfections of their knowledge and belief. Just as life itself, in its constantly unfolding creativity, is far richer than any conception we are able to form of it, so with the human self. Man not merely builds but lives better than he knows.

At the same time, it should be plain that a great measure of man's potential energy and vitality and creativity has been dissipated, because he has not been fully oriented to every aspect of reality, outward and inward. His various historic selves have served as fine meshes that rejected far more than they admitted. We can hardly yet picture the transformation that would be wrought if every part of man's experience were hospitably received; and if every part of the inner world were as accessible and as subject to conscious direction as the outer world. So far we have lived mainly in partial worlds; and they have allowed only a small share of our energies to be directly employed. Neither the loose subjective wholeness achieved by primitive man nor, at the other extreme, the accurate, piece-meal objectivity now sought by science could do justice to every dimension of human experience. If the first was limited by its caprices, which recognised no external order or causality, the latter is equally limited by its compulsions, which recognise no inner flow of purpose and make no account of free creativity or potential divinity. Living in half-worlds, it is hardly strange that we have produced only half-men, or creatures even more distorted than these homunculi, 'inverted cripples,' magnified ears, eyes, bellies, or brains, whose other parts have shrunk away.

Perhaps an even better figure for the state of man, as disclosed by history, would be that of a series of experimental plants, each fed with some of the elements necessary for full growth, but none yet supplied with all of them : here an excess of nitrogen has favoured a leggy growth of stem, there the absence of water has withered the whole plant : and, to make the figure even more accurate, in addition to these natural defects, the horticulturist himself has often clipped and pruned the growing plant or pinched its buds. What the experiment shows, if we may at last draw a lesson, is that man requires a sounder diet, including minute trace elements, than any self-enclosed historic culture has supplied him. He needs both a fuller exposure to sunlight above ground and a richer soil in the unconscious.

The ideal of wholeness itself is what has been lacking in the culture of man : his specialities and particularities have gotten the better of him. But from occasional periods, like the Renaissance, when the ideal of the whole man has commanded the foremost representatives of the age, we have a hint of the immense energising that may take place when every aspect of life is open to cultivation, when the instinctual life is no longer cut off from rational development, and when order and reason are not impoverished by torpid emotions or listless routines or limited purposes.

But even in unpropitious periods, individual figures, who had reached some degree of maturity in every department of life, may have appeared from time to time, only to be rejected by the society they transcended. At more than one moment in history, indeed, the effort to achieve wholeness, balance, universality, brought a measure of fulfilment. Greek culture, from the sixth century to the fourth, was remarkably peopled by such whole men : Solon, Socrates, Sophocles, were outstanding examples, but not rare ones : indeed, the proportion of highly developed persons in relation to the total population seems to have been greater than at possibly any other place and time.

These examples of wholeness may account for the attraction that Greek culture has exercised on the best minds of the West.

To a degree that few other cultures could claim, the Greek self seems to stand for the truly and fully human. The development of any individual might show flaws: witness Socrates' serious failure to connect man in the city with man in nature. But in the main, no part of life was closed to them, and no part of the self claimed such exclusive respect that it crippled other capacities or closed other avenues of experience. Sophocles' readiness to do his duty as citizen, in service as a general, did not incapacitate him as a tragic playwright: for in both roles he was first of all a man. The ultimate mysteries and irrationalities of existence—symbolised by Chance, Fate, the Furies, Eros—entered their consciousness without upsetting their composure or undermining the real values they had won.

Yet even at its fullest development, this Hellenic self, so finely poised, so admirably complete within its own cultural boundaries, its own favoured habitat, lacked universality. Their best representatives did not realise that the unity and balance they sought needed the help of other cultures and other types of personality: that in fact the barbarian they despised had had experiences and had produced values that might, for example, have kept one of their most creative minds, Plato, from conceiving such static and stultifying utopias as those he pictured in the *Republic* and the *Laws*. From the Jews, the Greeks needed to learn about the meaningfulness of time, change, and history; from the Persians, the fact that tension and struggle are essential to human growth, so that a polity that sought only a vegetative perfection, free from dialectic oppositions of good and evil, would be founded on illusion.

The example of the Greeks shows that the ideal possibilities of our own day have historic roots: their failures show that it is only by our accepting the realities of a contemporary world society, instead of seeking a more limited province for a more limited self, that we can find a new foundation for our own further development. The self we seek, one that will have a heightened consciousness of its own still-unused resources, has still to be created. To the shaping of that self we must give no small part of the energies that we have so far recklessly squandered on our misdirected and muddled 'conquest of nature.' Only by a concentration on our inner world, sufficient to counterbalance our present externalism, can we hope in time to achieve the balance and wholeness which will permit a steady flow of energies back and forth between inner and outer. In the fullness of time, a unified self will bring a world culture into existence, and that world culture will in turn sustain and bring to a higher pitch of development this new self.

4

Every transformation of man, except that perhaps which produced neolithic culture, has rested on a new metaphysical and ideological base; or rather, upon deeper stirrings and intuitions whose rationalised expression takes the form of a new picture of the cosmos and the nature of man. Even neolithic man may have been no exception; for who can say what images of fertility, what intuitions of the relation of seed and soil, phallus and womb, may not have been the prelude to that order? Our hope of creating one world within and without, accessible in all its reaches to all men, prompting a life more copious, vehement, and bold than any that has appeared before, rests upon a corresponding ideological change. To achieve unity between men, we must cultivate unity without ourselves: to enact that unity, we must have a vision of it before our eyes.

We have need, therefore, for a rational framework that will itself have the varied attributes of life: it must be capable of reconciling persistence with change, unity with variety, the internal with the external, the causal with the teleological, process with purpose. Many attempts to formulate such a philosophy during the last two centuries have been handicapped by the traditional tendency of philosophy itself to create a single watertight system, too confidently complete to admit repair or enlargement by other minds. We see this plainly in the early efforts at synthesis made by Hegel, Comte, Marx, Spencer, each of which, in excluding every rival system, undermined its own pretence to unity. Even the sciences themselves, which can modify their foundations and make additions to the superstructure without undermining the sound parts already built, have no place for any kind of experience except that which can be ratified by their methods, which exclude non-intellectual modes of creativity.

Certainly it would be presumptuous to attempt to rectify these errors by creating still another system; but it would be even more stultifying to follow the path taken by most contemporary philosophers and abandon the search for synthesis and unity as beyond human power. To effect a new transformation of man, we must be informed by a philosophy capable of uniting every aspect of human experience, and directing human development through every phase. Whilst the personless and purposeless *Weltbild* of seventeenth-century physics is already partly discredited in the sciences where it originated, the great corpus of scientific knowledge was largely formed under its influence. Most of our positive knowledge has passed through a filter devised to eliminate those aspects of experience that reveal autonomous and purposeful activities, not characteristic of purely physical systems. Even in the human sciences the same limitation holds. The reductive technique of conventional science, interpreting the complex in terms of the simple, the higher in terms of the lower, the whole in terms of the part, is useless for revealing movement in the opposite direction. It has no method for working forward toward the future, following the path of integration and development and emergence: so it fails to understand those organic processes in which the end or goal plays a part in determining the earlier sequence of events, even though the end, as imagined or projected, is itself subject in the very act of realisation to further changes in its own structure. In the case of organic or human development the reductive technique conceals the one characteristic that, above all others, signifies development as opposed to random change: namely, the continued forward movement toward a goal, or, at a lower stage, toward the completion of an organic sequence, like the life cycle of a species. With man, this movement toward a consciously projected ideal goal, though constantly modified by external conditions, has its origin in unconscious urges and dreams; and with the growth of knowledge and experience it takes in a much larger world than any visible environment suggests.

If ordered knowledge is to be at the service of man's further transformation, the sciences themselves will have to overcome the naïve bias against teleology they have inherited from the seventeenth century. At that time advanced thinkers like Galileo, Descartes, and even Spinoza found themselves constrained, in the pursuit of truth, to shake off the dogmatic finalism of axial thought. Theological dogma, which presumed to know the mind of God and the ultimate destination of man, on the basis of 'revelation,' had discredited itself by its very presumption. Though no finite mind can claim insight into the over-all processes of evolution and history, though, as Spinoza rightly said, 'Nature has no fixed end in view,' that is not to say that proximate ends and tentative goals are not visible and definable.

Doubtless the route that both nature and man have taken was not rigidly laid out at the beginning: indeed at every stage of the voyage we are greeted, as Columbus was, by unexpected landfalls and strange ports. But this does not say that the entire journey has been aimless and will never get one anywhere. A bottle thrown into the ocean may be carried, by the accidents of the tides and ocean currents, to a distant shore: but the great voyages of discovery were not conducted on the same terms, nor would they have succeeded without a purpose, a direction, and a goal. On the contrary, the end in view selectively controls and orders the sequence that brings about its accomplishment; and the better that end is interpreted, the more direct the voyage is likely to be. Organic activities create their own occasions, instead of being entirely at the mercy of nature's offerings.

Fortunately, biological knowledge has laid a fresh foundation for the teleological principle. Man has long known that the flow of life is directional and irreversible: corpses do not turn into embryos. Likewise, for a good part of an organism's existence, living processes oppose the tendency of energy to run downhill and disperse. The reversal of the natural trajectory of life is unbuilding and disintegration. We know, too, that certain attributes of organic existence have over long periods gained: that there was far more mind in existence at the point when man emerged than there had been a hundred million years before. Since man started on his career, there has not been merely an increase in the quantity of mind, but also in its qualitative attributes: in man's sensitiveness, his feeling, his capacity for love, and in his ability to encompass with the aid of symbols a larger and fuller sense of the whole. In man, the blind forces that stirred through matter and organic life have now achieved, as never before, a consciousness that reaches ever further back into origins and ever further forward into possible choices and possible destinies. Despite many setbacks and diversions, mind has matured, and love, which first sprang out of the needs of reproduction and nurture, has widened its domain. No theory of human development is adequate that does not include this widening of the province of love: it is this, rather than intelligence and the division of labour (which man shares with rats and termites), that marks man's full emergence into the human estate. In the act of maturation man has made existence more lovable by multiplying the objects and the ways of love.

As intuitions and scattered fragments of knowledge, all these facts and possibilities have been known to man at other times. But the growth of systematic thought has worked them into a unified body of knowledge. From Darwin to Freud, from Humboldt to Geddes, from Schliemann to Petrie and Evans, from Vico to Toynbee and Teilhard de Chardin, the disciplines that describe organic and human development have replaced guess and myth with accurate observation and a more comprehensive insight: though much of our existing knowledge needs the correction and amplification that only a more unified experience will be able to give it.

If life, in its fullness and wholeness, is to furnish our criterion for all development, then our philosophy must respect the main attributes of life, balance and growth, freedom and choice, persistence and variation, adaptation and insurgence, above all, the tendency to self-actualisation and self-transcendence. In the interest of wholeness, we must counter-balance inhibition with expression, etherealisation with materialisation, extroversion with introversion, automatism with renewed creativity. For the new person, as for William James, 'the real and the ideal are dynamically continuous.' And only in the act of living can that dynamic interplay be maintained.

This new orientation does not merely declare the primacy of life: even more decisively, it challenges the one-sided reductive and analytic technique by placing the highest term in conscious existence, the human person, in a position of responsibility for interpreting and directing the course of life, in so far as that now lies increasingly within his hands. Instead of devaluating the person by reducing him to his animal lusts and drives, or to his even lower physico-chemical components, it attaches a fresh value to all natural events by bringing them within the purview of the person.

5

This polarisation of thought around the concept of the person, as the highest emergent of known life, has been going on in many different minds during the past generation; but in a different sense than that of the axial religions. One means here, not the particular illumined person, the singular incarnation of axial religion, but the generic person, the last term in the development of the physical universe, the organic world, and the human community. As such, the person is endowed with the energies and vitalities of each earlier emergence. But he transcends his creaturely limitations by his capacity to interpret natural events, to conserve forms and values, to plan and project new goals and new destinies, to hold together in consciousness a meaningful world and to transform by action ever wider reaches of life, in accordance with that meaning.

The philosophy of the person includes every aspect of experience: the reality of love no less than the reality of power, the reality of the unique and the individualised no less than the reality of the repeated and the standardised. In the person both immanence and transcendence, necessity and freedom, are facts of experience. When we begin with the person we penetrate life at every level, not merely the past and the known, but the potential and the conceivable: that which still lies beyond our knowing. This is the polarising idea that will presently radiate into every department of thought, quickening the perception of interrelations and integrations, and giving a new value to truths that would otherwise remain inert.

A world built up conceptually from the atom might remain forever in fragments and unfinished sequences: in such a world, if uncorrected by a theory of organic development, even the phenomena of life might seem disjointed and accidental, without direction, without ultimate value. Whereas a world penetrated downward from the person begins with the fact of integration, with values and goals already embodied and incarnated. From that beginning one may interpret otherwise dispersed and aimless events in the light of the goal toward which they have moved and achieved conscious existence. Such a world assumes no preestablished harmony and no fixed destination. What it reveals is a multitude of organic patterns, which, in relation to further human designs, become cumulatively significant. The increase of creativity becomes accordingly man's measure of his success in life.

As man has gone on with his own development, he has become more conscious both of the general process of organic transformation and of the important role he himself has come to play. The concept of the person, associated with creativity and divinity, was originally confined to a single individual, the supreme ruler of the land, identified and worshipped as a god. Now it has become the essential mark of human development, in which all men share. Instead of man in person bowing himself out of the picture, as he did when he followed the old canons of the physical sciences, he now takes a central position on the stage, knowing that the performance itself, in the theatre of consciousness at least, cannot go on without him. Without man's intervention it would be meaningless dumb show.

Man begins as an actor, detached from his animal colleagues, already something of a star performer, but uncertain of what part he shall learn. In time, he becomes a scene painter, modifying the natural background and finding his own part modified by it, too: and he is driven to be a stagehand, likewise, shifting the 'properties' to make his entrances and exits more manageable. Only after much practice in all these roles, as scene painter, stagehand, costumer, make-up artist, actor, does man discover that his main function is to write and direct the drama. In composing the play itself man uses, in Shakespearean fashion, many of the old plots left by nature, but he gives them a new turn of the imagination and works the events up to a climax that nature, without his aid, might not have blundered upon for countless million years.

In its early stages, this intensification of creativity is represented, not in man's actual acts, but in the attributes of his gods, to whom he at first fearfully attributed the omniscience and omnipotence he secretly coveted for himself. Only late in man's development did he find it necessary to project, in his conception of divinity, an attribute that would offset the grave threat to life hidden in this all-knowingness and all-powerfulness: a divine all-lovingness.

Love, like mind itself, has been slowly gathering momentum through the organic world: by reason of its late introduction into the drama conceived and enacted by man, it has absorbed only a small share of man's working and learning activities. But in the development of the person love is actually the central element of integration: love as erotic desire and procreativeness, love as passion and aesthetic delight, lingering over images of beauty and shaping them anew, love as fellow feeling and neighbourly helpfulness, bestowing its gifts on those who need them, love as parental solicitude and sacrifice, finally, love with its miraculous capacity for overvaluing its own object, thereby glorifying it and transfiguring it, releasing for life something that only the lover at first can see. Without a positive concentration upon love in all its phases, we can hardly hope to rescue the earth and all the creatures that inhabit it from the insensate forces of hate, violence, and destruction that now threaten it. And without a philosophy of the person, who dares to talk of love?

What is ideally desirable, at this stage of man's development, does not exist in any past form of man, either biological or social: not cerebral man, muscular man, or visceral man: not the pure Hindu, the pure Mohammedan, the pure Christian, nor yet the pure Marxist or the pure Mechanist: not Old World man or New World man. The unity we seek must do justice to all these fragments, and lovingly include them in a self that shall be capable of transcending them. Any doctrine of wholeness that does not begin with love itself as the symbol and agent of this organic wholeness can hardly hope to produce either a unified self or a united world; for it is not in the detached intellect alone that this transformation must be effected.

6

This radical transvaluation of values is a necessary prelude to the next phase of man's development. Up to the present the chief activity of mankind has been confined to its biological ambit— to keep alive and reproduce itself. The quantity of time and attention that man could give to art and play, to ritual and religion, to philosophy and science, in short, to the central drama of existence, was only a modicum of that which he was forced to devote to the preparatory economic processes. What was achieved in meaning and value was almost surreptitiously filched from the so-called serious business of life. But almost within the memory of living men, a radical change in the human condition has come about. This change rivals that brought in by neolithic culture, and far outstrips that produced by earlier forms of mechanical organisation, for it brings with it the promise of release from compulsory labour and every form of external slavery. Thanks mainly to advances in science, almost unlimited energies are now at man's disposal; and in most of the servile modes of work, the automatic machine is capable of performing functions that heretofore were performed only at an immense sacrifice of human life.

Because the current activities of our society continued to flow into obsolete moulds, this change at first produced only industrial crises and dislocations; and even now, only a small part of its benefits is available. But already, in advanced industrial countries, the number of hours in the working week has been almost halved, and the proportion of people in the professions and in the services not devoted to agriculture or industrial production has risen steadily. As this change proceeds, a fact unknown outside the most primitive cultures comes once again into existence: no longer the domination of life by work, but the possible integration of work into a more abundant and significant life.

This relief from the demand that life shall be grimly subordinated to work holds out two great promises. The first of these is that work itself, at least that which remains outside the province of the automatic machine, may itself become an educative process, evoking intelligence and feeling, giving back even to mechanical functions the freedom the old craftsman used to exercise. This kind of creativity is largely lacking in the meretricious art of the market place, but has long been prophetically visible in art, such as the sculptures of Naum Gabo or the architecture of Frank Lloyd Wright. At this point, Le Play's great dictum, that the most important product that comes out of the mine is the miner, will apply to every occupation. Even more, we may now favour certain types of products and certain systems of production, and reject others, with reference to the effect that the work has upon the human personality: we shall weigh its influence upon love, fellowship, family life, citizenship, not merely upon mechanical efficiency.

The other great benefit of the transformation of the industrial process is the fact that its outcome need not be a plethora of material goods and gadgets, nor yet of instruments of warfare and genocide. Once we revamp the institutions of the market, and distribute goods mainly on the basis of need, rather than in proportion to toil or sacrifice or privileged status, our gains will be gains in leisure. In fact, without leisure, our expansion in industrial production would be almost meaningless; for we need a plenitude of time if we are to select and assimilate all the genuine goods that modern man now commands. *Schola* means leisure; and leisure makes possible the school. The promise of a life economy is to provide schooling for the fullest kind of human growth—not for the further expansion of the machine.

This does not mean simply that more of our lives will be devoted to education: it means rather that education will constitute the principal business of life. This change promises to be so profound that one must emphasise it by bestowing on it a new name, to indicate that the processes of infusing value and meaning into every phase of life will not stop with the formal school.

The words education, self-development, character formation,

conversion all bear upon the process; but they carry with them the limited references of their original use. That of education is still tied to the bookish training that used to begin with the mastery of the ABC's and even now lasts no longer, formally, than the attainment of the highest professional degree. The concept of self-development carries with it, if not a hint of humanistic priggishness or romantic wilfulness, the general axial belief that the welfare of the self can be secured in separation from that of society, or at least that its cultivation has no public concerns: thus the personal is falsely identified with the private.

As for character formation, it recalls the stern protestant discipline, with its daily assessment of weaknesses, its aesthetically repressive regimen; and that flavour of narrowness and negation remains, though in classic British education it mingled with a strong humanist influence that promoted manly athletic exercises and nourished physical beauty. Finally, conversion, the axial term for the birth of the second self, might be considered the most decisive of educational influences: yet in its formative stages it indicates only a change of attitude and direction and does not provide the social context. One needs a term to indicate not alone these traditional aspects of education, but something that world culture itself will add to the process.

The word for this larger conception of education is the Greek term *paideia*, which Werner Jaeger reintroduced in his brilliant and exhaustive study of Greek education. *Paideia* is education looked upon as a life-long transformation of the human personality, in which every aspect of life plays a part. Unlike education in the traditional sense, *paideia* does not limit itself to the conscious learning processes, or to inducting the young into the social heritage of the community. *Paideia* is rather the task of giving form to the act of living itself: treating every occasion of life as a means of self-fabrication, and as part of a larger process of converting facts into values, processes into purposes, hopes and plans into consummations and realisations. *Paideia* is not merely a learning: it is a making and a shaping; and man himself is the work of art that *paideia* seeks to form.

We are too easily tempted today, by habits that belong to past moments of civilisation, into thinking of the kind of unity that might be achieved by a formal assembly of specialists, by an organisation of 'interdisciplinary activities,' by an intellectual synthesis based upon some logical scheme for uniting the sciences. But *paideia* demands far more than that kind of formal synthesis:

the unity it seeks must be sought in experience, and it demands a readiness to interchange roles, even at a sacrifice of expertness, for the sake of the greater gain to learning and life. The lesson of *paideia* is fundamentally the prime lesson of democracy: growth and self-transformation cannot be delegated. What is more, the achievement of the human whole—and the achievement of the wholly human—take precedence over every specialised activity, over every narrower purpose. Though this new person will still doubtless cherish and develop the skills associated with specialised vocations, he will tend to be multi-occupational as a citizen, nourishing other interests and pursuing other activities, in harmony with a larger plan of life. To exercise all the capacities of a man will become more important than to earn the identifying badge of a vocation or an office; for the day will come, as Emerson predicted, 'when no badge, uniform, or star will be worn.'

This gives a new significance to Karl Marx's conception of the future society, which he threw out in passing in *Capital*, despite his own strict aversion to any kind of utopian prophecy. In this society, as Marx defined it, 'the "fragmentary man" would be replaced by the "completely developed individual," one for whom different social functions are but alternative forms of activity. Men would fish, hunt, or engage in literary criticism without becoming professional fishermen, hunters, or critics.' That moment of insight, based chiefly on his admiration for the freedom and human balance of American culture during the Golden Day, offsets, indeed nullifies, the more characteristic absolutism of Marx's dialectic. To complete it, one should perhaps add his master Hegel's admirable definition of an educated man: One who can do what any other man can do.

One may say of One World man, then, that he is no longer the incarnation of his class, his trade, his profession, or his religious faith, any more than he is the incarnation of his exclusive national group. He is, in fact, just the opposite of the competent technician—the impersonal, neutral functionary, obedient only to the science governing his métier, incurious about any process beyond his limited range: he whom Max Weber singled out as the type that would finally dominate the modern world. The bureaucrat and the technocrat are rather the ideal prototypes of post-historic man. One World man will gladly sacrifice their mechanical efficiency, along with their cocksureness and complacency, in order to enhance the quality of life itself.

The conquering hero, the suffering saint, the ardent lover, the reckless adventurer, the patient scientist, in short all the ideal types of previous cultures, took on their personalities for a whole lifetime. They were committed to their particular virtues, as soldiers, merchants, and craftsmen were dedicated to their single vocation. Each was imprisoned by his role in a cramped chamber and never had the run of the house. The saint could not remain a saint if he became a lover, nor the sage a sage if he became an adventurer. This fixation in permanent roles, vocational and moral, brought about an arrest of life itself; and its correction will be one of the happy tasks of One World personalities. While he is open to any of these possible roles, when the moment demands, a unified man would no more think of playing them throughout life than a capable actor would play only Hamlet. The historic function of these ideal images was to intensify and widen the capacities of man.

Though no single life can make use of all its opportunities or reveal all its potentialities, though restriction and concentration are in fact necessary for any full creative expression, the openness of the One World self will widen the area of its transactions and energise all its activities. It was such a widening of medieval Christian culture, by contact with the ideal world of Greece and Rome and the actual world of China, India, Africa, and America, that made possible the brilliant achievements of the Renaissance. Similarly, personal acquaintance has taught me, people like Patrick Geddes and Ananda Coomaraswamy, who actively participated in both Western and Eastern cultures, brought into the common human focus all that they touched. Even reading can do much to break through the parochialism of culture, as Emerson and Thoreau proved by their early use of Hindu texts; and when travel becomes more than mere sightseeing, when it brings about an interchange of experiences, it will multiply the number of those who are capable of reaching full human stature.

This basic ideological change and personal transformation have long been under way. But the obstacles in the way of a world-wide emergence of unified man are formidable; for the energies that will make it possible cannot be brought to the surface by any purely rational means. As with the early Christians one must prayerfully watch and wait, making every possible conscious preparation, yet realising that no cold act of will suffices. When the favourable moment comes and its challenge is accepted, thousands and tens of thousands will spontaneously respond to it, stirred by the sense of fellowship the moment will produce. In that act forces that were neutral or antagonistic to any larger plan or purpose will likewise undergo polarisation and become actively helpful. Then a new self will be born.

Ripeness is the condition for any organic transformation. The change to One World man was not possible, certainly, at an earlier stage of human development. When the inner ripening had taken place, as it did more than once under the axial religions, the lack of technical facilities and organs of communication alone was enough to impose a veto on the most generous dreams. Again, when technical facilities had brought about physical intercourse on the widest scale, the lack of adequate moral ideas and social purposes largely emptied this intercourse of ideal content and kept it from contributing to the common development. Today, neither the technical means nor the relevant social pressures are absent : it is rather the inner readiness that is lacking. Our generation needs faith in the processes of life sufficient to bring about a willing surrender to life's new demands.

Yet in isolated persons, like Albert Schweitzer in the present day, like Peter Kropotkin or Patrick Geddes in an earlier day, and Goethe and Emerson even earlier, the kind of self that the moment demands has actually been incarnated. Schweitzer, for example, has transcended the specialisations of vocation and nationality and religious faith. In deliberately choosing an uninviting region in Africa as the seat of his life-work, and the ministry of medicine as a means of translating his Christian ethic into practice, he sacrificed the opportunities that his special talents as theologian, musician, and philosopher seemed to demand. Seemingly under the most hostile conditions, he has demonstrated the possibility of actualising a unified personality; and the course of life he chose, which involved the heaviest of renunciations, has proved richer in its fruits than one that would have conformed to more orthodox patterns of Old World culture.

To reach full human stature, at the present stage of development, each of us must be ready, as opportunity offers, to assimilate the contributions of other cultures; and to develop, for the sake of wholeness, those parts of his personality that are weakest. Not least, he must renounce perfection in any single field for the sake of balance and continued growth. He who belongs exclusively to a single nation, a single party, a single religion, or a single vocation without any touch or admixture from the world beyond is not yet a full man, still less can he take part in this transformation. This is a fundamental lesson of human growth, always true—but now imperatively true. In its critical moment of integration, Christianity took in Persian and Egyptian myths, Greek philosophy, and Roman organisation, just as Mohammedanism took in the lessons of Moses and Zoroaster and Jesus. So One World man will embrace an even wider circle; and the whole person so created will cast aside the series of masks, some weakly benign, some monstrous, that so long concealed the living features of man.

In his very completeness, One World man will seem ideologically and culturally naked, almost unidentifiable. He will be like the Jain saints of old, 'clothed in space,' his nakedness a sign that he does not belong exclusively to any nation, group, trade, sect, school, or community. He who has reached the level of world culture will be at home in any part of that culture : in its inner world no less than its outer world. Everything that he does or feels or makes will bear the imprint of the larger self he has made his own. Each person, no matter how poorly endowed or how humble, is eligible to take part in this effort, and indeed is indispensable; yet no matter how great any individual's talents may be, the results will always be incomplete; for the equilibrium we seek is a dynamic one and the balance we promote is not an end in itself but a means to further growth. 'It is provided in the essence of things,' as Walt Whitman said, 'that from any fruition of success, no matter what, shall come forth something to make a greater struggle necessary.'

7

So we stand on the brink of a new age : the age of an open world and of a self capable of playing its part in that larger sphere. An age of renewal, when work and leisure and learning and love will unite to produce a fresh form for every stage of life, and a higher trajectory for life as a whole. Archaic man, civilised man, axial man, mechanised man, achieved only a partial development of human potentialities; and though much of their work is still viable and useful as a basis for man's further development, no mere quarrying of stones from their now-dilapidated structures will provide material for building the fabric of world culture. No less important than the past forces that drive men on are the new forms, dimly emerging in man's unconscious, that begin to beckon him and hold before him the promise of creativity: a life that will not be at the mercy of chance or fettered to irrelevant necessities. He will begin to shape his whole existence in the forms of love as he once only shaped the shadowy figments of his imagination—though, under the compulsions of his post-historic nihilism he now hardly dares thus to shape even purely aesthetic objects. But soon perhaps the dismembered bones will again knit together, clothed in flesh.

In carrying man's self-transformation to this further stage, world culture may bring about a fresh release of spiritual energy that will unveil new potentialities, no more visible in the human self today than radium was in the physical world a century ago, though always present. Even on its lowest terms, world culture will weld the nations and tribes together in a more meaningful network of relations and purposes. But unified man himself is no terminal point. For who can set bounds to man's emergence or to his power of surpassing his provisional achievements? So far we have found no limits to the imagination, nor yet to the sources on which it may draw. Every goal man reaches provides a new starting point, and the sum of all man's days is just a beginning.

THE END

WORLD PERSPECTIVES

What This Series Means

It is the thesis of *World Perspectives* that man is in the process of developing a new consciousness which, in spite of his apparent spiritual and moral captivity, can eventually lift the human race above and beyond the fear, ignorance, and isolation which beset it today. It is to this nascent consciousness, to this concept of man born out of a universe perceived through a fresh vision of reality, that *World Perspectives* is dedicated.

My Introduction to this Series is not of course to be construed as a prefatory essay for each individual book. These few pages simply attempt to set forth the general aim and purpose of the Series as a whole. They try to point to the principle of permanence within change and to define the essential nature of man, as presented by those scholars who have been invited to participate in this intellectual and spiritual movement.

Man has entered a new era of evolutionary history, one in which rapid change is a dominant consequence. He is contending with a fundamental change, since he has intervened in the evolutionary process. He must now better appreciate this fact and then develop the wisdom to direct the process toward his fulfillment rather than toward his destruction. As he learns to apply his understanding of the physical world for practical purposes, he is, in reality, extending his innate capacity and augmenting his ability and his need to communicate as well as his ability to think and to create. And as a result, he is substituting a goal-directed evolutionary process in his struggle against environmental hardship for the slow, but effective, biological evolution which produced modern man through mutation and natural selection. By intelligent intervention in the evolutionary process man has greatly accelerated and greatly expanded the range of his possibilities. But he has not changed the basic fact that it remains a trial and error process, with the danger of taking paths that lead to sterility of mind and heart, moral apathy and intellectual inertia; and even producing social dinosaurs unfit to live in an evolving world.

Only those spiritual and intellectual leaders of our epoch who have a paternity in this extension of man's horizons are invited to participate in this Series: those who are aware of the truth that beyond the divisiveness among men there exists a primordial unitive power since we are all bound together by a common humanity more fundamental than any unity of dogma; those who recognize that the centrifugal force which has scattered and atomized mankind must be replaced by an integrating structure and process capable of bestowing meaning and purpose on existence; those who realize that science itself, when not inhibited by the limitations of its own methodology, when chastened and humbled, commits man to an indeterminate range of yet undreamed consequences that may flow from it.

Virtually all of our disciplines have relied on conceptions which are now incompatible with the Cartesian axiom, and with the static world view we once derived from it. For underlying the new ideas, including those of modern physics, is a unifying order, but it is not causality; it is purpose, and not the purpose of the universe and of man, but the purpose *in* the universe and *in* man. In other words, we seem to inhabit a world of dynamic process and structure. Therefore we need a calculus of potentiality rather than one of probability, a dialectic of polarity, one in which unity and diversity are redefined as simultaneous and necessary poles of the same essence.

Our situation is new. No civilization has previously had to face the challenge of scientific specialization, and our response must be new. Thus this Series is committed to ensure that the spiritual and moral needs of man as a human being and the scientific and intellectual resources at his command for *life* may be brought into a productive, meaningful and creative harmony.

In a certain sense we may say that man now has regained his former geocentric position in the universe. For a picture of the

Earth has been made available from distant space, from the lunar desert, and the sheer isolation of the Earth has become plain. This is as new and as powerful an idea in history as any that has ever been born in man's consciousness. We are all becoming seriously concerned with our natural environment. And this concern is not only the result of the warnings given by biologists, ecologists and conservationists. Rather it is the result of a deepening awareness that something new has happened, that the planet Earth is a unique and precious place. Indeed, it may not be a mere coincidence that this awareness should have been born at the exact moment when man took his first step into outer space.

This Series endeavors to point to a reality of which scientific theory has revealed only one aspect. It is the commitment to this reality that lends universal intent to a scientist's most original and solitary thought. By acknowledging this frankly we shall restore science to the great family of human aspirations by which men hope to fulfill themselves in the world community as thinking and sentient beings. For our problem is to discover a principle of differentiation and yet relationship lucid enough to justify and to purify scientific, philosophic and all other knowledge, both discursive and intuitive, by accepting their interdependence. This is the crisis in consciousness made articulate through the crisis in science. This is the new awakening.

Each volume presents the thought and belief of its author and points to the way in which religion, philosophy, art, science, economics, politics and history may constitute that form of human activity which takes the fullest and most precise account of variousness, possibility, complexity and difficulty. Thus *World Perspectives* endeavors to define that ecumenical power of the mind and heart which enables man through his mysterious greatness to re-create his life.

This Series is committed to a re-examination of all those sides of human endeavor which the specialist was taught to believe he could safely leave aside. It attempts to show the structural kinship between subject and object; the indwelling of the one in the other. It interprets present and past events impinging on human life in our growing World Age and envisages what man may yet attain when summoned by an unbending inner necessity to the quest of what is most exalted in him. Its purpose is to offer new vistas in terms of world and human development while refusing to betray the intimate correlation between universality and individuality, dynamics and form, freedom and destiny. Each author deals with the increasing realization that spirit and nature are not separate and apart; that intuition and reason must regain their importance as the means of perceiving and fusing inner being with outer reality.

World Perspectives endeavors to show that the conception of wholeness, unity, organism is a higher and more concrete conception than that of matter and energy. Thus an enlarged meaning of life, of biology, not as it is revealed in the test tube of the laboratory but as it is experienced within the organism of life itself, is attempted in this Series. For the principle of life consists in the tension which connects spirit with the realm of matter, symbiotically joined. The element of life is dominant in the very texture of nature, thus rendering life, biology, a transempirical science. The laws of life have their origin beyond their mere physical manifestations and compel us to consider their spiritual source. In fact, the widening of the conceptual framework has not only served to restore order within the respective branches of knowledge, but has also disclosed analogies in man's position regarding the analysis and synthesis of experience in apparently separated domains of knowledge, suggesting the possibility of an ever more embracing objective description of the meaning of life.

Knowledge, it is shown in these books, no longer consists in a manipulation of man and nature as opposite forces, nor in the reduction of data to mere statistical order, but is a means of liberating mankind from the destructive power of fear, pointing the way toward the goal of the rehabilitation of the human will and the rebirth of faith and confidence in the human person. The works published also endeavor to reveal that the cry for patterns, systems and authorities is growing less insistent as the desire grows stronger in both East and West for the recovery of a dignity, integrity and self-realization which are the inalienable rights of man who may now guide change by means of conscious purpose in the light of rational experience.

The volumes in this Series endeavor to demonstrate that only in a society in which awareness of the problems of science exists can its discoveries start great waves of change in human culture, and in such a manner that these discoveries may deepen and not erode the sense of universal human community. The differences in the disciplines, their epistemological exclusiveness, the variety of historical experiences, the differences of traditions, of cultures, of languages, of the arts, should be protected and preserved. But the interrelationship and unity of the whole should at the same time be accepted.

The authors of *World Perspectives* are of course aware that the ultimate answers to the hopes and fears which pervade modern society rest on the moral fibre of man, and on the wisdom and responsibility of those who promote the course of its development. But moral decisions cannot dispense with an insight into the interplay of the objective elements which offer and limit the choices made. Therefore an understanding of what the issues are, though not a sufficient condition, is a necessary prerequisite for directing action toward constructive solutions.

Other vital questions explored relate to problems of international understanding as well as to problems dealing with prejudice and the resultant tensions and antagonisms. The growing perception and responsibility of our World Age point to the new reality that the individual person and the collective person supplement and integrate each other; that the thrall of totalitarianism of both left and right has been shaken in the universal desire to recapture the authority of truth and human totality. Mankind can finally place its trust not in a proletarian authoritarianism, not in a secularized humanism, both of which have betrayed the spiritual property right of history, but in a sacramental brotherhood and in the unity of knowledge. This new consciousness has created a widening of human horizons beyond every parochialism, and a revolution in human thought comparable to the basic assumption, among the ancient Greeks, of the sovereignty of reason; corresponding to the great effulgence of the moral conscience articulated by the Hebrew prophets; analogous to the fundamental assertions of Christianity; or to the beginning of the new scientific era, the era of the science of dynamics, the experimental foundations of which were laid by Galileo in the Renaissance.

An important effort of this Series is to re-examine the contradictory meanings and applications which are given today to such terms as democracy, freedom, justice, love, peace, brotherhood and God. The purpose of such inquiries is to clear the way for the foundation of a genuine *world* history not in terms of nation or race or culture but in terms of man in relation to God, to himself, his fellow man and the universe, that reach beyond immediate self-interest. For the meaning of the World Age consists in respecting man's hopes and dreams which lead to a deeper understanding of the basic values of all peoples.

World Perspectives is planned to gain insight into the meaning of man, who not only is determined by history but who also determines history. History is to be understood as concerned not only with the life of man on this planet but as including also such cosmic influences as interpenetrate our human world. This generation is discovering that history does not conform to the social optimism of modern civilization and that the organization of human communities and the establishment of freedom and peace are not only intellectual achievements but spiritual and moral achievements as well, demanding a cherishing of the wholeness of human personality, the "unmediated wholeness of feeling and thought," and constituting a never-ending challenge to man, emerging from the abyss of meaninglessness and suffering, to be renewed and replenished in the totality of his life.

Justice itself, which has been "in a state of pilgrimage and crucifixion" and now is being slowly liberated from the grip of social and political demonologies in the East as well as in the West, begins to question its own premises. The modern revolutionary movements which have challenged the sacred institutions of society for protecting social injustice in the name of social justice are here examined and re-evaluated.

In the light of this, we have no choice but to admit that the *un-freedom* against which freedom is measured must be retained with it, namely, that the aspect of truth out of which the night view appears to emerge, the darkness of our time, is as little abandonable as is man's subjective advance. Thus the two sources of man's consciousness are inseparable, not as dead but as living and complementary, an aspect of that "principle of complementarity" through which Niels Bohr has sought to unite the quantum and the wave, both of which constitute the very fabric of life's radiant energy.

There is in mankind today a counterforce to the sterility and danger of a quantitative, anonymous mass culture; a new, if sometimes imperceptible, spiritual sense of convergence toward human and world unity on the basis of the sacredness of each human person and respect for the plurality of cultures. There is a growing awareness that equality may not be evaluated in mere numerical terms but is proportionate and analogical in its reality. For when equality is equated with interchangeability, the human person is negated and individual identity transmuted into a faceless mask.

We stand at the brink of an age of a world in which human life presses forward to actualize new forms. The false separation of man and nature, of time and space, of freedom and security, is acknowledged, and we are faced with a new vision of man in his organic unity and of history offering a richness and diversity of quality and majesty of scope hitherto unprecedented. In relating the accumulated wisdom of man's spirit to the new reality of the World Age, in articulating its thought and belief, *World Perspectives* seeks to encourage a renaissance of hope in society and of pride in man's decision as to what his destiny will be.

World Perspectives is committed to the recognition that all great changes are preceded by a vigorous intellectual re-evaluation and reorganization. Our authors are aware that the sin of *hubris* may be avoided by showing that the creative process itself is not a free activity if by free we mean arbitrary, or unrelated to cosmic law. For the creative process in the human mind, the developmental process in organic nature and the basic laws of the inorganic realm may be but varied expressions of a universal formative process. Thus *World Perspectives* hopes to show that although the present apocalyptic period is one of exceptional tensions, there is also at work an exceptional movement toward a compensating unity which refuses to violate the ultimate moral power at work in the universe, that very power upon which all human effort must at last depend. In this way we may come to understand that there exists an inherent independence of spiritual and mental growth which, though conditioned by circumstances, is never determined by circumstances. In this way the great plethora of human knowledge may be correlated with an insight into the nature of human nature by being attuned to the wide and deep range of human thought and human experience.

Incoherence is the result of the present disintegrative processes in education. Thus the need for *World Perspectives* expresses itself in the recognition that natural and man-made ecological systems require as much study as isolated particles and elementary reactions. For there is a basic correlation of elements in nature as in man which cannot be separated, which compose each other and alter each other mutually. Thus we hope to widen appropriately our conceptual framework of reference. For our epistemological problem consists in our finding the proper balance between our lack of an all-embracing principle relevant to our way of evaluating life and in our power to express ourselves in a logically consistent manner.

Our Judaeo-Christian and Greco-Roman heritage, our Hellenic tradition, has compelled us to think in exclusive categories. But our *experience* challenges us to recognize a totality richer and far more complex than the average observer could have suspected—a totality which compels him to think in ways which the logic of dichotomies denies. We are summoned to revise fundamentally our ordinary ways of conceiving experience, and thus, by expanding our vision and by accepting those forms of thought which also include nonexclusive categories, the mind is then able to grasp what it was incapable of grasping or accepting before.

In spite of the infinite obligation of men and in spite of their finite power, in spite of the intransigence of nationalisms, and in spite of the homelessness of moral passions rendered ineffectual by the scientific outlook, beneath the apparent turmoil and upheaval of the present, and out of the transformations of this dynamic period with the unfolding of a world consciousness, the purpose of *World Perspectives* is to help quicken the "unshaken heart of well-rounded truth" and interpret the significant elements of the World Age now taking shape out of the core of that undimmed continuity of the creative process which restores man to mankind while deepening and enhancing his communion with the universe.

RUTH NANDA ANSHEN

WORLD PERSPECTIVES

WORLD PERSPECTIVES

Volumes already published

ḣarper ⚡ ʇorchbooḳs

American Studies: General

HENRY ADAMS Degradation of the Democratic Dogma. ‡ *Introduction by Charles Hirschfeld.* TB/1450

LOUIS D. BRANDEIS: Other People's Money, *and How the Bankers Use It. Ed. with Intro. by Richard M. Abrams* TB/3081

HENRY STEELE COMMAGER, Ed.: The Struggle for Racial Equality TB/1300

CARL N. DEGLER: Out of Our Past: *The Forces that Shaped Modern America* CN/2

CARL N. DEGLER, Ed.: Pivotal Interpretations of American History
Vol. I TB/1240; Vol. II TB/1241

A. S. EISENSTADT, Ed.: The Craft of American History: *Selected Essays*
Vol. I TB/1255; Vol. II TB/1256

LAWRENCE H. FUCHS, Ed.: American Ethnic Politics TB/1368

MARCUS LEE HANSEN: The Atlantic Migration: 1607-1860. *Edited by Arthur M. Schlesinger. Introduction by Oscar Handlin* TB/1052

MARCUS LEE HANSEN: The Immigrant in American History. *Edited with a Foreword by Arthur M. Schlesinger* TB/1120

ROBERT L. HEILBRONER: The Limits of American Capitalism TB/1305

JOHN HIGHAM, Ed.: The Reconstruction of American History TB/1068

ROBERT H. JACKSON: The Supreme Court in the American System of Government TB/1106

JOHN F. KENNEDY: A Nation of Immigrants. *Illus. Revised and Enlarged. Introduction by Robert F. Kennedy* TB/1118

LEONARD W. LEVY, Ed.: American Constitutional Law: *Historical Essays* TB/1285

LEONARD W. LEVY, Ed.: Judicial Review and the Supreme Court TB/1296

LEONARD W. LEVY: The Law of the Commonwealth and Chief Justice Shaw: *The Evolution of American Law, 1830-1860* TB/1309

GORDON K. LEWIS: Puerto Rico: *Freedom and Power in the Caribbean. Abridged edition* TB/1371

RICHARD B. MORRIS: Fair Trial: *Fourteen Who Stood Accused, from Anne Hutchinson to Alger Hiss* TB/1335

GUNNAR MYRDAL: An American Dilemma: *The Negro Problem and Modern Democracy. Introduction by the Author.*
Vol. I TB/1443; Vol. II TB/1444

GILBERT OSOFSKY, Ed.: The Burden of Race: *A Documentary History of Negro-White Relations in America* TB/1405

CONYERS READ, Ed.: The Constitution Reconsidered. *Revised Edition. Preface by Richrd B. Morris* TB/1384

ARNOLD ROSE: The Negro in America: *The Condensed Version of Gunnar Myrdal's An American Dilemma. Second Edition* TB/3048

JOHN E. SMITH: Themes in American Philosophy: *Purpose, Experience and Community* TB/1466

WILLIAM R. TAYLOR: Cavalier and Yankee: *The Old South and American National Character* TB/1474

American Studies: Colonial

BERNARD BAILYN: The New England Merchants in the Seventeenth Century TB/1149

ROBERT E. BROWN: Middle-Class Democracy and Revolution in Massachusetts, 1691-1780. *New Introduction by Author* TB/1413

JOSEPH CHARLES: The Origins of the American Party System TB/1049

HENRY STEELE COMMAGER & ELMO GIORDANETTI, Eds.: Was America a Mistake? *An Eighteenth Century Controversy* TB/1329

WESLEY FRANK CRAVEN: The Colonies in Transition: 1660-1712† TB/3084

CHARLES GIBSON: Spain in America † TB/3077

CHARLES GIBSON, Ed.: The Spanish Tradition in America + HR/1351

LAWRENCE HENRY GIPSON: The Coming of the Revolution: 1763-1775. † *Illus.* TB/3007

JACK P. GREENE, Ed.: Great Britain and the American Colonies: 1606-1763. + *Introduction by the Author* HR/1477

AUBREY C. LAND, Ed.: Bases of the Plantation Society + HR/1429

JOHN LANKFORD, Ed.: Captain John Smith's America: *Selections from his Writings* ‡ TB/3078

LEONARD W. LEVY: Freedom of Speech and Press in Early American History: *Legacy of Suppression* TB/1109

PERRY MILLER: Errand Into the Wilderness TB/1139

PERRY MILLER T. H. JOHNSON, Eds.: The Puritans: *A Sourcebook of Their Writings*
Vol. I TB/1093; Vol. II TB/1094

---

† The New American Nation Series, edited by Henry Steele Commager and Richard B. Morris.
‡ American Perspectives series, edited by Bernard Wishy and William E. Leuchtenburg.
α History of Europe series, edited by J. H. Plumb.
§ The Library of Religion and Culture, edited by Benjamin Nelson.
‖ Researches in the Social, Cultural, and Behavioral Sciences, edited by Benjamin Nelson.
Σ Harper Modern Science Series, edited by James A. Newman.
° Not for sale in Canada.
+ Documentary History of the United States series, edited by Richard B. Morris.
# Documentary History of Western Civilization series, edited by Eugene C. Black and Leonard W. Levy.
Λ The Economic History of the United States series, edited by Henry David et al.
¶ European Perspectives series, edited by Eugene C. Black.
** Contemporary Essays series, edited by Leonard W. Levy.
* The Stratum Series, edited by John Hale.

EDMUND S. MORGAN: The Puritan Family: *Religion and Domestic Relations in Seventeenth Century New England*   TB/1227
RICHARD B. MORRIS: Government and Labor in Early America   TB/1244
WALLACE NOTESTEIN: The English People on the Eve of Colonization: 1603-1630. † *Illus.*   TB/3006
FRANCIS PARKMAN: The Seven Years War: *A Narrative Taken from* Montcalm and Wolfe, The Conspiracy of Pontiac, *and* A Half-Century of Conflict. *Edited by John H. McCallum*   TB/3083
LOUIS B. WRIGHT: The Cultural Life of the American Colonies: 1607-1763. † *Illus.*   TB/3005
YVES F. ZOLTVANY, Ed.: The French Tradition in America +   HR/1425

American Studies: The Revolution to 1860

JOHN R. ALDEN: The American Revolution: 1775-1783. † *Illus.*   TB/3011
MAX BELOFF, Ed.: The Debate on the American Revolution, 1761-1783: *A Sourcebook*   TB/1225
RAY A. BILLINGTON: The Far Western Frontier: 1830-1860. † *Illus.*   TB/3012
STUART BRUCHEY: The Roots of American Economic Growth, 1607-1861: *An Essay in Social Causation. New Introduction by the Author.*   TB/1350
WHITNEY R. CROSS: The Burned-Over District: *The Social and Intellectual History of Enthusiastic Religion in Western New York, 1800-1850*   TB/1242
NOBLE E. CUNNINGHAM, JR., Ed.: The Early Republic, 1789-1828 +   HR/1394
GEORGE DANGERFIELD: The Awakening of American Nationalism, 1815-1828. † *Illus.*   TB/3061
CLEMENT EATON: The Freedom-of-Thought Struggle in the Old South. *Revised and Enlarged. Illus.*   TB/1150
CLEMENT EATON: The Growth of Southern Civilization, 1790-1860. † *Illus.*   TB/3040
ROBERT H. FERRELL, Ed.: Foundations of American Diplomacy, 1775-1872   HR/1393
LOUIS FILLER: The Crusade against Slavery: 1830-1860. † *Illus.*   TB/3029
DAVID H. FISCHER: The Revolution of American Conservatism: *The Federalist Party in the Era of Jeffersonian Democracy*   TB/1449
WILLIAM W. FREEHLING, Ed.: The Nullification Era: *A Documentary Record* ‡   TB/3079
WILLIM W. FREEHLING: Prelude to Civil War: *The Nullification Controversy in South Carolina, 1816-1836*   TB/1359
PAUL W. GATES: The Farmer's Age: *Agriculture, 1815-1860* ∆   TB/1398
FELIX GILBERT: The Beginnings of American Foreign Policy: *To the Farewell Address*   TB/1200
ALEXANDER HAMILTON: The Reports of Alexander Hamilton. ‡ *Edited by Jacob E. Cooke*   TB/3060
THOMAS JEFFERSON: Notes on the State of Virginia. ‡ *Edited by Thomas P. Abernethy*   TB/3052
FORREST MCDONALD, Ed.: Confederation and Constitution, 1781-1789 +   HR/1396
BERNARD MAYO: Myths and Men: *Patrick Henry, George Washington, Thomas Jefferson*   TB/1108
JOHN C. MILLER: Alexander Hamilton and the Growth of the New Nation   TB/3057
JOHN C. MILLER: The Federalist Era: 1789-1801. † *Illus.*   TB/3027

RICHARD B. MORRIS, Ed.: Alexander Hamilton and the Founding of the Nation. *New Introduction by the Editor*   TB/1448
RICHARD B. MORRIS: The American Revolution Reconsidered   TB/1363
CURTIS P. NETTELS: The Emergence of a National Economy, 1775-1815 ∆   TB/1438
DOUGLASS C. NORTH & ROBERT PAUL THOMAS, Eds.: *The Growth of the American Economy to 1860* +   HR/1352
R. B. NYE: The Cultural Life of the New Nation: 1776-1830. † *Illus.*   TB/3026
GILBERT OSOFSKY, Ed.: Puttin' On Ole Massa: *The Slave Narratives of Henry Bibb, William Wells Brown, and Solomon Northup* ‡   TB/1432
JAMES PARTON: The Presidency of Andrew Jackson. *From Volume III of the* Life of Andrew Jackson. *Ed. with Intro. by Robert V. Remini*   TB/3080
FRANCIS S. PHILBRICK: The Rise of the West, 1754-1830. † *Illus.*   TB/3067
MARSHALL SMELSER: The Democratic Republic, 1801-1815 †   TB/1406
TIMOTHY L. SMITH: Revivalism and Social Reform: *American Protestantism on the Eve of the Civil War*   TB/1229
JACK M. SOSIN, Ed.: The Opening of the West +   HR/1424
GEORGE ROGERS TAYLOR: The Transportation Revolution, 1815-1860 ∆   TB/1347
A. F. TYLER: Freedom's Ferment: *Phases of American Social History from the Revolution to the Outbreak of the Civil War. Illus.*   TB/1074
GLYNDON G. VAN DEUSEN: The Jacksonian Era: 1828-1848. † *Illus.*   TB/3028
LOUIS B. WRIGHT: Culture on the Moving Frontier   TB/1053

American Studies: The Civil War to 1900

W. R. BROCK: An American Crisis: *Congress and Reconstruction, 1865-67* °   TB/1283
T. C. COCHRAN & WILLIAM MILLER: The Age of Enterprise: *A Social History of Industrial America*   TB/1054
W. A. DUNNING: Reconstruction, Political and Economic: 1865-1877   TB/1073
HAROLD U. FAULKNER: Politics, Reform and Expansion: 1890-1900. † *Illus.*   TB/3020
GEORGE M. FREDRICKSON: The Inner Civil War: *Northern Intellectuals and the Crisis of the Union*   TB/1358
JOHN A. GARRATY: The New Commonwealth, 1877-1890 +   TB/1410
JOHN A. GARRATY, Ed.: The Transformation of American Society, 1870-1890 +   HR/1395
HELEN HUNT JACKSON: A Century of Dishonor: *The Early Crusade for Indian Reform.* † *Edited by Andrew F. Rolle*   TB/3063
ALBERT D. KIRWAN: Revolt of the Rednecks: *Mississippi Politics, 1876-1925*   TB/1199
ARTHUR MANN: Yankee Reforms in the Urban Age: *Social Reform in Boston, 1800-1900*   TB/1247
ARNOLD M. PAUL: Conservative Crisis and the Rule of Law: *Attitudes of Bar and Bench, 1887-1895. New Introduction by Author*   TB/1415
JAMES S. PIKE: The Prostrate State: *South Carolina under Negro Government.* ‡ *Intro. by Robert F. Durden*   TB/3085
WHITELAW REID: After the War: *A Tour of the Southern States, 1865-1866.* ‡ *Edited by C. Vann Woodward*   TB/3066
FRED A. SHANNON: The Farmer's Last Frontier: *Agriculture, 1860-1897*   TB/1348

VERNON LANE WHARTON: The Negro in Mississippi, 1865-1890   TB/1178

American Studies: The Twentieth Century

RICHARD M. ABRAMS, Ed.: The Issues of the Populist and Progressive Eras, 1892-1912 + HR/1428
RAY STANNARD BAKER: Following the Color Line: American Negro Citizenship in Progressive Era. ‡ Edited by Dewey W. Grantham, Jr. Illus.   TB/3053
RANDOLPH S. BOURNE: War and the Intellectuals: Collected Essays, 1915-1919. ‡ Edited by Carl Resek   TB/3043
A. RUSSELL BUCHANAN: The United States and World War II. † Illus.
        Vol. I TB/3044; Vol. II TB/3045
THOMAS C. COCHRAN: The American Business System: A Historical Perspective, 1900-1955   TB/1080
FOSTER RHEA DULLES: America's Rise to World Power: 1898-1954. † Illus.   TB/3021
JEAN-BAPTISTE DUROSELLE: From Wilson to Roosevelt: Foreign Policy of the United States, 1913-1945. Trans. by Nancy Lyman Roelker   TB/1370
HAROLD U. FAULKNER: The Decline of Laissez Faire, 1897-1917   TB/1397
JOHN D. HICKS: Republican Ascendancy: 1921-1933. † Illus.   TB/3041
ROBERT HUNTER: Poverty: Social Conscience in the Progressive Era. ‡ Edited by Peter d'A. Jones   TB/3065
WILLIAM E. LEUCHTENBURG: Franklin D. Roosevelt and the New Deal: 1932-1940. † Illus.   TB/3025
WILLIAM E. LEUCHTENBURG, Ed.: The New Deal: A Documentary History +   HR/1354
ARTHUR S. LINK: Woodrow Wilson and the Progressive Era: 1910-1917. † Illus. TB/3023
BROADUS MITCHELL: Depression Decade: From New Era through New Deal, 1929-1941 ʌ   TB/1439
GEORGE E. MOWRY: The Era of Theodore Roosevelt and the Birth of Modern America: 1900-1912. † Illus.   TB/3022
WILLIAM PRESTON, JR.: Aliens and Dissenters: Federal Suppression of Radicals, 1903-1933   TB/1287
WALTER RAUSCHENBUSCH: Christianity and the Social Crisis. ‡ Edited by Robert D. Cross   TB/3059
GEORGE SOULE: Prosperity Decade: From War to Depression, 1917-1929 ʌ   TB/1349
GEORGE B. TINDALL, Ed.: A Populist Reader: Selections from the Works of American Populist Leaders   TB/3069
TWELVE SOUTHERNERS: I'll Take My Stand: The South and the Agrarian Tradition. Intro. by Louis D. Rubin, Jr.; Biographical Essays by Virginia Rock   TB/1072

Art, Art History, Aesthetics

CREIGHTON GILBERT, Ed.: Renaissance Art ** Illus.   TB/1465
EMILE MALE: The Gothic Image: Religious Art in France of the Thirteenth Century. § 190 illus.   TB/344
MILLARD MEISS: Painting in Florence and Siena After the Black Death: The Arts, Religion and Society in the Mid-Fourteenth Century. 169 illus.   TB/1148
ERWIN PANOFSKY: Renaissance and Renascences in Western Art. Illus.   TB/1447
ERWIN PANOFSKY: Studies in Iconology: Humanistic Themes in the Art of the Renaissance. 180 illus.   TB/1077

JEAN SEZNEC: The Survival of the Pagan Gods: The Mythological Tradition and Its Place in Renaissance Humanism and Art. 108 illus.   TB/2004
OTTO VON SIMSON: The Gothic Cathedral: Origins of Gothic Architecture and the Medieval Concept of Order. 58 illus.   TB/2018
HEINRICH ZIMMER: Myths and Symbols in Indian Art and Civilization. 70 illus. TB/2005

Asian Studies

WOLFGANG FRANKE: China and the West: The Cultural Encounter, 13th to 20th Centuries. Trans. by R. A. Wilson   TB/1326
L. CARRINGTON GOODRICH: A Short History of the Chinese People. Illus.   TB/3015
DAN N. JACOBS, Ed.: The New Communist Manifesto and Related Documents. 3rd revised edn.   TB/1078
DAN N. JACOBS & HANS H. BAERWALD, Eds.: Chinese Communism: Selected Documents   TB/3031
BENJAMIN I. SCHWARTZ: Chinese Communism and the Rise of Mao   TB/1308
BENJAMIN I. SCHWARTZ: In Search of Wealth and Power: Yen Fu and the West   TB/1422

Economics & Economic History

C. E. BLACK: The Dynamics of Modernization: A Study in Comparative History   TB/1321
STUART BRUCHEY: The Roots of American Economic Growth, 1607-1861: An Essay in Social Causation. New Introduction by the Author.   TB/1350
GILBERT BURCK & EDITORS OF Fortune: The Computer Age: And its Potential for Management   TB/1179
JOHN ELLIOTT CAIRNES: The Slave Power. ‡ Edited with Introduction by Harold D. Woodman   TB/1433
SHEPARD B. CLOUGH, THOMAS MOODIE & CAROL MOODIE, Eds.: Economic History of Europe: Twentieth Century #   HR/1388
THOMAS C. COCHRAN: The American Business System: A Historical Perspective, 1900-1955   TB/1180
ROBERT A. DAHL & CHARLES E. LINDBLOM: Politics, Economics, and Welfare: Planning and Politico-Economic Systems Resolved into Basic Social Processes   TB/3037
PETER F. DRUCKER: The New Society: The Anatomy of Industrial Order   TB/1082
HAROLD U. FAULKNER: The Decline of Laissez Faire, 1897-1917 ʌ   TB/1397
PAUL W. GATES: The Farmer's Age: Agriculture, 1815-1860 ʌ   TB/1398
WILLIAM GREENLEAF, Ed.: American Economic Development Since 1860 +   HR/1353
J. L. & BARBARA HAMMOND: The Rise of Modern Industry. || Introduction by R. M. Hartwell   TB/1417
ROBERT L. HEILBRONER: The Future as History: The Historic Currents of Our Time and the Direction in Which They Are Taking America   TB/1386
ROBERT L. HEILBRONER: The Great Ascent: The Struggle for Economic Development in Our Time   TB/3030
FRANK H. KNIGHT: The Economic Organization   TB/1214
DAVID S. LANDES: Bankers and Pashas: International Finance and Economic Imperialism in Egypt. New Preface by the Author TB/1412
ROBERT LATOUCHE: The Birth of Western Economy: Economic Aspects of the Dark Ages   TB/1290

W. ARTHUR LEWIS: Economic Survey, 1919-1939
TB/1446
W. ARTHUR LEWIS: The Principles of Economic
Planning. *New Introduction by the Author°*
TB/1436
ROBERT GREEN MC CLOSKEY: American Conservatism in the Age of Enterprise   TB/1137
PAUL MANTOUX: The Industrial Revolution in
the Eighteenth Century: *An Outline of the
Beginnings of the Modern Factory System in
England°*   TB/1079
WILLIAM MILLER, Ed.: Men in Business: *Essays
on the Historical Role of the Entrepreneur*
TB/1081
GUNNAR MYRDAL: An International Economy.
New Introduction by the Author   TB/1445
RICHARD S. WECKSTEIN, Ed.: Expansion of World
Trade and the Growth of National Economies **   TB/1373

Historiography and History of Ideas

HERSCHEL BAKER: The Image of Man: *A Study
of the Idea of Human Dignity in Classical
Antiquity, the Middle Ages, and the Renaissance*   TB/1047
J. BRONOWSKI & BRUCE MAZLISH: The Western
Intellectual Tradition: *From Leonardo to
Hegel*   TB/3001
EDMUND BURKE: On Revolution. Ed. by Robert
A. Smith   TB/1401
WILHELM DILTHEY: Pattern and Meaning in History: *Thoughts on History and Society.°
Edited with an Intro. by H. P. Rickman*
TB/1075
ALEXANDER GRAY: The Socialist Tradition: *Moses
to Lenin°*   TB/1375
J. H. HEXTER: More's Utopia: *The Biography of
an Idea. Epilogue by the Author*   TB/1195
H. STUART HUGHES: History as Art and as
Science: *Twin Vistas on the Past*   TB/1207
ARTHUR O. LOVEJOY: The Great Chain of Being:
A Study of the History of an Idea   TB/1009
JOSE ORTEGA Y GASSET: The Modern Theme.
Introduction by Jose Ferrater Mora   TB/1038
RICHARD H. POPKIN: The History of Scenticism
from Erasmus to Descartes. *Revised Edition*
TB/1391
G. J. RENIER: History: *Its Purpose and Method*
TB/1209
MASSIMO SALVADORI, Ed.: Modern Socialism #
HR/1374
BRUNO SNELL: The Discovery of the Mind: *The
Greek Origins of European Thought*   TB/1018
W. WARREN WAGER, ed.: European Intellectual
History Since Darwin and Marx   TB/1297
W. H. WALSH: Philosophy of History: *In Introduction*   TB/1020

History: General

HANS KOHN: The Age of Nationalism: *The
First Era of Global History*   TB/1380
BERNARD LEWIS: The Arabs in History TB/1029
BERNARD LEWIS: The Middle East and the
West °   TB/1274

History: Ancient

A. ANDREWS: The Greek Tyrants   TB/1103
ERNST LUDWIG EHRLICH: A Concise History of
Israel: *From the Earliest Times to the Destruction of the Temple in A.D. 70°*   TB/128

THEODOR H. GASTER: Thespis: *Ritual Myth and
Drama in the Ancient Near East*   TB/1281
MICHAEL GRANT: Ancient History °   TB/1190
A. H. M. JONES, Ed.: A History of Rome
through the Fifgth Century # *Vol. I: The
Republic*   HR/1364
Vol. II The Empire: HR/1460
SAMUEL NOAH KRAMER: Sumerian Mythology
TB/1055
NAPHTALI LEWIS & MEYER REINHOLD, Eds.:
Roman Civilization *Vol. I: The Republic*
TB/1231
Vol. II: The Empire   TB/1232

History: Medieval

MARSHALL W. BALDWIN, Ed.: Christianity
Through the 13th Century #   HR/1468
MARC BLOCH: Land and Work in Medieval
Europe. *Translated by J. E. Anderson*
TB/1452
HELEN CAM: England Before Elizabeth TB/1026
NORMAN COHN: The Pursuit of the Millennium:
*Revolutionary Messianism in Medieval and
Reformation Europe*   TB/1037
G. G. COULTON: Medieval Village, Manor, and
Monastery   HR/1022
HEINRICH FICHTENAU: The Carolingian Empire:
*The Age of Charlemagne. Translated with an
Introduction by Peter Munz*   TB/1142
GALBERT OF BRUGES: The Murder of Charles the
Good: *A Contemporary Record of Revolutionary Change in 12th Century Flanders.
Translated with an Introduction by James
Bruce Ross*   TB/1311
F. L. GANSHOF: Feudalism   TB/1058
F. L. GANSHOF: The Middle Ages: *A History of
International Relations. Translated by Rémy
Hall*   TB/1411
DENYS HAY: The Medieval Centuries °   TB/1192
DAVID HERLIHY, Ed.: Medieval Culture and Society #   HR/1340
J. M. HUSSEY: The Byzantine World   TB/1057
ROBERT LATOUCHE: The Birth of Western Economy: *Economic Aspects of the Dark Ages °*
TB/1290
HENRY CHARLES LEA: The Inquisition of the
Middle Ages. || *Introduction by Walter
Ullmann*   TB/1456
FERDINARD LOT: The End of the Ancient World
and the Beginnings of the Middle Ages. *Introduction by Glanville Downey*   TB/1044
H. R. LOYN: The Norman Conquest   TB/1457
GUIBERT DE NOGENT: Self and Society in
Medieval France: *The Memoirs of Guilbert de
Nogent.* || Edited by John F. Benton TB/1471
MARSILIUS OF PADUA: The Defender of Peace.
The Defensor Pacis. Translated with an Introduction by Alan Gewirth   TB/1310
CHARLES PETET-DUTAILLIS: The Feudal Monarchy
in France and England: *From the Tenth to
the Thirteenth Century °*   TB/1165
STEVEN RUNCIMAN: A History of the Crusades
Vol. I: The First Crusade and the Foundation of the Kingdom of Jerusalem. Illus.
TB/1143
*Vol. II: The Kingdom of Jerusalem and the
Frankish East 1100-1187. Illus.*   TB/1243
*Vol. III: The Kingdom of Acre and the
Later Crusades. Illus.*   TB/1298
J. M. WALLACE-HADRILL: The Barbarian West:
The Early Middle Ages, A.D. 400-1000
TB/1061

ALBERT GOODWIN, Ed.: The European Nobility in the Enghteenth Century TB/1313
ALBERT GOODWIN: The French Revolution TB/1064
ALBERT GUERARD: France in the Classical Age: *The Life and Death of an Ideal* TB/1183
JOHN B. HALSTED, Ed.: Romanticism # HR/1387
J. H. HEXTER: Reappraisals in History: *New Views on History and Society in Early Modern Europe* ° TB/1100
STANLEY HOFFMANN et al.: In Search of France: *The Economy, Society and Political System In the Twentieth Century* TB/1219
H. STUART HUGHES: The Obstructed Path: *French Social Thought in the Years of Desperation* TB/1451
JOHAN HUIZINGA: Dutch Civilisation in the 17th Century and Other Essays TB/1453
LIONAL KOCHAN: The Struggle for Germany: *1914-45* TB/1304
HANS KOHN: The Mind of Germany: *The Education of a Nation* TB/1204
HANS KOHN, Ed.: The Mind of Modern Russia: *Historical and Political Thought of Russia's Great Age* TB/1065
WALTER LAQUEUR & GEORGE L. MOSSE, Eds.: Education and Social Structure in the 20th Century. ° *Volume 6 of the* Journal of Contemporary History TB/1339
WALTER LAQUEUR & GEORGE L. MOSSE, Ed.: International Fascism, 1920-1945. ° *Volume 1 of the* Journal of Contemporary History TB/1276
WALTER LAQUEUR & GEORGE L. MOSSE, Eds.: Literature and Politics in the 20th Century. ° *Volume 5 of the* Journal of Contemporary History. TB/1328
WALTER LAQUEUR & GEORGE L. MOSSE, Eds.: The New History: *Trends in Historical Research and Writing Since World War II.* ° *Volume 4 of the* Journal of Contemporary History TB/1327
WALTER LAQUEUR & GEORGE L. MOSSE, Eds.: 1914: *The Coming of the First World War.* ° *Volume 3 of the* Journal of Contemporary History TB/1306
C. A. MACARTNEY, Ed.: The Habsburg and Hohenzollern Dynasties in the Seventeenth and Eighteenth Centuries # HR/1400
JOHN MCMANNERS: European History, 1789-1914: *Men, Machines and Freedom* TB/1419
PAUL MANTOUX: The Industrial Revolution in the Eighteenth Century: *An Outline of the Beginnings of the Modern Factory System in England* TB/1079
FRANK E. MANUEL: The Prophets of Paris: *Turgot, Condorcet, Saint-Simon, Fourier, and Comte* TB/1218
KINGSLEY MARTIN: French Liberal Thought in the Eighteenth Century: *A Study of Political Ideas from Bayle to Condorcet* TB/1114
NAPOLEON III: Napoleonic Ideas: *Des Idées Napoléoniennes, par le Prince Napoléon-Louis Bonaparte. Ed. by Brison D. Gooch* ¶ TB/1336
FRANZ NEUMANN: Behemoth: *The Structure and Practice of National Socialism, 1933-1944* TB/1289
DAVID OGG: Europe of the Ancien Régime, 1715-1783 ° α TB/1271
GEORGE RUDE: Revolutionary Europe, 1783-1815 ° α TB/1272
MASSIMO SALVADORI, Ed.: Modern Socialism # TB/1374
HUGH SETON-WATSON: Eastern Europe Between the Wars, 1918-1941 TB/1330

DENIS MACK SMITH, Ed.: The Making of Italy, 1796-1870 # HR/1356
ALBERT SOREL: Europe Under the Old Regime. *Translated by Francis H. Herrick* TB/1121
ROLAND N. STROMBERG, Ed.: Realism, Naturalism, and Symbolism: *Modes of Thought and Expression in Europe, 1848-1914* # HR/1355
A. J. P. TAYLOR: From Napoleon to Lenin: *Historical Essays* ° TB/1268
A. J. P. TAYLOR: The Habsburg Monarchy, 1809-1918: *A History of the Austrian Empire and Austria-Hungary* ° TB/1187
J. M. THOMPSON: European History, 1494-1789 TB/1431
DAVID THOMSON, Ed.: France: Empire and Republic, 1850-1940 # HR/1387
ALEXIS DE TOCQUEVILLE & GUSTAVE DE BEAUMONT: Tocqueville and Beaumont on Social Reform. *Ed. and trans. with Intro. by Seymour Drescher* TB/1343
G. M. TREVELYAN: British History in the Nineteenth Century and After: 1792-1919 ° TB/1251
H. R. TREVOR-ROPER: Historical Essays TB/1269
W. WARREN WAGAR, Ed.: Science, Faith, and MAN: *European Thought Since 1914* # HR/1362
MACK WALKER, Ed.: Metternich's Europe, 1813-1848 # HR/1361
ELIZABETH WISKEMANN: Europe of the Dictators, 1919-1945 ° α TB/1273
JOHN B. WOLF: France: 1814-1919: *The Rise of a Liberal-Democratic Society* TB/3019

Literature & Literary Criticism

JACQUES BARZUN: The House of Intellect TB/1051
W. J. BATE: From Classic to Romantic: *Premises of Taste in Eighteenth Century England* TB/1036
VAN WYCK BROOKS: Van Wyck Brooks: The Early Years: *A Selection from his Works, 1908-1921 Ed. with Intro. by Claire Sprague* TB/3082
ERNST R. CURTIUS: European Literature and the Latin Middle Ages. *Trans. by Willard Trask* TB/2015
RICHMOND LATTIMORE, Translator: The Odyssey of Homer TB/1389
SAMUEL PEPYS: The Diary of Samual Pepys. ° *Edited by O. F. Morshead. 60 illus. by Ernest Shepard* TB/1007
ROBERT PREYER, Ed.: Victorian Literature ** TB/1302
ALBION W. TOURGEE: A Fool's Errand: *A Novel of the South during Reconstruction. Intro. by George Fredrickson* TB/3074
BASIL WILEY: Nineteenth Century Studies: *Coleridge to Matthew Arnold* ° TB/1261

Philosophy

HENRI BERGSON: Time and Free Will: *An Essay on the Immediate Data of Consciousness* ° . TB/1021
LUDWIG BINSWANGER: Being-in-the-World: *Selected Papers. Trans. with Intro. by Jacob Needleman* TB/1365
H. J. BLACKHAM: Six Existentialist Thinkers: *Kierkegaard, Nietzsche, Jaspers, Marcel, Heidegger, Sartre* ° TB/1002
J. M. BOCHENSKI: The Methods of Contemporary Thought. *Trans. by Peter Caws* TB/1377
CRANE BRINTON: Nietzsche. *Preface, Bibliography, and Epilogue by the Author* TB/1197

7

MIRCEA ELIADE: Myths, Dreams and Mysteries: *The Encounter Between Contemporary Faiths and Archaic Realities* § TB/1320
MIRCEA ELIADE: Rites and Symbols of Initiation: *The Mysteries of Birth and Rebirth* § TB/1236
HERBERT FINGARETTE: The Self in Transformation: *Psychoanalysis, Philosophy and the Life of the Spirit* || TB/1177
SIGMUND FREUD: On Creativity and the Unconscious: *Papers on the Psychology of Art, Literature, Love, Religion.* § *Intro. by Benjamin Nelson* TB/45
J. GLENN GRAY: The Warriors: *Reflections on Men in Battle. Introduction by Hannah Arendt* TB/1294
WILLIAM JAMES: Psychology: *The Briefer Course. Edited with an Intro. by Gordon Allport* TB/1034
C. G. JUNG: Psychological Reflections. *Ed. by J. Jacobi* TB/2001
KARL MENNINGER, M.D.: Theory of Psychoanalytic Technique TB/1144
JOHN H. SCHAAR: Escape from Authority: *The Perspectives of Erich Fromm* TB/1155
MUZAFER SHERIF: The Psychology of Social Norms. *Introduction by Gardner Murphy* TB/3072
HELLMUT WILHELM: Change: *Eight Lectures on the I Ching* TB/2019

Religion: Ancient and Classical, Biblical and Judaic Traditions

W. F. ALBRIGHT: The Biblical Period from Abraham to Ezra TB/102
SALO W. BARON: Modern Nationalism and Religion TB/818
C. K. BARRETT, Ed.: The New Testament Background: *Selected Documents* TB/86
MARTIN BUBER: Eclipse of God: *Studies in the Relation Between Religion and Philosophy* TB/12
MARTIN BUBER: Hasidism and Modern Man. *Edited and Translated by Maurice Friedman* TB/839
MARTIN BUBER: The Knowledge of Man. *Edited with an Introduction by Maurice Friedman. Translated by Maurice Friedman and Ronald Gregor Smith* TB/135
MARTIN BUBER: Moses. *The Revelation and the Covenant* TB/837
MARTIN BUBER: The Origin and Meaning of Hasidism. *Edited and Translated by Maurice Friedman* TB/835
MARTIN BUBER: The Prophetic Faith TB/73
MARTIN BUBER: Two Types of Faith: *Interpenetration of Judaism and Christianity* ° TB/75
MALCOLM L. DIAMOND: Martin Buber: *Jewish Existentialist* TB/840
M. S. ENSLIN: Christian Beginnings TB/5
M. S. ENSLIN: The Literature of the Christian Movement TB/6
ERNST LUDWIG EHRLICH: A Concise History of Israel: *From the Earliest Times to the Destruction of the Temple in A.D. 70* ° TB/128
HENRI FRANKFORT: Ancient Egyptian Religion: *An Interpretation* TB/77
ABRAHAM HESCHEL: The Earth Is the Lord's & The Sabbath. *Two Essays* TB/828
ABRAHAM HESCHEL: God in Search of Man: *A Philosophy of Judaism* TB/807
ABRAHAM HESCHEL: Man Is not Alone: *A Philosophy of Religion* TB/838
ABRAHAM HESCHEL: The Prophets: *An Introduction* TB/1421

T. J. MEEK: Hebrew Origins TB/69
JAMES MUILENBURG: The Way of Israel: *Biblical Faith and Ethics* TB/133
H. J. ROSE: Religion in Greece and Rome TB/55
H. H. ROWLEY: The Growth of the Old Testament TB/107
D. WINTON THOMAS, Ed.: Documents from Old Testament Times TB/85

Religion: General Christianity

ROLAND H. BAINTON: Christendom: *A Short History of Christianity and Its Impact on Western Civilization. Illus.*
Vol. I TB/131; Vol. II TB/132
JOHN T. MCNEILL: Modern Christian Movements. *Revised Edition* TB/1402
ERNST TROELTSCH: The Social Teaching of the Christian Churches. *Intro. by H. Richard Niebuhr* Vol. TB/71; Vol. II TB/72

Religion: Early Christianity Through Reformation

ANSELM OF CANTERBURY: Truth, Freedom, and Evil: *Three Philosophical Dialogues. Edited and Translated by Jasper Hopkins and Herbert Richardson* TB/317
MARSHALL W. BALDWIN, Ed.: Christianity through the 13th Century # HR/1468
W. D. DAVIES: Paul and Rabbinic Judaism: *Some Rabbinic Elements in Pauline Theology. Revised Edition* ° TB/146
ADOLF DEISSMANN: Paul: *A Study in Social and Religious History* TB/15
JOHANNES ECKHART: Meister Eckhart: *A Modern Translation by R. Blakney* TB/8
EDGAR J. GOODSPEED: A Life of Jesus TB/1
ROBERT M. GRANT: Gnosticism and Early Christianity TB/136
WILLIAM HALLER: The Rise of Puritanism TB/22
GERHART B. LADNER: The Idea of Reform: *Its Impact on the Christian Thought and Action in the Age of the Fathers* TB/149
ARTHUR DARBY NOCK: Early Gentile Christianity and Its Hellenistic Background TB/111
ARTHUR DARBY NOCK: St. Paul ° TR/104
GORDON RUPP: Luther's Progress to the Diet of Worms ° TB/120

Religion: The Protestant Tradition

KARL BARTH: Church Dogmatics: *A Selection. Intro. by H. Gollwitzer. Ed. by G. W. Bromiley* TB/95
KARL BARTH: Dogmatics in Outline TB/56
KARL BARTH: The Word of God and the Word of Man TB/13
HERBERT BRAUN, et al.: God and Christ: *Existence and Province. Volume 5 of Journal for Theology and the Church, edited by Robert W. Funk and Gerhard Ebeling* TB/255
WHITNEY R. CROSS: The Burned-Over District: *The Social and Intellectual History of Enthusiastic Religion in Western New York, 1800-1850* TB/1242
NELS F. S. FERRE: Swedish Contributions to Modern Theology. *New Chapter by William A. Johnson* TB/147
WILLIAM R. HUTCHISON, Ed.: American Protestant Thought: *The Liberal Era* ‡ TB/1385
ERNST KASEMANN, et al.: Distinctive Protestant and Catholic Themes Reconsidered. *Volume 3 of Journal for Theology and the Church,*

8

C. V. DURELL: Readable Relativity. *Foreword by Freeman J. Dyson* TB/530
GEORGE GAMOW: Biography of Physics. Σ *Illus.* TB/567
F. K. HARE: The Restless Atmosphere TB/560
J. R. PIERCE: Symbols, Signals and Noise: *The Nature and Process of Communication* Σ TB/574
WILLARD VAN ORMAN QUINE: Mathematical Logic TB/558

Science: History

MARIE BOAS: The Scientific Renaissance, 1450-1630 ° TB/583
STEPHEN TOULMIN & JUNE GOODFIELD: The Architecture of Matter: *The Physics, Chemistry and Physiology of Matter, Both Animate and Inanimate, as it has Evolved since the Beginnings of Science* TB/584
STEPHEN TOULMIN & JUNE GOODFIELD: The Discovery TB/576
STEPHEN TOULMIN & JUNE GOODFIELD: The Fabric of the Heavens: *The Development of Astronomy and Dynamics* TB/579

Science: Philosophy

J. M. BOCHENSKI: The Methods of Contemporary Thought. *Tr. by Peter Caws* TB/1377
J. BRONOWSKI: Science and Human Values. *Revised and Enlarged. Illus.* TB/505
WERNER HEISENBERG: Physics and Philosophy: *The Revolution in Modern Science. Introduction by F. S. C. Northrop* TB/549
KARL R. POPPER: Conjectures and Refutations: *The Growth of Scientific Knowledge* TB/1376
KARL R. POPPER: The Logic of Scientific Discovery TB/1376
STEPHEN TOULMIN: Foresight and Understanding: *An Enquiry into the Aims of Science. Foreword by Jacques Barzun* TB/564
STEPHEN TOULMIN: The Philosophy of Science: *An Introduction* TB/513

Sociology and Anthropology

REINHARD BENDIX: Work and Authority in Industry: *Ideologies of Management in the Course of Industrialization* TB/3035
BERNARD BERELSON, Ed.: The Behavioral Sciences Today TB/1127
JOSEPH B. CASAGRANDE, Ed.: In the Company of Man: *Twenty Portraits of Anthropological Informants. Illus.* TB/3047
KENNETH B. CLARK: Dark Ghetto: *Dilemmas of Social Power. Foreword by Gunnar Myrdal* TB/1317
KENNETH CLARK & JEANNETTE HOPKINS: A Relevant War Against Poverty: *A Study of Community Action Programs and Observable Social Change* TB/1480
LEWIS COSER, Ed.: Political Sociology TB/1293
ROSE L. COSER, Ed.: Life Cycle and Achievement in America ** TB/1434
ALLISON DAVIS & JOHN DOLLARD: Children of Bondage: *The Personality Development of Negro Youth in the Urban South* || TB/3049
PETER F. DRUCKER: The New Society: *The Anatomy of Industrial Order* TB/1082
CORA DU BOIS: The People of Alor. *With a Preface by the Author*
Vol. I *Illus.* TB/1042; Vol. II TB/1043
EMILE DURKHEIM et al.: Essays on Sociology and Philosophy: *with Appraisals of Durkheim's Life and Thought.* || *Edited by Kurt H. Wolff* TB/1151

LEON FESTINGER, HENRY W. RIECKEN, STANLEY SCHACHTER: When Prophecy Fails: *A Social and Psychological Study of a Modern Group that Predicted the Destruction of the World* || TB/1132
CHARLES Y. GLOCK & RODNEY STARK: Christian Beliefs and Anti-Semitism. *Introduction by the Authors* TB/1454
ALVIN W. GOULDNER: The Hellenic World TB/1479
ALVIN W. GOULDNER: Wildcat Strike: *A Study in Worker-Management Relationships* || TB/1176
CESAR GRANA: Modernity and Its Discontents: *French Society and the French Man of Letters in the Nineteenth Century* TB/1318
L. S. B. LEAKEY: Adam's Ancestors: *The Evolution of Man and His Culture. Illus.* TB/1019
KURT LEWIN: Field Theory in Social Science: *Selected Theoretical Papers.* || *Edited by Dorwin Cartwright* TB/1135
RITCHIE P. LOWRY: Who's Running This Town? *Community Leadership and Social Change* TB/1383
R. M. MACIVER: Social Causation TB/1153
GARY T. MARX: Protest and Prejudice: *A Study of Belief in the Black Community* TB/1435
ROBERT K. MERTON, LEONARD BROOM, LEONARD S. COTTRELL, JR., Editors: Sociology Today: *Problems and Prospects* ||
Vol. I TB/1173; Vol. II TB/1174
GILBERT OSOFSKY, Ed.: The Burden of Race: *A Documentary History of Negro-White Relations in America* TB/1405
GILBERT OSOFSKY: Harlem: The Making of a Ghetto: *Negro New York 1890-1930* TB/1381
TALCOTT PARSONS & EDWARD A. SHILS, Editors: Toward a General Theory of Action: *Theoretical Foundations for the Social Sciences* TB/1083
PHILIP RIEFF: The Triumph of the Therapeutic: *Uses of Faith After Freud* TB/1360
JOHN H. ROHRER & MUNRO S. EDMONSON, Eds.: The Eighth Generation Grows Up: *Cultures and Personalities of New Orleans Negroes* || TB/3050
ARNOLD ROSE: The Negro in America: *The Condensed Version of Gunnar Myrdal's An American Dilemma. Second Edition* TB/3048
GEORGE ROSEN: Madness in Society: *Chapters in the Historical Sociology of Mental Illness.* || *Preface by Benjamin Nelson* TB/1337
PHILIP SELZNICK: TVA and the Grass Roots: *A Study in the Sociology of Formal Organization* TB/1230
PITIRIM A. SOROKIN: Contemporary Sociological Theories: *Through the First Quarter of the Twentieth Century* TB/3046
MAURICE R. STEIN: The Eclipse of Community: *An Interpretation of American Studies* TB/1128
EDWARD A. TIRYAKIAN, Ed.: Sociological Theory, Values and Sociocultural Change: *Essays in Honor of Pitirim A. Sorokin* ° TB/1316
FERDINAND TONNIES: Community and Society: *Gemeinschaft und Gesellschaft. Translated and Edited by Charles P. Loomis* TB/1116
SAMUEL E. WALLACE: Skid Row as a Way of Life TB/1367
W. LLOYD WARNER: Social Class in America: *The Evaluation of Status* TB/1013
FLORIAN ZNANIECKI: The Social Role of the Man of Knowledge. *Introduction by Lewis A. Coser* TB/1372

DATE DUE

OC 12 77			
DE 14 77			
OC 3 0 '80			
SE 2 3 '81			
SE 2 8 '82			
OC 1 9 '82			
AP 2 7 '83			
OC 1 1 '83			
NOV 1 3 '83			
OC 2 '84			
GAYLORD			PRINTED IN U.S.A.